MOBILE SELVES

SOCIAL TRANSFORMATIONS IN
AMERICAN ANTHROPOLOGY
General Editor: Ida Susser

*The Sounds of Latinidad: Immigrants Making Music and Creating
Culture in a Southern City*
Samuel K. Byrd

Mobile Selves: Race, Migration, and Belonging in Peru and the U.S.
Ulla D. Berg

Mobile Selves

*Race, Migration, and Belonging in
Peru and the U.S.*

Ulla D. Berg

NEW YORK UNIVERSITY PRESS
New York and London

NEW YORK UNIVERSITY PRESS
New York and London
www.nyupress.org

References to Internet websites (URLs) were accurate at the time of writing. Neither the author nor New York University Press is responsible for URLs that may have expired or changed since the manuscript was prepared.

ISBN: 978-1-4798-0346-0

ISBN: 978-1-4798-7570-2 (PB)

For Library of Congress Cataloging-in-Publication data, please contact the Library of Congress.

New York University Press books are printed on acid-free paper, and their binding materials are chosen for strength and durability. We strive to use environmentally responsible suppliers and materials to the greatest extent possible in publishing our books.

Manufactured in the United States of America

10 9 8 7 6 5 4 3 2 1

Also available as an ebook

For Sissel and Linus

CONTENTS

FIGURES

ACKNOWLEDGMENTS

This book is the product of more than ten years of work thinking, reading, talking, and writing about migration and mobility and about the attachments and aspirations of people in flux. Above all else I wish to extend my deepest thanks to the many Peruvians who have contributed to this study from different latitudes and vantage points, sharing their experiences and their views, and letting me participate in their lives, travels, and daily activities over a number of years. I cannot acknowledge my interlocutors by their real names, because I promised them anonymity, but I am deeply grateful to those whose stories and experiences are reflected in this book's pages. Their struggles to produce and maintain social relations while coping with the difficulties of migration and the challenges of living across many borders and boundaries continue to humble and inspire me.

The research upon which this book is based was made possible by generous funding from the Danish Research Agency, the Wenner-Gren Foundation for Anthropological Research, a McCracken Fellowship from New York University, Rutgers Research Council, and travel grants from New York University and the Center for Latin American Studies at Rutgers. Write-up of the materials was generously supported by a fellowship at the International Center for Advanced Studies (ICAS) at NYU and years later by a Richard Carley Hunt Postdoctoral Fellowship from the Wenner-Gren Foundation, which funded my academic leave from Rutgers during the last stretch of bringing the manuscript to publication.

Ambulant ethnographic work produces many debts in multiple locations. In Paterson, New Jersey, Roberto Bustamante and Luis Aranguren helped me get this project off the ground by providing important contacts and sharing a wealth of information. Manuel Angulo also endorsed my project and offered me institutional support through AIPEUC. In Miami, I am particularly indebted to the Jiménez and Alva families for spending valuable time and for sharing their everyday lives and their fiestas with me. Consul Jorge Román and the members of the Advisory Council (Consejo de Consulta) at the Peruvian consulate in Miami provided useful testimony and perspectives on migrant-state relationships. My dear friends Fernando Calzadilla and Elaiza Irizarry offered me a lovely home away from home during fieldwork in Miami. In Washington, D.C., and Maryland, many Urcumarquinos shared their food, fiestas, and valuable time teaching me about the importance of maintaining long-distance social and affective relationships across many borders. My debt to all of them remains irredeemable.

In Peru, countless individuals and institutions have helped make this research possible. At La Católica—my alma mater in Peru—I owe much to Teófilo Altamirano, Gisela Cánepa Koch, Raúl Romero, Manuel Raez, Makena Ulfe, and especially Alex Huerta-Mercado for being my unconditional interlocutor and close friend since we first met in Lima in 1997 and during our time together at NYU. I am also grateful to Martín Tanaka and Carolina Trivelli for welcoming me as an affiliated scholar at the Instituto de Estudios Peruanos (IEP) in 2004, and to Ramón Pajuelo, Javier Avila, and the late Carlos Iván Degregori for stimulating conversations. Lucho and Renata Millones deserve special mention for their constant encouragement, cariño, and continued support of my work. In Huancayo (and later Lima), my comadre and fellow anthropologist on the move, Carla Tamagno, has inspired this research in more ways than I can possibly account for. The Tamagno, Jiménez, and Caso families also facilitated my shorter and longer stays in Huancayo and in Matahuasi by putting me up in their homes, and I am grateful *siempre* for their hospitality and friendship. José Luis Alvarez first introduced me to Jauja and its surrounding communities and has been a frequent interlocutor about the history and anthropology of El Valle del Mantaro. In Lima, Carlos Cueva and Manuel Mendieta provided me with a place to live and acted as my family in Peru since my first extended stay there in 1997–98. My friend, the Peruvian poet Domingo de Ramos, distracted me in productive ways from writing this book and made *Lima, la horrible* a poetic and adventurous place to live and work. Zenaida Meza Vargas and Yobani González Jauregui provided valuable research assistance in Huancayo and Lima, respectively, and I am grateful for their time and dedication to this project. During a brief follow-up research trip in the summer of 2011, I was fortunate to count on valuable research assistance from

Alex Tavara Aranibar, José David Cotrina, and Jhoan Jorge Alva. Javier Avila, Rosemary Boltan, and Soledad Chacón transcribed several of my interviews.

I am indebted to several key mentors, colleagues, and friends who at different stages of my journey have been important interlocutors, pushing me toward critical analysis, and inspiring me to claim ownership over an unruly project and develop my authorial voice. Norman Long supervised my first ethnographic fieldwork and taught me much of what I know about agency and social change. His mentorship continues to influence my outlook on social science research. Karsten Paerregaard continues to be a wonderful mentor, enthusiastic colleague, academic collaborator, and dear friend. A deep gratitude goes to Thomas Abercrombie at NYU, whose complex and profound thinking on Andean life—past and present—inspired me in ways too many to name here. From the very moment when I learned that "my hat was in the ring," he believed in my project and provided me with invaluable guidance and mentorship, intellectual challenges, and enduring friendship. The guidance of Faye Ginsburg, Bambi Schieffelin, Arlene Dávila, Fred Myers, Don Kulick, Diana Taylor, and Deborah Poole have also been central to this project and I am grateful to all of them for their support.

While I take full responsibility for what this book has become, including any errors, many colleagues have read and commented on specific parts of the manuscript and offered suggestions on how to improve it. In addition to those already named above, I am grateful for comments on earlier versions of individual chapters from Ninna Nyberg Sørensen, Luis Guarnizo, Sarah Mahler, Richard Kernaghan, Zoila Mendoza, Elana Zilberg, Marcial Godoy-Anativia, Ayumi Takenaka, Angeles Escrivá, Elena Sabogal, Suzanne Oboler, Robyn Rodriguez, Alyshia Gálvez, Nina Siulc, Amikole Maraesa, Carlos Vargas-Ramos, and Sherene Seikaly. I have also benefited from presenting my ideas in several seminar venues over the years. Thanks to an invitation from Thomas Bender and Tim Mitchell, I was lucky enough to participate in a yearlong seminar titled "Reconfiguring the Social" under their superb intellectual stewardship at NYU's International Center for Advanced Studies during 2006–07. In 2007–08, the Institute for Research on Women (IRW) at Rutgers provided a stimulating and nurturing academic environment to further develop my arguments thanks to a generous invitation from

Dorothy Hodgson. The "Economies of Affect" working group—a joint effort between Rutgers and CUNY in 2010–11—provided a productive and supportive forum, as did the "Whiteness in the Americas" workshop at Baruch College-CUNY in 2013–14. In all these spaces, I have benefited from insightful feedback from scholars too many to list here, but I am grateful to every one of them for their engagement with my work. A special thanks goes to Ana Ramos-Zayas and Edgar Rivera-Colón, who both played a titanic role as interlocutors in my final stages of writing and in helping me "add spunk" to my writing. Gracias familia! This would not have happened without you.

At Rutgers, I want to thank my colleagues in various departments and centers for engaging conversations, excellent feedback, and crucial support at several stages of this project. In particular, I thank Aldo Lauria-Santiago, Zaire Dinzey-Flores, Carlos Decena, Kathy López, Yolanda Martínez-San Miguel, Nelson Maldonado-Torres, Camilla Stevens, Michelle Stevens, Yarimar Bonilla, Fran Mascia-Lees, Louisa Schein, Angelique Haugerud, Daniel Goldstein, Parvis Ghassem-Fachandi, David Hughes, Rocío Magaña, and Joanna Regulska, as well as the Rutgers graduate students who participated in and enriched my graduate seminar on "Personhood" in Spring 2011 with lively and important discussions.

Finally, I am deeply appreciative of the valuable feedback offered by the anonymous reviewers from NYU Press, two of whom—Jessaca Leinaweaver and Jeff Cohen—"outed" themselves to me. Their comments have improved this manuscript tremendously and I am honored to have been the recipient of such productive and collegial engagement. I am also very grateful for the enthusiastic support of my editor, Jennifer Hammer, for seeing this book through to publication with admirable professionalism, and to her assistant Constance Grady. In earlier stages of revising the manuscript I have relied on the superb editorial assistance of Cecelia Cancellaro and Julie Bleha and on the always efficient and skillful research assistance of Deniz Daser. Brenda D. Allen competently created the maps and Carlos Tamagno helped me reproduce photographic materials and I am grateful to them too.

The transnational connections I continue to sustain with my own extended family in Denmark, France, London, Spain, Brazil, Lebanon, and Puerto Rico have taught me much about the challenges of "doing kinship" across borders and about the existential importance of family and belonging. My parents, Lene Dalum and Ole Visti Petersen, and my father, Mogens Berg, have nurtured, supported, and encouraged me for as long as I can remember and for this I am forever grateful. Over the years, I have been lucky to rely on my New York, Copenhagen, and San Juan "chosen family" who have listened to my countless deliberations as I went through the project's various stages: Javier Cardona, Larry Schulze, Alejandra Martorell, Mia Morales, Marlene Ramírez-Cancio, Urayoán Noel, Monxo López, Libertad Guerra, Ana Ramos-Zayas, Zaire Dinzey-Flores, Ariel Rojas, Julie Bleha, Galina Draiby, Martha Gutiérrez, Lucía Stacey, Niels Ole Sørensen, Rasmus Boserup, and Sine Plambech. Many have shifted geographical coordinates along the way but are still in my life from their present latitudes. Last but certainly not least, I want to thank Rebio Díaz who has been my *compañero* for as long as this project has been in the works. Together we have learned to straddle the difficult balance between academic and family life, raising two *chiquitines* in New York City—*eso no es poca cosa. Para ti Rebio, gracias totales!* Finally, our children Sissel and Linus with their presence and intensity, joy, curiosity, and loudest voices in the neighborhood have put writing this book in healthy perspective, reminding me daily that life is so much more than words on a page. I dedicate this book to them.

Introduction

In early October 2004, I was rushing through Miami airport just off the plane from Lima. A local hurricane warning had delayed flights out of Lima and passengers were worried about making connecting flights. Rounding a corner, I saw to my despair that in the passage ahead was a mass of international travelers, which a U.S. Immigration (USCIS) officer was trying to divide into a "citizens and residents only" line and another line for everyone else. She explained that because of the hurricane warning the lines for immigration were unusually long and requested that all passengers wait patiently in line.

A group of Limeños in front of me, with all the typical markers of class entitlement, style, and embodied affect that in Peru defines a *pituco*—or upper-class Peruvian—started to joke amongst themselves about the Puerto Rican USCIS officer. They laughed about her looks and her *español masticado* ("chewed" or broken Spanish). One woman from the Peruvian group said: "And Puerto Ricans, where do they go?" The comment amused her friends because it played on common stereotypes among Latin Americans about U.S.-born Puerto Ricans as culturally and linguistically deficient (cf. Ramos-Zayas 2003).

Soon, a second USCIS officer—also Latino—appeared onsite to enforce the ordering of the two lines and to help the citizen line to move forward. The people in my line (noncitizens) were restless and started voicing complaints. The same Peruvian woman stepped out of line to stretch her back but was immediately asked by the second immigration officer to remain in line. She turned to her husband and said indignantly: "*Paul, imagínate, hasta aquí hemos venido para que nos traten como cholos*" ("Imagine Paul, we have come all this way to be treated as cholos"). A cholo in Peru generally refers to a person of indigenous origins in the urban environment who has adopted urban manners and lifestyles, but the term carries a derogatory connotation because of its "in betweenness" in ethnic and political terms (Larson 2005). Behind me, a man I'd talked to briefly at the Lima airport asked for permission to come through; Jorge, a long-term Miami resident, was originally from the highland city of Huancayo, and had an undeniable phenotypic "Indianness." He sported expensive baggy jeans, a Tommy Hilfiger shirt, and a designer watch. He was waving his U.S. passport to get to the proper line; while passing through he accidentally bumped into the woman in front of me. Her immediate and visceral reaction said it all: "¡Y este, qué se cree, cholo de miércoles!" ("And this guy, who does he think he is, piece-of-shit cholo!").[1] It was inconceivable to an upper-class white Peruvian that a "simple cholo" could access the preferential treatment of the citizenship line, while she herself had to stand with her *pituco* friends in the line of alien others. I do not know if Jorge heard the woman's comment and if so, how he felt about it, but the incident stayed with me for the duration of my fieldwork and long after. It is a constant reminder of the barriers faced by those Peruvians who trace their origins to the Andean highlands when striving to reinvent themselves as cosmopolitan and transnational subjects. Most migrants do not end up, like Jorge, in the citizens and residents line, but all run afoul of the resentments of the Lima elites who experience the new upward and outward mobility of Andean Peruvians, which is the subject of this book, as a kind of "passing" and a threat and affront to their own presumed whiteness and their long-term and "higher class" cosmopolitanism.

* * *

This book examines the experiences, practices, and imaginaries of transnational migration and mobility among Andean Peruvians who between the late 1980s and around 2010 sought to extend their livelihoods, first from rural villages to Peru's cities, and then beyond Peru's borders. Based on ethnographic research carried out over a period of several years in rural communities of the Mantaro Valley in Peru's central highlands, and following migrants from that area, in the Peruvian cities of Huancayo, Lima, and the U.S. destinations of Miami, Washington, D.C., and Paterson, New Jersey, I depict here the experiences of those persons I came to know well. Drawing on this material as a series of extended case studies and upon more general social theory and scholarship on migration, mobility, circulation, and exchange, I examine the social organization of migration, the forces driving it, and the images that migrants produce and circulate of themselves through communicative practice and exchange between Peru and the United States. Focusing on the relationship of social practice and cultural and technological mediation, I argue that social relations among transnational migrants and those with whom they engage throughout the migration process are mediated by images, objects, practices, and by an expanding reach of Andean cultural forms. I demonstrate how the difficulty of maintaining meaningful transnational lives in today's world is embedded in the form and process of always-partial communication between migrants, their families, their communities, and the state. The situated representations of self and Other that are produced within these relationships operate centrally in shaping how indigenous and rural migrants strive to become mobile and are also key to how these migrants reenvision their communities and themselves in the contemporary global and interconnected world through migration.

While globalization since the 1970s has facilitated the circulation of goods and of privileged subjects, it has also brought about constraints on the mobility of laboring men and women, making the global circulation of human bodies inherently limited and contingent. This development is evident in the increased policing of international borders and in the production of new racialized boundaries both in migrant-sending and receiving contexts (De Genova 2002, 2010; Fassin 2011; Inda 2006; Chávez 2008). Within this global scenario only some bodies can circulate without major obstacles to their mobility. Others constantly evoke suspicion and are perceived as threats. Yet the ideological and moral coding of the mobility of the subaltern as negative is hardly novel.[2] Since colonial times the mobility of the indigenous subject within the colonial and later republican social order and imagination has been perceived as deeply problematic. Framed as the antithesis first of Spanishness, then of whiteness, indigenous migrants in cities were deliberately excluded from "decent" city centers and from participating as citizens in urban political life (Larson 2005). Relegated to precarious lives in peripheral neighborhoods, and tolerated only because of the need for their labor, migrants in cities were largely treated as contaminants, as "matter out of place" (Douglas 1978), and a threat to civilized society (Weismantel 2001; Wilson 2004). Such images of Andean indigenous subjects as quintessentially "antimodern" and "antiurban" were revived during the massive rural-to-urban migration from the Andes to Lima starting in the mid-twentieth century and again by the threat of violence during the 1980s era of Sendero Luminoso (Shining Path) during which the displacement of Andean peasants to Peru's cities was regarded as a burden on the nation and a problem to be solved. A structurally similar coding of the mobility of the subaltern as profoundly unsettling also appears in contemporary contexts of Latin American migration to metropolitan centers in the United States and Europe. Here, Latin American migrants are frequently portrayed, in the words of anthropologist Jonathan Xavier Inda, as "parasite[s] intruding on the body of the host nation, drawing nutrients from it, while providing nothing to its survival and even threatening its well-being" (2000:47).

This book shows that such long-standing encodings of mobility figure centrally in the particular articulations through which recent Andean migrants from the central highlands of Peru remake themselves and are remade through transnational migration by larger structures, institutions, and technologies. Often unsuccessful in obtaining visas on their own via official bureaucratic procedures, lower class and indigenous Peruvians from the Andean highlands pursue transnational mobility within this political and racial global economy by turning to the services of "migration professionals" to help them get their migration projects off the ground. These services include help with acquiring bank accounts, passports, visas, and guidance on how to camouflage their rural or marginal urban demeanor that otherwise would place them squarely on the rejection list when applying for a U.S. visa in Lima. This involves cultivating the ability to embody the ease that comes with the taken-for-granted privilege of state-authorized mobility. Aspiring migrants who seek to travel to international destinations in the post-9/11 political and racial economy are well aware of this need to compensate for their ostensible excess of rural or marginal urban markers and the alleged liability of their claims to mobility, citizenship, and belonging. They constantly evaluate the friction produced by the mobility of their bodies through space as they navigate multiple social positionings within larger power dynamics that shape the transnational circulation of human bodies.

Peruvians migrate to foreign destinations for a variety of reasons, including economic ones. Yet for many of the Peruvians from the Mantaro

Valley I have come to know over the course of the research process, the quest for transnational migration and mobility is much more than just an economic project. It is a cultural and class aspiration, and a demand for citizenship status and belonging which is at the very center of the always-unfinished process of social becoming. This aspiration to mobility, I argue, aims to overcome centuries-old urban constructions of indigenous Peruvians and their urban cholo counterparts as rural, backward, and essentially unfit for citizenship, metropolitan modernity, and international travel, which until recent decades was monopolized by Peru's elites. The possibility for Andean Peruvians of modest means to migrate to distant countries is relatively new and constitutes an important practice through which migrants attempt to not just reproduce but also transform their predicament.

Peruvian Migration and Its Contexts

For most of the twentieth century the migration of indigenous and working-class Peruvians occurred *within* Peru. These Peruvians left their rural towns and communities to search for new opportunities, education for their children, and more modern lifestyles in the mining centers, the provincial capitals of the Andes, or in the nation's capital, Lima. Over time their mobility transformed the face of Lima and of Peru itself. The Peruvian anthropologist José Matos Mar ([1984] 2004) has referred to this process as a *desborde popular*, or popular overflow; a transformative process through which Andean Peruvians could no longer be ignored as social and historical actors. The *desborde popular* importantly also changed the categories through which Peruvians of different class backgrounds make sense of self and Other.

While Andean Peruvians moved extensively within the national territory it was not until the late 1980s that international migration became a significant practice or even remote possibility for nonelite Andean Peruvians. Indeed, since colonial times overseas mobility had only been available to well-traveled Spanish and *criollo* (American-born Spaniard) elites, those who later came to call themselves "whites." Central to these elites' self-definition was cosmopolitanism in taste, consumption patterns, and educational experience, made possible by their relative wealth and access to political power, ID papers, and travel opportunities. Yet to

Figure I.1. Map of Peru. (Map by Brenda D. Allen)

become mobile within the transatlantic colonial societies, new-world criollo elites had to send "proofs of service" and "clean blood" to the Spanish king, hoping to take up administrative posts in Spain after having served their terms in the colonies (Abercrombie 1998; Pratt 1992). After independence in 1821, Peru's self-styled and now "white" upper classes, who could no longer call themselves "Spaniards," traveled for business and leisure and sent their children to study at exclusive universities in Europe and the United States.[3] Such passport-and-visa-enabled international travel only became available to Andean Peruvians at a much more recent historical juncture, not as "vacation," but as the next step in labor migration.

Beginning in the 1970s, countries in Latin America (along with Europe and the United States) went through yet another stage of profound social and economic change variously referred to as globalization, late capitalism, neoliberal globalization, or simply neoliberalism (Harvey 1989, 2007; Sassen 1998).[4] Over the course of a few decades, the old political and economic elites increasingly lost their monopolistic hold over land, labor, national industries, businesses, and political life, ceding it to transnational corporations, foreign capital, neopopulist politicians, and an always-emergent class of entrepreneurs, many of Andean background (Tapia 1998). Many of the changes of that era were imposed through World Bank and International Monetary Fund "packages" that required Latin American countries seeking foreign debt repayment loans to demonstrate free-market policy performance (McClintock and Vallas 2003:109–10). Among them were free trade agreements and massive cuts in government spending to already meager social services, policing, and infrastructural funding, leading to an overall "shrinking of the state." Furthermore, the end of import substitution industrialization (ISI) in Peru in 1987, and the opening of national markets to cheap commodities (generally from East Asia) also contributed to an immediate spike in poverty and unemployment (Gonzáles de Olarte 2007). These intertwined Washington Consensus policies asked Latin American countries to decentralize government, and aimed at propelling the growth of "civil society" and political participation at the grassroots level (McClintock and Vallas 2003; Tanaka 2002). In Peru, they coincided with the escalation of the PCP-SL (Sendero Luminoso) insurgency across the national territory—not the sort of grassroots political action that Washington had sought.

Escape from the violence of the Sendero Luminoso insurgency/counterinsurgency and rural poverty were the main push factors that propelled rural-to-urban migration and urban middle-class transnational migration in the 1980s. Democratic instability and growing inequality as a result of Peru's transition to a full-blown neoliberal economic regime in the 1990s produced unprecedented and upwardly spiraling emigration which continued through the first half of the decade of 2000 to 2010 not just from countryside to city, but away from Peru, of Peruvians of all regional backgrounds and social classes (Berg and Paerregaard 2005; Durand 2010; Massey and Capoferro 2006; Takenaka et al. 2010). According to numbers from the National Institute for Statistics and Information (INEI), 2,444,634 Peruvians left the country between 1990–2011 without coming back; this number represents 8.2 percent of the total population in 2011 (IOM 2012:81).[5] Meanwhile, Andean rural communities were largely neglected by the state, left to resolve their own problems as they best could—often with the help of remittances from migrants abroad. Yet these communities simultaneously enjoyed several benefits from globalization; in particular the greatly enhanced global communication infrastructure which allowed people to communicate transnationally and access information previously unavailable to them. These articulations through new technology worked to broaden the horizon and aspirations of many and soon these Peruvians would impinge on what national elites historically had seen as their exclusive entitlement: the right to overseas travel and to the kind of cosmopolitan modernity and transnational subjectivity associated with it.

Yet, as I argue in this book, Andean Peruvians cannot freely access international destinations via state-authorized travel because of long-lived racial and class hierarchies in Peru that code their mobility negatively. While this prevailing social and racial order had already been partially destabilized by rural-to-urban migration and by the rise of the figure of the cholo as a political subject, it has been challenged anew in recent years with the migration of nonelite Andean Peruvians to foreign destinations. This book demonstrates how—when making claims to the transnational mobility embodied in overseas travel—nonelite Andean Peruvians produce friction and provoke elite policing of the boundar-

ies of what constitutes proper and legitimate "transnational mobility."
When traveling abroad and encountering other Peruvians in foreign
cities, these migrants are largely regarded with suspicion in the context
of cross-class social relations, thus reviving the "cultural conflict" of
the cholo from an earlier era (Quijano 1980), but now projected onto
a transnational scale. Further, when these provincial Peruvians return
"Americanized" from abroad, like Jorge in the opening vignette, they are
ridiculed by elites for their multiple and intertwined lacks and excesses
and, perhaps most of all, for their wrongful belief that money alone can
"whiten" them and give them access to elite social spaces and symbolic
capital.

The research presented in this book depicts a moment in time when
international migration from Peru was still spiraling upwards. I draw
on ethnographic fieldwork in Peru and among Peruvian migrants in
the United States conducted between 1998 and 2005, but most intensely
during a period of eighteen months of dissertation fieldwork between
March 1, 2004 and September 1, 2005. Two short research trips to Peru
in the summer of 2011 and spring of 2013, and ongoing periodic visits to
the U.S. locations of Paterson, New Jersey; Miami, Florida; and Washington, D.C., have allowed me to update my original long-term research
and bring the life histories and migration histories up to date. Yet as
the Peruvian economy in more recent years has continued to grow, the
odds of migration, the motivations for leaving, and the dominant representations of mobility are shifting. After the global financial crisis of
2008, some Peruvians, including friends and informants from Paterson,
Washington, D.C., and Miami, returned from abroad (IOM 2012), but
in the bigger picture the number of return migrants is still insignificant
relative to the number of Peruvians who continue to leave. I address
these recent shifts and tendencies in the book's conclusion, but for now
I invite the reader to enter an ethnographic present in which staying in
Peru had become tantamount with stagnation and lack of opportunities
for survival, economic advancement, and self-improvement, in contrast
to travel to foreign destinations—preferably outside Latin America—
which has been imagined to be full of possibilities for realizing a promising and exciting future. But in order for this future to be actualized in
real and tangible migration projects of outward and upward mobility,
migrants had to continuously communicate to others who they were

and what they would like to become. Attention to these communicative practices is central to the approach to transnational migration, circulation, and mobility that I propose in this book.

Producing Mobility: Transnational Migration as Communicative Practice

For more than two decades, scholars interested in the increased circulation and flows of people, money, and goods emerging from a new global system of production and from increased travel opportunities and electronic mediation have documented and theorized how a variety of practices that span borders and straddle more than one nation-state have come to shape the consciousness, family forms, communities, and daily lives of people on the move around the world.

Much of the early globalization literature was quick to assert the decline of the nation-state, including its role in categorizing populations within this new social field characterized by global flows and deterritorialization of social, cultural, and political forms (Appadurai 1996). Anthropologists interested in international migration intervened in these broader debates by proposing what they called the transnational approach to migration (Glick Schiller et al. 1992, 1995). This approach studied "the process by which immigrants forge and sustain simultaneous multi-stranded social relations that link together their societies of origin and settlement" (1995:48). This intervention spurred a vigorous debate about the kind, density, directionality, durability, and newness of migrants' transnational ties.[6] Initially based mostly on case studies of migration flows and circulation within sociocultural systems between Caribbean islands (e.g., Grasmuck and Pessar 1991; Glick-Schiller et al. 1992), the transnational approach advanced important critiques of earlier U.S. immigration scholarship which had focused on *im*migration as a one-directional movement of cultural and racial outsiders coming in (i.e., "*im*migrants") and on the ensuing processes of assimilation, acculturation, and integration that were supposed to make these newcomers into Americans.[7] These latter studies had failed to account for migrants' agency and for how the social contexts from which migrants' actions also derived meaning might be located outside the United States, often in countries with dense histories of U.S. colonial, imperial, and transnational entanglements that complicated assumptions of a unidirectional process of assimilation. The transnational approach quickly gained traction in migration studies, especially amongst anthropologists and sociologists, but some voiced concern with the approach's *a priori* emphasis on the "national" in the "trans*national*" and the assumption that the national scale was the main frame of identification and reference for people on the move. Such an assumption, scholars argued, overlooked the complexity and meaning of migrants' varied extralocal sociocultural relations, for example within dispersed global family networks (Olwig 2003), "migrant circuits" (Rouse 1991), "transnational communities" (Al-Ali and Koser 2002) or migrants' varied social actions within the context of "transborder" or "translocal" lives (Stephen 2007).[8] Roger Rouse (1995), for example, noted the methodological and epistemological problem of paying too much attention to struggles over collective identities without referencing the related processes by which people are made individual within the multiple constraints of the migration process. This book builds on Rouse's still pertinent critique and uses the case of Andean migration and circulation to establish that there is nothing inherently homogeneous about national categories to begin with—whether "Peruvians," "the Peruvian community abroad," or "Peruvians in the United States"—because people inhabit such categories in radically dissimilar ways. Yet unlike scholars such as Wimmer and Glick Schiller (2002) who criticize the "methodological nationalism"—that is, the persistent assumption that the nation-state is the most central frame for empirical studies of international migration—in migration studies that focus on national origin groups and retain a claim on the centrality of the state (e.g., Waldinger and Fitzgerald 2004), I side with governmentality scholars who focus not so much on the power of the nation-state *per se* as on the limits of its claims to coherence, impartiality, and legibility (Fassin 2011). In doing so, I offer an alternative strategy against methodological nationalism by focusing on the various stratifications that make national identification differentiated, partial, and incomplete in the first place. This is particularly relevant in a country like Peru with its long and persistent legacy of discrimination, racialization, and even criminalization of the mobility of the subaltern.

Over the course of this book, I show that migrants from the Mantaro Valley did not arrive at the U.S. border or port of entry or in U.S. towns and cities with a ready-made "Peruvian identity" in their possession or a coherent "inner self" upon which a secondary "outer self" could be modeled. I demonstrate that the global economy and the migration process itself launch these migrants into complicated and continuous exercises of self and boundary making, through which they continuously attempt to act upon their predicament in order to transform it. These processes of self-definition, identification, boundary drawing, and subject making at play do, of course, not occur unilaterally or in a political vacuum. Numerous scholars from various theoretical orientations have argued that social boundaries and identifications are always coconstructed, relational; and always made against external and hegemonic definitions (Barth 1969; Battaglia 1995; Bourdieu 1989; Jenkins 1996; Nelson 1999), and shaped by historical processes and institutions, including colonialism, religion, the state, and the law (Brubaker and Cooper 2000:14–17). This book, then, offers an analysis of how migrants who act upon a world in movement and through movement construct themselves as social beings while they also simultaneously are being "produced" by larger structures, institutions, processes, and technologies.

My focus on mobility as social and communicative practice and embodied experience invites the analytical approach of practice theory and places this study in dialogue with central concerns in anthropology and social theory. Practice theory, particularly Bourdieu's development of Marcel Mauss's notion of *habitus*, has influenced generations of anthropologists since the 1960s (Ortner 1984).[9] For Bourdieu, the concept of *habitus* links structure and action by making action a result of the embodiment of structure, which can also subsequently re-create structure (1990:53). Habitus is thus acquired through the activities and embodied experiences of everyday life in the form of values, dispositions, and sensibilities. It is important to highlight that social agents, according to Bourdieu, do not operate by making explicit calculations according to economic or other "rational" criteria—something that Bourdieu argued strongly against—but rather according to an implicit practical and bodily logic through which the individual can mobilize various strategies, albeit always within the generative capacities of his or her habitus and the social worlds he or she inhabits. Critics, however, have argued that Bourdieu's framework is too rigid to account for the way in which people's actions upon the world also has the potential to transform the world through action. Social actors, many have noted, do not just mind-lessly reproduce the world without becoming aware of its contradictions and of their own predicament (cf. Comaroff 1985). Ortner has famously argued for the need to add gender, history, and culture to practice theory to make it convincing to anthropologists and to truly turn one's back on the functionalism of an earlier era (2006:16–18).[10]

In this book, I combine a theory of social practice with one of signi-fication through cultural and technological mediation to demonstrate how the transnational mobility of Peruvians is both a social and a signi-fying embodied practice that links the individual to the social collectiv-ity. Jean Comaroff defines a "signifying practice" as "the process through which persons acting upon an external environment construct them-selves as social beings" (1985:6). In contexts of migration, the migrant body is the center of these processes of signification; it is that which is read by others—for example, migration officers, Anglo Americans, and nonmigrant relatives—and that which in the most fundamental sense mediates all action upon the world and simultaneously constitutes new subjectivities within wider webs of social relations, structures, and in-stitutions. Drawing upon this definition and upon recent insights about the technological mediation of social relationships in a broad sense, I demonstrate that migrants over the course of the migration process en-gage in a variety of communicative practices—from using and embody-ing phony documents to calling their children from abroad and from performing "Peruvianness" in U.S. public spaces to circulating videos within their own transnational kin and family networks—to constitute the self in movement and produce the world of social relations within which they operate. For example, I show how visual and oral forms of communication not only extend but also complicate and in their own way expose the inherent tensions and ambiguities of the migrant/trans-national condition of Andean Peruvians.

Broadly understood, then, these communicative practices that use visual, rhetorical, and material resources and cues are central to the way Andean Peruvians over the course of migration—whether temporary or permanent, internal and transnational—become increasingly conscious of their own social positioning within a larger social and racial order and within the multiple social relationships they maintain and create across borders. I show that the larger constraints of the migration process constantly prompt migrants to communicate to others—elite Peruvians, people in migrants' home towns and urban neighborhoods in Peru, U.S. immigration officials, employers, and wider publics—an image of what one is and who one wishes or is expected to be. Such images are necessarily partial; indeed, they deny any facile claims to legibility embedded in normative and ideal-typical representations of who "Peruvians" or "Peruvian migrants" are, yet as mediations that operate across multiple contexts and scales they are centrally shaping how Andean Peruvians construct, experience, and embody their mobility. They are also key to the way migrants reenvision their communities and themselves in a contemporary global and interconnected world.

The challenge for many anthropologists who study transnational and global migration is how to maintain a sense of fluidity and process from the ground up while also acknowledging the heightened role of nation-states and other regimes of power that categorize populations by imposing new forms of governance and control and in turn shape the production and experience of mobility. Using a transnational and multisited approach, this volume explicitly addresses this challenge as it exposes the productive tension between the lives of Andean migrants who through the circulation of images, objects, and embodied performances produce their own mobility, creating partial representations of who they are and wish to become, with accounts of the relevant structures, institutions, and technologies that shape and constrain their efforts. The applicability of the conclusions drawn from this study go beyond the Peruvian and Latin American context and offer a new analytic frame for considering the exasperated relationships between race, mobility, and global formations today. The book's broader question about how personhood gets distributed, questioned, and challenged in contexts of migration exposes how in contemporary societies goods and money may flow relatively unhindered across international borders, but the mobility of men and women of various backgrounds continues to be constrained and coded in ways that have profound consequences in migrants' everyday lives.

The Transgressiveness of Andean Mobility

Peru presents a particularly interesting case for the study of migrant personhood because of the ways in which larger colonial and imperial projects for centuries have informed judgments about Peruvians and their mobile practices. Despite the fact that cities in Latin America have never existed without Indian labor, the "out-of-placeness" of Indians in the urban environment has since the colonial period simultaneously produced the mobility of the Andean indigenous subject and the cultural hybridity emerging from it as fundamentally transgressive. This transgression is embodied in the figure of the cholo itself. Since the early days of the colonial period, indigenous and mestizo migrants settled in Spanish towns and cities where they were registered as *indios criollos* (creole Indians, i.e., cholos) working in urban trades (Graubart 2009) or as *yanaconas* ("helpers" or "dependants") who became essential to the social reproduction of white Spaniard and *criollo* households. However, their presence in urban public spaces was undeniably met with suspicion because they embodied what Abercrombie calls a "pernicious form of debased Indianhood" (1991:114). Historians have reported that colonial authorities complained when Indians adopted Spanish and *mestizo* clothing and hairstyles, attitudes, language, and lifestyle because it made them problematically indistinguishable from their Spanish and mestizo associates (Spalding 1970:647). Such complaints were informed by a broader and predominant view in the colonial society of cities as the natural habitat of the cosmopolitan and world-knowing urban elites, whereas Indians belonged in the mountains unless hidden as invisibilized labor in the kitchens or bedrooms of elite households.

Lack of literacy, formal education, and knowledge of urban lifestyles was understood first by Spaniards and later whitened *criollo* elites, as well as by *indigenista* intellectuals and republican nationalists, as preventing the rural person in the city labeled cholo from successfully acquiring their kind of urban skills and behaving like whitened, privileged city dwellers. The word cholo is said to emerge in this colonial context, according to historian Magnus Mörner, as "an expression of the suspicion that an individual claiming mestizo status was merely an Indian trying to escape his oppressed condition" (Mörner 1985:63).[11] In fact, the Quechua noble Guaman Poma de Ayala already described the figure of the cholo in *El Primer Nueva Crónica y Buen Gobierno,* a 1,200-page chronicle written between 1600 and 1615 for King Philip III of Spain.

The politics of colonial subjugation and its criteria of difference changed the economy of identification within Latin America's new nation-states after independence in 1821. With the emergence of nineteenth-century racial theory, the hierarchy reigning in the urban spheres of the Andean republics was simplified into *blancos* (whites), *mestizos* (mixed race), and *cholos* (i.e., the urban Indian). Abercrombie (1996:95, 96) has shown that the categories of "criollo" and "españoles criollos" ceased to make sense as categories of self-identification in the new Andean republics. He argues that it was now the claim to a superior "whiteness," backed by "scientific" theories of race, which became the postcolonial elites' access point to disproportionate wealth and the power to disenfranchise others on the basis of race.

Modern race making in Peru paralleled a political process of place-making within the new nation-state following evolutionary logics and distributions of power across the national territory. Several scholars have demonstrated that the racialization of geography gave rise to a pervasive image of the existence of "two Perus": one coastal and white/mestizo, which ranked higher in the social order, and the other, Andean and indigenous, which ranked lower (Cueto 1989; De la Cadena 2000:21; Méndez 2011; Orlove 1993, 1998; Poole 1997).[12] This image of the two Perus was widely circulated by Peru's intellectual elites. De la Cadena writes about how José de la Riva Agüero, one of Peru's best known thinkers and one of the few Limeño intellectuals to venture to the highlands in the 1910s, depicted this social, racial, and geographical divide in his travel writings: "The coast has represented innovation, swiftness, joy, and pleasure; the highlands, have symbolized an almost backward conservatism, a seriousness that approaches sadness, a discipline that approximates civility and an endurance leading virtually to torpidness" (Riva Agüero 1995:225, quoted in De la Cadena 2000:21). The spatialization of race across the national territory—along with the attribution of particular forms of racialized affect to inhabitants of the "two Perus"—has provided continued legitimacy to Peru's highly stratified class structure and social and racial order and persistently justified the control, exploitation, and differential classification of members of society into ranks of racial, social, and moral superiority (De la Cadena 2000; Poole 1997; Quijano 2007).[13]

The spatialization of race across the national territory had clear implications for the negative moral coding of the mobility of the Andean Indian within Peru. When Andean peasants migrated to cities and adopted urban lifestyles they were seen as invading urban space and encroaching on the privileges of urban elites. "Indians in cities" and along with them the urban figure of the "cholo" became the key threat to urban elites because of their in betweenness in political, economic, and cultural terms.[14] In order to prevent the invasion of the city produced by "Indian mobility" and preclude the further incursion of the cholo into the social and political domains of the urban lettered elites, rural-urban migration had to be curbed, disciplined, regulated, and contained. The late nineteenth and early twentieth centuries saw numerous public policy initiatives, many phrased in the language of health, hygiene, and public order, aimed at keeping indigenous migrants out of Peru's cities and preventing them from participating as citizens in urban political and social life. In the provinces, the newly fashioned postcolonial and provincial elites, as shown by Fiona Wilson (2004) in the case of Tarma, also attempted to separate the modernizing towns from their prior colonial embeddedness in indigenous customs, by drawing new racial distinctions and social boundaries to effectively reorder urban society and redefine citizenship around constricting notions of whiteness. This included attempts to deny the indigenous guilds the right to process and dance in the center of town and regulate the burial practices of the town's Indians (Wilson 2004:173–76). In Lima, these exclusionary policies continued into the twentieth century and included everything from bans on the construction of affordable housing in the 1930s, making it more difficult for migrant families to settle in the capital, to proposed legislation that directly sought to prohibit people from the provinces from entering the capital and by requiring them to carry an internal passport (De Soto 1986). Progressive social reformers in the early twentieth century were also contemplating how to resolve Peru's "Indian problem" (i.e., how to integrate the indigenous rural population in the national community.) Some advocated for the transformative power of industrialization, as shown by Paulo Drinot (2011), and hoped that industrialization could transform Peru's backward indigenous population into de-Indianized and civilized modern workers. Others highlighted education as central to the modernizing state's project of making Indians into de-Indianized modern subjects (cf. De la Cadena 2000).

But whereas the Indian at the turn of the century across the Andean republics was perceived by political elites as being potential material for improvement and civilization who could be redeemed through education, the real villains of Andean modernity, as Brooke Larson (2005:232) has convincingly argued, remained the provincial mestizo, who was regarded by urban elites as an economic parasite and a political despot, and the urban cholo who was viewed as semi-acculturated, politically volatile, vice-ridden, and socially and sexually transgressive. These long-standing social and racial stereotypes which had a significant impact on the way migrants from the central highlands were perceived when they began arriving in Lima in the early to mid-twentieth century, were revived when Andean Peruvians started to migrate abroad in larger numbers at the end of the twentieth century.

As Peru continues to change, Peruvians of Andean background are carving out important social, economic, and political spaces within and beyond Peruvian society. Some white Limeños now jokingly yet ambiguously proclaim: "We're all cholos now." While such claims are mostly parasitical on the success of the much-touted entrepreneurial cholo as a new neoliberal subject and less a validation of the legacy of rural-to-urban migrants and their new Limeño children (Portocarrero 1993), they do indicate that something is in flux in the Peruvian social order. The entrance of racialized working-class Peruvians into global migration streams in larger numbers has also contributed to fostering an aspirational class mobility among Andean Peruvians who associate their image of "middle-classness" with material capital, global mobility, and a vernacular kind of cosmopolitan lifestyle that combines local cultural forms and social mores with global patterns of mobility. One of the best places to observe these dynamics ethnographically is in the Mantaro Valley whose inhabitants for centuries have been systematically drawn into colonial, regional, and global labor markets and whose contemporary inhabitants in many ways are the "living embodiments" of centuries-long contradictory processes of articulation through mobility and circulation.

Between the Two Perus: The Mantaro Valley of the Central Highlands

The Mantaro Valley in the central highlands of Peru where I conducted most of my fieldwork occupies a particular in-between space in Peru's social and racial geography, which in many ways challenges the typical binary pairs (e.g. coastal/Andean, mestizo/Indian, rural/urban) that historically have characterized the pervasive construction of the "two Perus." Since very early on in the colonial period the Mantaro Valley has been tied into global processes of circulation and exchange, which produced a particular history of *mestizaje*, or racial mixing, that scholars have interpreted as unique to the area (Arguedas 1953, 1975; Romero 2001, 2004). This history, along with the irreversible wave of "modernization" that hit the valley in the early twentieth century, has fundamentally shaped the views on mobility in this area and created particular conditions for the production of mobile subjectivities. This regional variability is important to consider when discussing what is specific about Andean transnational migration vis-à-vis other transnational migration flows and processes. In contrast to theories of transnationalism that posit similar conditions shaping migrant exchanges regardless of local cultural context and specific historical and materialist contexts, I propose that the particular history of exchange and circulation in which the Mantaro region is articulated continues to shape people's outlook on transnational migration and mobility today.

The Mantaro Valley is located in the Department of Junín, east of the Central Cordillera of the Andes, and is split in two by the Mantaro River, which runs northwest–southeast between the cities of Jauja and Huancayo—the former, once the first capital of Peru and now a quiet provincial town, and the latter the largest and most important city in the area with a bustling commercial center, several universities, and a total population of 357,279 (INEI 2013). The city of Huancayo has grown exponentially since the 1980s with the arrival of internal migrants displaced by the violent conflict from their communities in the nearby departments of Huancavelica and Ayacucho and also from the more distant departments of Huánuco and Apurimac (Tamagno 1998). Huancayo is also the center of gravity for the inhabitants of the valley's sixty-four rural districts on the plains surrounding the river and in the

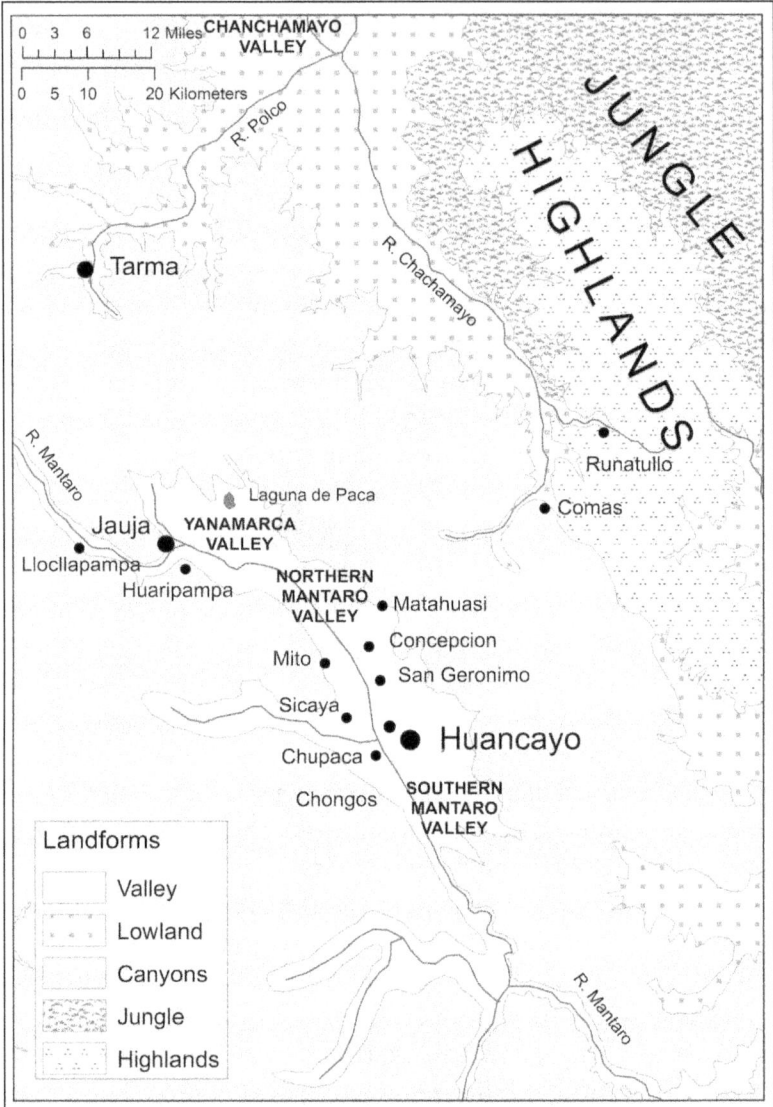

Figure I.2. Map of the Central Highlands. (Map by Brenda D. Allen)

highlands surrounding the actual valley who often frequent the city's markets, schools, and government offices.

The intense circulation of people, goods, and cultural forms and an accelerated process of mestizaje have shaped this area of the Peruvian highlands over many centuries and made it a unique region within Peru which, in a way that is atypical compared to the other regions in the country, combines strong integration into the global economy with a dedicated effort at cultural distinction from the national society. The Peruvian novelist, poet, and anthropologist José Maria Arguedas always highlighted the Mantaro Valley in his essays for its high degree of economic and cultural independence with regard to the dominant culture of national elites. When Arguedas arrived in Huancayo in 1928, he described the city as a typical mestizo town but where any Indian could be integrated "because the city offers prospects for all, without requiring anyone to surrender their gods for admission to its premises" (Arguedas 1975:139).

Yet in the Peruvian Andes, as elsewhere in Latin America (cf. Nelson 1999), it is impossible to distinguish between "Indians" and "mestizos" in any meaningful way because of the very nature of the colonial process itself. In an attempt to undo the common view of a presumptive unidirectional historical process which made the Indians into mestizos, Marisol de la Cadena (2005) has masterfully argued that the term mestizo itself is "doubly hybrid." Eighteenth- and nineteenth-century racial taxonomies, she argues, defined "mestizos" as nonindigenous individuals as the result of biological or cultural mixture and in this sense made the mestizo "empirically hybrid." But she also shows that the mestizo category since early on in the colonial period denoted transgression of the rule of faith and its statuses of purity, which produced a different kind of hybridity, one in which indigeneity could be retained. This historical complexity makes the mestizo a "doubly" hybrid category—one which, according to De la Cadena, reveals several subordinate options for mestizo subject positions, including various forms of indigeneity (2005:263–264). Romero (2004:33) has argued that rather than binary racial categories of Indians and whites, it was economic stratification coupled with the area's particular history of *mestizaje* that became the most important criteria for social distinction in the twentieth century. This point is corroborated by the anthropological scholarship on the many festivals, musical traditions, dances, and indigenous rituals in the area that show that the mestizos of the valley have continued to practice and deliberately cultivate a strong regional cultural identity—in Huancayo, frequently glossed as "la identidad wanka"—which in turn has bolstered the area's strong sense of Andean cultural autonomy vis-à-vis the national criollo society (Arguedas 1953; Romero 2001; Vilcapoma 1995). This "reinvented" and inherently modern cultural identity, as also noted by Romero (2004:44–47), is a source of pride for many inhabitants in the valley and, indeed, I saw many of these cultural practices and religious symbols mobilized by Mantaro Valley migrants abroad. Yet I am here less concerned with the reproduction of any preexisting identity or cultural form as with the ongoing processes through which mobility is embodied, experienced, and imbued with meaning by Mantaro Valley residents.

Residents of the Mantaro Valley have been migrating since the turn of the twentieth century. Wealthier peasants typically migrated to Lima and cultivated strong social and economic networks in the capital, some settling in the capital on a more permanent basis. Peasants from less well-off families went to the nearby mining areas or to the coast, but their migration was seldom a unidirectional movement toward permanent and irreversible settlement on the coast. Many retained their family homes and small land holdings in the area. Scholars have contended that such patterns of mobility allowed the peasants in this area to resist proletarization as miners. Instead they used their migration earnings to fuel the local fiesta circuit and economy (Bonilla 1974; Long and Roberts 1978; Mallon 1983; Romero 2001). This tendency is repeated in contemporary transnational migration; however, here the duration of migration trips is much longer and return to the home community is seldom permanent.

The escalating political violence and the restructuring of the Peruvian economy in the 1980s and 1990s prompted not just Mantaro Valley residents to migrate abroad; indeed, many nonelite Andean Peruvians who were not part of the small segment of Peruvian society standing to benefit from neoliberal economic reforms and the state's repressive counterinsurgency strategy increasingly opted to extend their livelihood beyond Peru's borders. From the 1990s and onward, transnational migration became a key strategy for people from the Mantaro Valley to circumvent the barriers against social and class mobility in Peru and to act upon their desire for transnational mobility and modernity still largely denied to them within Peru today. Many chose the United States as their most desired destination. It is with this history of striving for outward and upward mobility—and the emergence of new Andean subjectivities within it—that I am primarily concerned here.

Despite Mantaro Valley residents' self-image as modern, industrious, and culturally autonomous within Peru, when migrating to the United States they are instantly perceived through the images and dominant prototypes through which the majority of Latinos are typically racialized in the United States. How working-class and indigenous Latin American migrants are perceived and racialized under U.S. nativism as part of the larger anti-immigration and anti-Latino narrative—what Leo Chávez has called "the Latino Threat" (2008)—is in many ways homologous to the way indigenous and mestizo migrants of rural origins historically have been perceived in Latin American urban life and still are today, as much for the identities they have not fully realized as for those they have failed to leave behind. Thus, along with the migration of actual bodies, this book also examines the transnational circulation of such dominant tropes of urban life and their complicity in shaping the way migrants both embody mobility and negotiate race, class, and gendered subjectivities in national and transnational contexts.

Peruvian Migrants in the U.S. Racial Economy

Peruvians and other South American migrants have until recently received little attention in the scholarship on migration to the United States and in studies of U.S. Latinos. Oboler (2005a) has suggested that their numerical and political presence has not been deemed significant enough to merit more serious scholarly attention in comparison to other geopolitically more "important" migrant groups such as Cubans, Mexicans, and Central Americans of various national origins who have been widely studied in the literature on U.S.-bound migration (cf. Boehm 2012; Coutin 2007; Dreby 2010; García 2006; Massey et al. 2003; R. C. Smith 2005; Stephen 2007). Moreover, as Oboler also notes (2005a), since South Americans until the 1990s were largely either elite or middle-class skilled professionals and, in Elsa Chaney's words, "aliens by choice" (1976), they had largely remained under the radar in U.S. academic discussions about Latinos, Latinismo, and Latinidad, either because they had inserted themselves as "honorary whites" into mainstream U.S. society, facilitated by their education and class status, or because they experienced their own migration as a temporary period in a longer life trajectory, which would end with a return to the homeland (cf. Pellegrino 2003). This return may or may not have happened, but the idea of it shaped these earlier migrants' politics of identification in the United States.[15]

According to official 2100 U.S. census data, there are 556,000 Hispanics of Peruvian origin residing in the United States, making Peruvians the 11th largest Hispanic group in the country accounting for 1.1% of the Hispanic population (the Hispanic population overall in the U.S. is 51.9 million, or 16.5% of the total U.S. population) (Pew Hispanic Center 2013).[16] In comparison, the Peruvian government and the International Organization of Migration (IOM) estimated in 2010 that 939,855 Peruvians were living in the United States that year and that roughly 50% of them were likely to have irregular migratory statuses (INEI, DIGEMIN, and IOM 2010).[17] The majority of Peruvians in the U.S. is foreign-born (ca. two-thirds) and arrived in the U.S. in 1990 or later. Indeed, in recent years, Peru, with Colombia and Ecuador, has become one of the three major migrant-sending nations from South America to the United States (Tienda and Sánchez 2013).

This changing demographic landscape has also shifted the politics of identification among Peruvians abroad as more and more working-class and indigenous Peruvians are now migrating to the United States, and to a greater extent than prior cohorts of migrants are being subjected to racialization as Latinos in the United States. Omi and Winant (1994) first proposed the concept of racialization to grasp the way that racial identity gets assigned and assumed by people in the context of everyday experience, especially in societies like the United States where race in very fundamental ways structures both the state and everyday life in communities. Adding to this discussion, sociologist Eduardo Bonilla-Silva (1997) notes that although the perspective of Omi and Winant represented a major breakthrough in theorizing about race, it does not sufficiently regard race as "social collectivities." Bonilla-Silva proposes in turn the more general concept of "racialized social systems," which he uses to refer to societies in which "economic, political, social, and ideological levels are partially structured by the placement of actors in racial categories or races" (Bonilla-Silva 1997:469). Following Bonilla, when migrants arrive in the United States they are placed in such racial categories, which in turn have consequences for how they fare in the country. Race is of course not the only structural factor that conditions migrants' possibilities of reinventing themselves in new settings and other scholars have shown that gender, class, sexuality, and illegality are equally important to consider when looking at the factors that constrain Latin American migrant experiences (Abrego 2014; Boehm 2012; Decena 2011; Vasquez del Aguila 2013). Although recognizing that race is produced at the intersection of other systems of power, we cannot disregard its fundamental importance given that so many migrants in the United States today live as racialized and undocumented workers whose self-definition strategies are limited in multiple ways by labor exploitation, discrimination, institutionalized racism, and contradictory immigration policies (De Genova 2005; Ramos-Zayas 2012; Durand and Massey 2003; Chávez 2008).

This book also demonstrates that the migration process itself complicates racialization processes as migrants move between and are located within several national and racial projects. The entrance of working-class and indigenous Latin Americans into a global labor market has produced a new and aspirational cosmopolitanism and a homogenization of the image of "middle class" among these populations, associated with material capital (cf. Werbner 2008). Within this larger global context, racialization necessarily gets redefined, and this requires a more dynamic structural perspective on race because mobility is constitutive of how individuals assume race and how they are accommodated—socially and racially—as they cross boundaries and social worlds. Racialization processes that are seen as generated solely from one "national context" are therefore inadequate because migrants' actions—the way they imagine themselves and others—often derive meaning from multiple social and historical contexts, some of which are located outside the United States, in the home country. Indeed, the discussions presented in this book highlight the fact that the intersection between racial formations in Peru and the subject positions that are produced through migration and transnational practices prompt racialized Peruvians in the United States to "become Peruvian" in ways that they could not have been prior to migration because of entrenched racism and enduring class bias.

Peruvian migration to the United States was first studied anthropologically by Teófilo Altamirano (1988, 1990), who in two volumes described the social, cultural, and psychological dynamics of Peruvian migrants to the country via the communities and migrant organizations they formed there in the 1980s. More recently, Paerregaard (2008) has tracked the global dispersion of Peruvians, including to the United States, where he examines the tensions between migrants' transnational links and the structures of opportunity they encounter in their destination countries. Studies based on larger scale demographic survey data studies, such as Princeton University's Latin American Migration Project (LAMP), have offered demographic profiles highlighting different aspects of the changing nature of Peruvian emigration (Durand 2010; Massey and Capoferro 2006; Takenaka and Pren 2010). Jorge Durand, for example, has concluded that Peruvian migration is composed of older and better educated individuals than is typical of comparable international migrations, that it tends to involve a wider variety of destinations, and that it has evolved into a multiclass phenomenon over the past decades as a result of Peru's overlapping economic and political crisis of the 1980s (2010:25–26). Durand also suggests that the highly urban composition reported in the available studies reflects that most of them are based on surveys and fieldwork in Lima and that these findings are still to be corroborated by studies from other regions of Peru.

This book offers an ethnographic study of a migrant-sending region in the central highlands and also draws on research with migrants who left that area between the late 1980s and around 2005 to seek work and opportunities in the United States.[18] While migrants from the central highlands can be found in many communities across the United States, this volume draws on research with migrants from the Mantaro Valley in Paterson, New Jersey, Miami, Florida, and the Washington, D.C./Maryland area. These sites were originally chosen as U.S. field sites because they reflect the different moments and conditions of departure as well as the way in which Peru's class structure is reproduced, distributed, and mapped onto particular U.S. urban and suburban spaces.[19]

Peruvians started to arrive in Paterson in the 1950s and 1960s, when a moderate number of migrants from Lima's working-class neighborhoods came to New Jersey to work in the textile industry (Altamirano 1990). Like most Americans at the time, Peruvians who arrived at Paterson in the early 1960s believed that the United States was standing at the dawn of a golden age. Work was still plentiful in Paterson's factories and by mid-decade the immigration reforms of 1965 further favored Latin American migration. Postwar-era deindustrialization and rising unemployment in the 1970s and 1980s gave rise to common urban problems like poverty, crime, racial tension, and white flight and the earlier generations of immigrants (mostly white ethnics, but also some Peruvians) started leaving the city and moving to the surrounding suburbs and more affluent towns. [20] Peruvians in New Jersey today live in many different towns, although the largest number continue to live in Paterson. Miami also became a preferred destination for Peruvian exile elites who fled the left-wing military dictatorship of General Juan Velasco Alvarado (1968–75) and his successor Francisco Morales Bermudez (1975–1980); they settled in the affluent areas of Key Biscayne and Coral Gables, among other places.[21]

These early migration streams of both elite and working-class urban migrants were later followed by large numbers of middle-class Peruvians, also urban, who fled the economic crisis and political violence in Peru of the 1980s and 1990s. Sarah Mahler, for example, has noted that the South Americans she encountered on Long Island in the late 1980s (many of them Peruvians) were better off economically, more educated, and overwhelmingly urban when compared to the Central Americans in her study (1995:23). When observing a Spanish-language mass at a Catholic church, Mahler noted that, in contrast to the Central Americans, the South Americans would enter and sit at the front of the sanctuary; they were "conspicuous" and "dressed for success" (Mahler 1995:15,17).[22] Yet many middle-class Peruvians experienced downward mobility upon their arrival. Elena Sabogal (2005) has shown that Peruvian middle-class professionals who migrated to Miami in the 1990s, many without legal status, language skills, or employment sponsorship, experienced a great deal of anxiety and worked hard to reconcile their downward social mobility with their professional backgrounds and personal aspirations.

Lower-class and indigenous migration from the Mantaro Valley and other parts of the central and southern highlands of Peru to Washington, D.C., and its environs took place starting in the late 1960s and 1970s and unfolded in two phases. The first was facilitated by changes in U.S. immigration law after 1965, when women from the central and southern highlands of Peru—all with prior migration experience as *empleadas domesticas*, or domestic workers, in Lima—came to Maryland and the District of Columbia to work as housekeepers and child care providers in the homes of Washington, D.C.'s diplomatic and professional families (Gelles 2005).[23] When the political violence in Peru escalated toward the end of the 1980s, the second phase of migration took place, comprised of male relatives (sons, husbands, and siblings) traveling with help from their female precursors.[24] Many of these male relatives did not qualify for family reunification, as their female relatives had often overstayed their employment visas and had also not met the cut-off date for the 1986 Immigration Reform and Control Act (IRCA), the last amnesty to see the light of day in recent U.S. immigration history. Instead they traveled via unauthorized routes, often assisted by migration professionals. But in contrast to Mexican and Central American labor migrants, Peruvians cannot simply pay a coyote or human smuggler to walk or drive them across an adjacent border at a relatively moderate (though rising) cost (Spener 2009). Instead, they must pay astronomical amounts to access the "services" of increasingly expensive and specialized migration professionals in Lima to reach their faraway destinations by a combination of air and overland routes. Those who successfully "pass" the heightened scrutiny of background checks and immigration checkpoints are still likely to end up without permanent legal status in low-paid entry-level service-sector jobs at the bottom of the U.S. labor market.

While this book relies partly on fieldwork among Peruvian migrants I encountered in these U.S. cities and suburbs, who happen to embody multiple and heterogeneous experiences, it is not a conventional immigration study about "Peruvians in the United States" from the perspective of the receiving society. Rather, the story it tells is about transnational circulation and the notions of person and self operating in the social and temporal space that spans the Peruvian highlands, Lima, various U.S. cities and suburbs, and the transit spaces that migrants inhabit in between. The experiences abroad of Andean Peruvians who migrated to the United States in the 1990s and 2000s constitute an important aspect of this book, but it is only one aspect of the story of circulation I wish to tell. Equally important is the unsettling friction produced by Andean migrants' presence and practices when they return to Peru as "Americanized cholos" displaying a particular kind of transnational and cosmopolitan sensibility, or when intervening in local and national affairs from abroad. By returning the analytical gaze to Peru at the end of the book, I want to remind the reader of the perseverance of the ethnic, racial, class, and gender hierarchies that condition nonelite Andean migrants' access to transnational mobility in the first place, but also of the transformative power of migrant practices which refract and make untenable the forms of personhood historically accorded to Andean migrants within Peru's traditional race and class hierarchies.

Ambulant Ethnography

This project was originally inspired by George Marcus's conceptualizations of multisited ethnography (1995) and is profoundly influenced by his invitation to methodological innovation for fieldwork in global and transnational settings.[25] Yet the project's multisitedness did not emerge as an attempt at methodological virtue *per se*; rather, it was the empirical realities of the subjects' lives that motivated the choice of various ethnographic sites and made the project "multisited."

The scope of this project and its geographical dispersion involved me being constantly on the move and in a transient state, whether on board one of the Peruvian-owned *combis* shuttling between New York's Penn Station and downtown Paterson, or descending from the Andes on the night bus from Huancayo to Lima accompanying informants on their way to fix paperwork for an upcoming trip (*tramitar papeles*), pick up remittances or *encomiendas* from a migrant relative, do business errands, or visit family. I call this fieldwork modality "ambulant ethnography." I use the term ambulant here not just to indicate a mode of fieldwork based on tracking the movement of people and objects through space, which is what Marcus suggested when he proposed to "follow the people" (1995:106), but also in specific reference to the Spanish noun *ambulante* (from the Latin *ambulare*, i.e., "walking"), which in Peru means a street vendor, often a migrant woman of Andean origins who peddles goods on the streets or at the market. The *ambulante* is the epitome of a mobile, malleable, boundary transgressing, and highly agentive character who must adapt to the rhythm of urban life, to traveling far, and to the ever-present possibility of uncertain payoff. So too is the work of the ambulant ethnographer, whose sensibilities are oriented toward situating agency in the multiple spatial and temporal contexts in which people move, dwell, or fashion themselves; while not all these contexts involve the crossing of national borders, they are all firmly situated in the larger framework of political and racial economies and regimes of mobility.[26]

Ambulant ethnography is grounded in an anthropological perspective on migration and mobility that sees migration as social practice and as a profoundly generative process for other social forms and categories, including self and personhood. I use the term mobility to indicate that migration as experience and embodied social practice is centrally imbued with meaning and power. Here, I build on the work of Tim Cresswell (2006), who surveys how mobility in the Western world is historically variable and grounded in particular contexts and calls upon scholars to be aware of how mobility may be shaped by either "sedentarist" or "nomadic" metaphysics that code mobility—and by extension mobile subjects—in particular ways (2006:38). Yet I also side with scholars who critique the facile and celebratory view of "new mobilities studies," including the assumed newness frequently ascribed to such mobilities. Glick Schiller and Salazar (2013), for example, indicate that current conceptions that conflate and normalize various forms of movement into one single category (see, for example, Urry 2007) are inadequate for understanding the particular complexities of human migration and the regimes of mobility that shape them. Others have argued that despite the heightened currency of "mobility," "movement," and "flow" which have become ever more popular in academic discourse and relevant in the world at large to describe the conditions of life under late capitalism, such "mobilities" and "flows" should not be taken as an indication, as this study also confirms, that the ontological status of places and of belonging in people's experience of their own mobility is in any way diminishing (Rockefeller 2010, 2011).

Ambulant ethnography thus seeks to provide ethnographic descriptions of the social, performative, and communicative practice that positions and connects migrants and their nonmigrating family members in relation to specific places, nationalist projects, border crossings, and within larger political and racial economies. In doing so, this mode of fieldwork considers how the meanings, experiences, and imaginaries of transnational migration and mobility are deeply intertwined with long-standing forms of *immobility* (Salazar and Smart 2011), based on racial and class hierarchies. Focusing on my interlocutors' own perceptions of who they are or would like to be and how they seek to belong in a world of movement and stasis has allowed me to understand their migration trajectories as part of a larger aspirational project that spans extensive time-spaces and generates new forms of subjectivity, but which is never inseparable from the persistent image of the rural indio or the urban cholo as quintessential anticosmopolitan subjects. I am not trying to claim that my ethnographic interlocutors understood their own self-fashioning strategies in the same way I did or even that they used the same terms to describe their actions and identifications. People often tell stories about themselves that may not be congruent with the also partial story that the anthropologist attempts to tell and so it is our role—indeed the staple of our discipline—to situate these narratives through the complex exercise of ethnographic contextualization.

A project of this nature required a polyfocal research strategy. I used a combination of methods including participant observation, ethnographic interviews, life histories, narrative analysis, social network analysis, photo and video elicitation, analysis of media objects and texts, and field notes constructed from memory to address the various and contradictory processes of articulation of which the inhabitants of the Mantaro Valley are "living embodiments" (Comaroff 1985:2). This included generating material about the experience and meaning of transnational migration and its links to ideas and histories of mobility in highland Peru; the role of various structures, institutions, and technologies in the migration process which shape migrant agency and link it to wider social, racial, and politicoeconomic contexts and regimes of mobility; and finally, the moral economy of transnational socialities including migrants' and nonmigrating family and community members' perceptions and management of long-distance social relations. Whenever possible I collected exemplary media objects and texts exchanged between migrants abroad and family members in Peru. These included photographs, videos, some older audiocassettes, letters, and some email correspondence. Analyzing these materials, along with listening in and taking notes on "presentations of self" (Goffman [1955] 2005, 1959; Bauman and Briggs 1990) through phone conversations, web chats, face-to-face visits, gift exchanges, and other mediated practices, allowed me to understand how participants in all sites strove to extend themselves through objects, technologies, and embodied skills to signal who they are as members of transnational families and communities and how they belong.

Needless to say, the challenging task of holding in juxtaposition the numerous sites so that a coherent overall argument could emerge, at times required acrobatic exercises of ethnographic contextualization, in addition to the intense multitasking needed over the course of the fieldwork period. The methodological challenges I faced are similar to those described by other anthropologists working with migrants in transnational settings (Coutin 2007; Zilberg 2011) or in what Karen Fog Olwig (2003) has termed "extended fieldsites." Indeed, the fantasy of fieldwork as a total immersion in a relatively bounded collectivity or in social relationships which are circumscribed to one locality is no longer feasible to entertain when researching transnationally mobile subjects whose lives are articulated and become meaningful within territorially dispersed and often highly fragmented social networks and through ephemeral and mediated forms of social and cultural belonging.

The question of how we are to immerse ourselves in social relations that are not contained within one or just a few localities, and are also often experienced either through their absence or through various forms of technological mediation, is less straightforward. The real challenge with multisited fieldwork is that due to the practical challenges of managing multiple sites we often have less time and fewer opportunities to "get to know" people, access their existential fields of experience, and understand their social dynamics in each site and through different media. Hence our ability to observe how people are constructing themselves in relation to others and the connections between their various narratives and the spaces they inhabit is somewhat limited (cf. Miller and Slater 2000). I am *not* claiming here that anthropologists at any point have been able to access the total fields of experiences of our informants, but rather that this task has become more complex as research sites become more dispersed and global forces harder to pin down ethnographically in terms of their concrete material and affective manifestations (although see Mintz 1998, who contends that the notion that transnationalism is a qualitatively different global phenomenon with implications for fieldwork is exaggerated). Consequently, anthropologists today who work with dispersed populations must rely methodologically a great deal more on the "media trails" from a variety of social media platforms that research subjects produce about their social lives and relations. These can yield important information about the strategies of self-fashioning that they employ.

The Anthropologist on the Move

A transnationally mobile, educated, and light-skinned European woman, I entered this fieldwork project from a very different vantage point and social positioning than the majority of my Peruvian interlocutors, and my own migration history, subjectivity, fieldwork trajectory, and multiple place attachments have shaped in important ways both my research practice and the conclusions I have reached. My Danish nationality and my claims to a privileged transnational mobility and cosmopolitan subjectivity were rarely questioned by the institutions and social groups monitoring it—in Peru, the United States, and the transit spaces in between—and my interlocutors in the central highlands of Peru perceived me at best with some ambiguity partly (from what I could judge) as a result of our vastly different class, racial, gendered, and institutional positionalities and the normative projects that shape them.

When I did my first fieldwork in the central highlands in the late 1990s, I was enrolled as an exchange student at La Pontificia Universidad Católica del Perú, then one of Lima's most expensive and exclusive universities.[27] La Católica is widely known across the country and any association with it almost immediately evokes the symbolic, social, and financial capital that characterize national elites in Peru. Yet my informants in the Mantaro Valley quickly noticed, as did my peers at the University in Lima, that I lacked coherence in my social and cultural comportment that would let me fit into the social categories that they each had available for me. My affiliation with marginal urban art scenes in Lima and my temporary residence in a boyfriend's family home in Matute (a low-income neighborhood in the district of La Victoria) left my academic and university acquaintances perplexed, at best a little amused, and some had the urge to reprimand and discipline me. Most middle- and upper-class Limeños associated Matute with petty criminals, assaults, and prostitution and would only go there to buy drugs or attend a game at the soccer stadium of Alianza Lima. While I never did any actual fieldwork in Matute and had no intention of using my affiliation with this neighborhood to fashion myself as a street-savvy urban ethnographer, my experiences there did help me to understand a great deal not just about what it meant to transgress social and class boundaries in Peru, but also about the privileges of whiteness operating in the Peruvian context. Ultimately, it was my position as an outsider to the Peruvian social and racial order that gave me the creative license and privileged positionality to transgress social boundaries without facing any major consequences.

In the Mantaro Valley, the presence of foreign students, researchers, NGO workers, and mining engineers was not at all uncommon at the time. My anthropological fascination with provincial ways of life, the migration trajectories of people from the area, and my fluency in Spanish yet lack of Limeño affect and symbolic capital, made me a perhaps less threatening interlocutor for provincial Peruvians who longed for the validation of their mobile projects and aspirations so often denied them within Peru's dominant social order. Still, through their mobility and performative self-fashioning, my informants constantly transgressed and subverted whatever categories I mobilized in my own attempt to understand their experiences and self-positioning to the point where I was always uneasy about what to finally call them in my ethnographic representations. Eventually, I chose to use the term "migrant," but occasionally I also use class- and place-based categories such as "nonelite Andean Peruvians," "Mantaro Valley residents," or, when referring to people from particular localities, terms such as Urcumarquinos, Matahuasinos, or Huancaínos. Well aware of its pejorative connotations, I use the term cholo to evoke the urban imaginary of invasion of the city by the common Indian and to indicate the profound uneasiness that urban elites historically have felt and continue to feel about the mobility of the subaltern.

When starting the research in the U.S. locations in 2004–05 my prior knowledge of the Peruvian context became both an asset and a menace, probably a general condition of research in transnational settings. When I readily participated in Urcumarquino festivities in Maryland, dressed as a Jaujina (a woman from Jauja) for the traditional *corta monte* dance which I had learned to dance in the valley, my Urcumarquino friends were generally pleased and took my gesture as an act of recognition not just of their "culture," but also of them as people. This in turn granted me some social legitimacy and recognition as a culturally competent subject, especially among rural migrants in Maryland and Washington, D.C. But my familiarity with particular transnational family networks or with particular persons' premigration life trajectories was also occasionally perceived with suspicion and unease, especially by migrants who were trying hard to start over, leave their rural Peruvian pasts behind, and produce themselves as "Americans" and as modern metropolitan subjects; it was almost as if they imagined that I would hold them accountable to their premigration selves and social obligations. Of course it was not my intention to "out" anyone from their claims to particular social identities and belongings, but such incidents served as a reminder of how the transnational circulation of people, information, and images has made social consciousness span various borders and social contexts; a reflexivity that many scholars attribute to modernity itself.

A Road Map

The book is divided into three parts which together illustrate the ways in which Andean migrants strive to become transnationally mobile and how they come to realize and reenvision themselves and their communities in the process. Part I, titled "Cosmopolitan Desires," focuses on the histories and current practices of mobility through which inhabitants of the central Andes of Peru imagine and produce themselves as mobile and cosmopolitan subjects even as they chart unauthorized and unconventional pathways to transnational mobility. Chapter 1 offers an overview of the Mantaro region's historic articulation with global markets and cosmopolitan ways of life, which produced various social and technological infrastructures that precede the more recent transnational circulation of labor migrants from this area and shaped valley inhabitants' experience and imaginings of modernity and transnational mobility in important ways. To illustrate how present-day transnational migration operates within this broader history of Andean modernity, circulation, mobility, and travel, I discuss the migration stories of two young women from different towns in the valley: Inés from Matahuasi and Domitila from Urcumarca. By examining these two stories I demonstrate that transnational mobility is variously imagined, experienced, practiced, and corporealized in contemporary Peru, but that it is never inseparable from long-standing moral and cultural imperatives about class mobility exemplified in expressions such as "getting ahead" (*salir adelante*) and "improving oneself" (*superarse*).

Despite the aspirations of many valley residents to travel abroad, transnational mobility in the post-9/11 era is not a resource all Peruvians can access equally. Migrants of provincial and lower-class backgrounds must often extend themselves through objects, technologies, and embodied skills to realize their migration projects and they do so with guidance and professional help from *tramitadores* (document fixers) and other service providers in Peru's growing and extremely profitable migration industry. Chapter 2 examines how aspiring migrants navigate the world of document fixers, loan sharks, travel agents, lawyers, notaries, and state bureaucrats, including consular staff and U.S. immigration officials, in preparation for international migration. As I detail these practices, interactions, and relationships, I also provide accounts of the institutions, technologies, social and cultural forms, and relationships that shape and constrain migrants' efforts. The chapter also discusses the complex politics of race and class that undergird the historically unequal access to mobility in Peru and in turn intersects with U.S. racialization of Latin American migrants that begins with their first encounters with U.S. consular staff in Lima.

The efforts of my informants to produce themselves in response to the demands of the migration process did not end once they had left Peru and arrived in the United States. Part II, titled "Transnational Socialities" focuses on the ongoing strivings of Peruvian migrants abroad to remain emotionally connected and relevant in the everyday lives of their families in Peru and socially visible in the communities they left behind. I examine the affective and moral economy that shapes migrants' gendered and racial social positioning within the context of transnational families and communities. Upon arrival in the United States most novice migrants were constantly preoccupied with maintaining the social bonds of kinship with family and relatives left behind. They did this via long-distance communication, remitting small amounts of money from their meager entry-level salaries in the U.S. service economy, and by circulating a variety of material and media objects. Chapter 3 examines how U.S.-based migrants forge affective ties with children, caregivers, and other dependents in the Mantaro Valley and in Lima through transnational communication. I evoke the concept of "remote sensing" and expand the standard technical and geographical definition of this term to name the attempts particularly of migrant parents to "feel" and "know" their children's lives and whereabouts from afar. This communicative, sensory, and mediated practice regularly played out against dominant social norms that cast migrants abroad in a favorable light back home as caring mothers, responsible fathers, dutiful daughters, and reliable and dependable "hijos ausentes," that is, the absent sons and daughters of their rural communities of origin. I contend that "remote sensing," in the context of the prolonged separation caused by migration, amplifies rather than ameliorates the social and emotional struggles of transnational families, because participants are often not able to perform according to the roles assigned them by gendered and intergenerational normative frameworks. The chapter ultimately shows how long-distance communication, as a form of social, cultural, and affective practice, is fraught with tension, uncertainty, and power inequalities.

Chapter 4 extends this inquiry into the realm of the visual by analyzing the circulation of three genres of "migrant videos" within one transnational migrant circuit. By examining questions of accountability and power in the cross-contextual circulation of image-objects and by highlighting the role of these mediated images in the making of self and community, I show how video production, consumption, and circulation figure centrally in migrants' staging of their own social visibility as "worldly" and "cosmopolitan" ex-*campesinos* in a larger "visual economy" (Poole 1997). Participants in my study were highly invested in monitoring, selecting, and negotiating the criteria by which images of migrant life abroad could be shared with those back in Peru and what in turn had to be made invisible and left out of circulation to avoid rumors, tensions, and accusations within transnational families or larger collectivities of fellow migrants and *paisanos*. The chapter offers an analysis of situations where particular image-objects escape intended networks of circulation and move beyond specific audiences, giving rise to "visual evidence" that feeds into and exposes particular rumors and secrets, which in turn may complicate migrants' efforts of self-fashioning. I show that such revelations have implications for the production of social cohesion within transnational migrant collectivities, and that they ultimately highlight circulating image-objects as a new form of social control and surveillance.

Part III, "Discrepant Publics," grapples with the tensions surrounding how migrants abroad make claims to membership, rights, and belonging from the realm of the intimate and familial to the ways in which they situate themselves and are situated by others as subjects worthy of citizenship, belonging, and social and cultural recognition within larger nationalist and racial projects and public spheres. Specifically, this last part shows that both home communities and the country of origin remain important contexts for the validation of migrants' projects of mobility. The two chapters in this section look at how Andean Peruvians both in Peru and in the United States inhabit the public sphere through attempts to situate themselves within ongoing national and racial projects of both countries. Just as when they first arrived in the capital Lima from the Peruvian highlands, Andean migrants in the United States must after years or even decades of living there still justify their migration projects, their presence in particular urban and suburban spaces, and the fact that they are worthy of citizenship and belonging within a larger transnational political and racial economy.

Chapter 5 exposes these issues by examining the yearly "Peruvian Parade" in Paterson, New Jersey. A large-scale public spectacle commemorating Peru's Independence Day (*Fiestas Patrias*), though in the standard U.S. format of ethnic parades, this yearly event is a key site for the ongoing resignifiability of "Peruvianness" in the United States. By analyzing issues regarding the parade's social organization, sponsorship, framing, and wider context, the chapter explores the way this public spectacle not only mediates links between subjectivity and nations (Peru and the United States), but also works to present an image of Peruvians as decent, worthy, and hardworking "immigrants" in the context of a larger post-9/11 political and racial economy in which some groups figure as more deserving of U.S. citizenship and recognition than others.

Chapter 6 approaches the issue of citizenship, membership, and belonging from a different angle. It takes as its point of departure a violent incident in the town of Urcumarca, to discuss how Urcumarquino migrants in Maryland and Washington, D.C., who historically have not enjoyed full citizenship in Peru, seek to reposition themselves as citizens from abroad within the larger neoliberal project of the Peruvian labor-exporting state.[28] In recent years, the Peruvian state has sought to incorporate its emigrant population into a redefined national imaginary that extends beyond Peru's borders. Yet not all Peruvians are heralded as "national heroes" and as valuable and productive citizens of what government officials call El Quinto Suyo ("the fifth region"), in reference to the Quechua term for the Inca Empire *Tawantinsuyu*, meaning "the four regions." But whereas transnational mobility for some has become a virtue, for others it remains a liability. The last chapter highlights how state officials' glamorization of a generic category of "Peruvians abroad" works to efface the actual and continued effects of profound social and racial inequalities that affect contemporary Peru as well as the mobility of its Andean population.

The Conclusion considers the general implications of this book for mobile populations worldwide and shows that the insights generated from this case study speak beyond the Peruvian-U.S. divide. I also ponder the possible future scenarios of migration in the Peruvian context. In this regard it is not unimportant that the bulk of the research conducted for this book was done before the global financial crisis, at a time when outward migration from Peru was still escalating. In recent years, as Peru has become one of the world's star economies and Latin America's posterchild of allegedly successful neoliberal economic development with an expanding urban middle class, researchers and state officials have been quick to announce the return of Peruvians and the end of massive out-migration as we saw it during the 1990s and early 2000s.[29] This book cautions against making quick assumptions about what Peru's economic boom might mean for migration flows long-term. To the eyes of this researcher laboring people from the Andes will continue to go abroad in significant numbers to take up entry-level jobs in deeply racially and socially segregated foreign labor markets—not only because they can no longer afford to eat the quinoa their communities produce for affluent health food chains in the United States and Europe—but because their past and present lives are intimately tied up in global and transnational processes of circulation through which they reimagine themselves and their communities in ways that are always contingent and inconclusive, but equally full of hope that life will unfold and flourish in a better time and place.

PART I

Cosmopolitan Desires

1

Salir Adelante

Mobility, Travel, and Aspirational Economies in the Central Andes

Modernity is what it is—an obsessive march forward—not because it always wants more, but because it never gets enough; not because it is more ambitious and adventurous, but because its adventures are bitter and its ambitions frustrated. The march must go on because any place of arrival is but a temporary station.
—Zygmunt Bauman, 1991

The contrast of the country and city is one of the major forms in which we become conscious of a central part of our experience and of the crises of our society.
—Raymond Williams, 1973

Postulantes de loteria de visas acuden a cabinas de Internet en mancha. [Visa lottery applicants storm the Internet cafés *en masse.*]
—*Ojo*, 2003

In June 2004, when I arrived in Peru to start my dissertation fieldwork, the country seemed on the surface to be recovering rapidly from the deep internal political crisis that led to the implosion of the Fujimori regime in 2000. President Alejandro Toledo—or el Cholo Toledo, as some Peruvians liked to call him—was now three years into his term. The Peruvian economy had reached one of the highest growth rates in Latin America at the time, inflation was reduced, and the deficit was at an all-time historic low (Gonzalez de Olarte 2007). Democracy had been restored and the Peruvian congress was debating the Truth and Reconciliation Commission's final report of recommendations for institutional reform and a comprehensive reparation program for the victim-survivors of the violent conflict between the Maoist guerilla *Sendero Luminoso* and the Peruvian state that had plagued the country for close to two decades.[1] At first glance Peru seemed to be on a fast track toward a new era in its social and political life.

Yet there is always more than meets the eye. The national media reported weekly, if not daily, about Peruvians leaving the country in growing numbers. A few weeks before my arrival in the field in 2004, the largest national newspaper, *El Comercio*, had published an opinion poll based on a survey conducted in Lima, which showed that 74 percent of young Limeños would migrate abroad if they could and 53 percent had concrete plans to migrate in the near future.[2] Scholars, politicians, and the national media at large participated in the production and circulation of an alarmist discourse of mass exodus, citing endless statistics of how many Peruvians had left that week or that month, and how many were likely to leave in the near future. Media images and popular culture references to people fleeing the country had circulated widely, perhaps not surprisingly, during the worst years of political violence. But why, now that Peru had supposedly become more economically stable and was generally safer for the average citizen, were images of exodus still so prevalent?

The panicky discourse about continued mass exodus in 2004 was not without material basis. Peruvians did in fact continue to migrate internationally in skyrocketing numbers throughout the first decade of the new century despite the country's economic upturn, much applauded by both economic analysts and the international community. The answer to this apparent paradox is to be found in the processes of network expansion that accompany most migration flows and, once established, make them self-perpetuating over time (Massey et al. 1993). Based on data from the Latin American Migration Project (LAMP), scholars have argued that whilst a decent paycheck that could sustain a family was still readily available to most people in Lima under the regime of import substitution industrialization (ISI), this scenario changed after the introduction of structural adjustment policies in 1987 when both secure employment and wages fell dramatically (Massey and Capoferro 2006).[3] Between 1988 and the early 2000s, more and more families in the capital responded to the economic dislocations produced by neoliberal economic policies and to the climate of violence and insecurity and relied increasingly on connections abroad to diversify their household income through international migration (Massey and Capoferro 2006). As a result, the number of migrants augmented dramatically post-1987, as did the variety of foreign destinations and the diversity of migrants' regional and class backgrounds (Takenaka et al. 2010).[4]

While it is clear that the social, economic, and political transformations that accompany the expansion of markets along with the enduring effects of almost two decades of political violence produced the ongoing migration flows from Peru throughout the early 2000s, migration studies that approach human mobility merely as a brute fact that can be observed, measured, and analyzed, while valuable in their own right, are less useful for understanding mobility as embodied practice imbued with meaning that is historically variable.

The operative principle in Lima at the beginning of the new millennium indeed seemed to be *sálvese quien pueda*, an expression that roughly translates as "every man for himself" (Durand in Massey and Capoferro 2006:126). But it was not only in Lima that Peruvians were looking to abandon ship. In the central highlands where most of my Peru-based fieldwork took place, many people I talked to—young and old, men and women, rural and urban—were also contemplating the possibility of migration to foreign destinations. They talked incessantly about their desire to leave and articulated this aspiration by evoking expressions like "getting ahead" (*salir adelante*) and "improving oneself" (*superarse*); terms that are simultaneously classically Peruvian and utterly neoliberal in their implication of bootstrap performativity.[5] Even Peruvians who had relatively stable jobs in local government offices in Huancayo or Jauja or owned small businesses were on the lookout for migration opportunities to foreign destinations which they hoped could put them on track toward greater future prosperity.

This chapter discusses how people in the Mantaro Valley and in Lima imagined migration to foreign destinations and what it meant to them. I suggest that these imaginaries are not unrealistic fantasies but are grounded in a broader history and political economy of travel, exchange, and expanding infrastructures that continue to shape the contemporary circulation of people, money, ideas, and cultural forms within and beyond the central highlands. This history is significant not only because it has shaped the identity of the Mantaro Valley as a particularly modern and prosperous region within Peru with a unique and vigorous popular culture (Romero 2001), but because it has produced shifting ideologies of mobility that in turn shape the production of contemporary mobile practices. To illustrate how present-day transnational migration operates within this broader history of Andean circulation, modernity, mobility, and travel, I discuss the migration histories of two young women, each from a different town in the area: Inés from Matahuasi and Domitila from Urcumarca. By examining the migration histories and experiences of women like Inés and Domitila and other migrants like them, I show that transnational mobility is variously imagined, experienced, practiced, and corporealized in contemporary Peru, but never inseparable from long-standing moral and cultural imperatives about class mobility which are exemplified in expressions such as "getting ahead" *(salir adelante)* and "improving oneself" *(superarse)*.

Anthropologists working on issues of poverty, education, and race/class mobility have noted that expressions such as "salir adelante" were often linked to education in Peru and elsewhere in Latin America. For most of the twentieth century education was viewed as the main strategy through which the indigenous population could escape poverty, reduce racial discrimination, and achieve social mobility (De la Cadena 2000; Leinaweaver 2008; Malkin 2004). Jessaca Leinaweaver, for example, describes how concepts such as "getting ahead" and "improving oneself" operate in the context of child circulation in the southern highlands of Peru, that is, the practice of moving children between households and placing them where parents think they will have the best life opportunities. Here, as in the context of rural-urban migration more generally, these expressions immediately evoke the class position that one *should* aspire to move out of, and therefore impose on poor people, an ideology of self-improvement that they must claim as their own if they are to escape poverty (Leinaweaver 2008:60). This moral connotation attached to the concept of "improving oneself" should be seen in a relational context; in fact, it only fully makes sense when evoked in the context of the family or the community where the notion of "self" refers to more than the individual and includes close kith and kin.[6]

This prevailing ideology of self-improvement through education as a means to get ahead in life is now increasingly intersecting with processes of transnational migration. Indeed, in some cases, as Inés and Domitila's stories will show, a key motivation for migration, especially for migrants who are a little older and have dependent children at the time of their migration, is either to be able to pay for a child's education in Peru (Domitila) or to eventually send for one's child or younger siblings to offer them an education abroad (Inés). Like education, transnational migration as a strategy for individual and familial progress and social mobility is imbued with hope for change and transformation; indeed, it is sometimes imagined as being capable of lifting entire families out of the shackles of poverty, immobility, and rural backwardness still largely associated with the Andean highlands and with Andean migrants in the capital and abroad.

Aspiring migrants in the Mantaro Valley had good material basis for imagining transnational migration as a stepping stone to a future full of possibilities. Many were already members of transnational migrant households and received monthly monetary remittances in U.S. dollars or Euros, birthday gifts, frequent phone calls, video letters, and home videos burned onto DVDs, from family members in the United States, Japan, Italy, Spain, or other countries. Simultaneously, they were returning photos or videos of home improvement projects and growing children left in their care and occasionally they shipped boxes with local food items, religious paraphernalia, handicraft souvenirs from the area, and DVDs featuring musical performances by local or regional artists. They also frequently visited Huancayo or Jauja's many Internet cafés, the characteristic *cábinas publicas* found on every street corner, to connect with their relatives in other countries or to work on getting their own mobile projects off the ground.

The circulation of people, goods, money, ideas, and images across space is facilitated by and indeed largely depends on both older and more contemporary forms of physical, digital, and electronic infrastructures. Brian Larkin has noted that infrastructures as physical form "comprise the architecture for circulation, literally providing the undergirding of modern societies" (2013:328). Larkin draws on media theorist Armand Mattelart who has argued that all ideas of progress from the Enlightenment and in liberalism are based on representations of a world in movement, a world where the free flow of ideas and goods is unrestrained by the fixed hierarchical relations that had characterized feudal

Figure 1.1. An Internet café (*cabina pública*) in Huancayo, 2013. (Photo by Author)

society (Mattelart 1996 in Larkin 2008:58–59; cf. Cresswell 2006). But for such movement to exist, Larkin notes, "it requires the constitution of technical systems of canals, roads, railways, and telegraphs, which create the material channels through which movement can occur" (2008:58). Understanding the *longue duree* of travel and mobility in this particular Andean region thus similarly requires attention to the changing infrastructure that has facilitated such movements over time and helped produce shifting representations of mobility, which in turn has shaped and continues to shape the production of mobile practices, including migration, in this part of Peru.

Routes, Travel, and Infrastructure in the Production of Andean Mobility

While infrastructures and the possibility of exchange over space that these enable are typically associated with industrial technological systems of the nineteenth century, they are not exclusive to modern societies.[7] From precolonial times, Andean livelihoods were based on spatial mobility and complex but well-integrated production, distribution, trade, and exchange systems were fundamental to connecting the highland communities with the coast and the jungle lowlands toward the eastern slopes of the Andes. Scholars have shown that forms of spatial circulation including transhumance, differentiated and seasonal agriculture, barter, and trade allowed most Andean populations to earn sustainable livelihoods under changing political and economic circumstances, climatic uncertainties, and shifting pressures and demands of the precolonial and later the colonial state (Cook 1990; Golte 1980; Mayer 2002; Rostworowski de Diez Canseco 1999). These spatial practices allowed populations in the Andes not only to meet their subsistence needs by controlling access to as many microclimates, altitude levels, and ecological environments as possible (Cole 1985, Condarco [1971] 1987), but also to develop the powerful centers and infrastructures of ancient Andean civilizations, which in turn relied on complex transfers and control of labor flows and resources as well as an extensive road and communication system (Murra [1972] 1987).

The most powerful of the Andean civilizations was the Inca Empire.[8] In the central highlands, the native inhabitants, the Wankas, had been

subjugated to the Inca rulers who from around 1460 had disciplined regional chieftains into complying with their imperial policies (Espinoza
Soriano 1973:68). Scholars have suggested that the arrival of the Spanish conquistadores to the area thus represented an opportunity for the
Wankas to rebel against their Inca oppressors by becoming allies of the
Spaniards. Some argue that this initial alliance is the reason why land
in the Mantaro Valley—in contrast to other areas of the Andes where
the Crown granted the colonial *encomenderos* or *corregidores* both land
and the right to the labor of the Indians living on it—remained largely
in the hands of the local population throughout the colonial period as a
reward to the Wankas for their alliance with and loyalty to the Spaniards
(Arguedas 1975; Espinoza Soriano 1973; Romero 2001).

Despite this early alliance with the Spaniards, the region suffered
deeply from the devastating effects of the European invasion. Like the
rest of Peru, the central highlands underwent dramatic demographic
and social changes throughout the seventeenth and eighteenth centuries and historians have documented the way sweeping epidemics and
out-migration of the population to participate in *mita* labor service,
road construction, and the building of churches and *reducciones* towns
profoundly changed the demography of the area (Mallon 1983; Stern
1982). This was further accentuated by the influx of population to work
in the *obrajes*—the colonial equivalent of today's sweatshops. Historian
Florencia Mallon has found that already by 1780, this region had one
of the highest percentages of mixed-race population in the Viceroyalty
(1983:11).

The colonial regimes of governmentality that attempted to fix and
confine the Indian population in the *reducciones* towns (except when
they were drafted to work for the colonial administration) not only
transformed older Andean practices of spatial mobility to gain access
to as many ecological environments as possible, but also gave rise to
new forms and shifting meanings of mobility. Within the place-based
logic of the *reducciones,* the Indians who became (or remained) mobile came to be seen as existing on the margins. According to Mörner
(1985), some tried to escape their Indian status and its corresponding
fiscal responsibilities simply by leaving their assigned communities and
adopting Spanish speech and customs elsewhere. This was possible, for
example, if they settled and registered as *yanaconas* ("helpers/depen-

Figure 1.2. A Spanish traveler mistreats his native carrier. Guamán Poma, El Primer Nueva Corónica y Buen Gobierno, 527[541]. (Courtesy of the Royal Library, Copenhagen, Denmark)

dents"), *forasteros* ("strangers/foreigners"), or even *mestizos* in a Spanish town, or if they entered the service of a landowner or miner as a *peon* (day laborer).[9]

Furthermore, as Saignes has shown, indigenous women in the Andes speculated on the future status of their children by registering them as illegitimately born to bypassing muleteers or llama-drovers (*arrieros*), thereby exempting their children from future tribute and labor obligations (Saignes 1995:184; Bouysse-Cassagne and Saignes 1992). These strategies for avoiding taxation and abuse from colonial authorities and taking advantage of the opportunities for social mobility and differentiation made possible through alliances with the Spaniards have frequently been interpreted in Andeanist scholarship under the rubric of resistance to the imposition of colonial rule. Luis Miguel Glave, for example, has argued that what before the conquest was a reproduction strategy (i.e., displacing the population to adapt to a rational use of space) had become "a movement of diaspora which manifests tactics of resistance to the colonial pressure" (Glave 1989:18; my translation). An exclusive focus on resistance, however, precludes an understanding of the aspirations and social agency of Andean societies and the often dynamic relationship between the colonial and indigenous society (Spalding 1970).

After independence in 1821, the control of mobility came under the purview of the new nation-state. The newly minted citizens could now at least in theory move without seeking permission, yet mobility was still organized along the lines of race, class, and gender and across the national territory. Social and economic stratification increased toward the end of the nineteenth century where new market and exchange opportunities gave rise to a new class of traders and town-based landholding *mestizo* elites (Adams 1959; Alberti and Sánchez 1974; Long and Roberts 1978; Mallon 1983). Peasants in turn engaged in subsistence and small-scale commercial agriculture and in seasonal labor migration to highland haciendas, coffee plantations in the lowlands, sugar and cotton plantations on the coast, and to the nearby mining areas which often recruited through the *enganche* system (Laite 1984:117) where pay is received in advance but the workers are locked into an obligation to the recruiter.[10]

Scholars of mobility have shown that technological developments in many places in the world have produced increased movement of people

Figure 1.3. Train arriving at Huancayo, ca. 1920. (Courtesy of Pío Altamirano)

on the national and global scale and also new ways of thinking about mobility (Cresswell 2006). The establishment of the U.S.-owned Cerro de Pasco Corporation in 1901 and the construction of the railroad, which arrived at Huancayo in 1908, produced an unprecedented expansion of internal and external markets (Bonilla 1974; Flores Galindo 1974). These developments began an irreversible wave of "modernization" in the valley and renewed the promise of the area's inclusion in an integrated national territory and project of modernity.[11] The railroad linked the region directly to external markets by connecting the valley with Lima and the port of El Callao and with the mining areas of Huancavelica, La Oroya, and Cerro de Pasco, and facilitated the transport of minerals and wool from the highlands to the coast. It also transported people and goods and served as a vehicle for new sensibilities, subjectivities, taste, and style. Moreover, it contributed importantly to changing previous views of mobility and imbued it with new ideas of liberty, freedom, and progress. As a result of the railroad, the region's epicenter shifted toward Huancayo, which became the economic and financial center for the prosperous agricultural villages in the southern part of the valley (Arguedas 1978; Alberti and Sánchez 1974). Unlike Jauja, Huancayo did not have a landowning aristocracy, but with the railroad European and Asian immigrants arrived in Huancayo and the city became more cosmopolitan in spirit (Pinilla 2004:40). As Huancayo continued to grow, the once prosperous city of Jauja lost its importance as a center of political power in the valley and in 1931 Huancayo became the capital of the Province of Junín (Romero 2001).

Over the following decades the migration and circulation patterns in the valley changed anew. The depression of the 1930s affected the regional economy, particularly the mining sector. Seasonal migration to the mines decreased and only resumed after World War II. Out-migration flows were instead redirected to Lima, and throughout the 1940s the department of Junín contributed the largest number of migrants to the Lima-Callao area (Long and Roberts 1978:33). The combination of a growing national industry protected by import substitution policies since 1961 and the overall breakup of Peru's agrarian structure produced from the 1970s and onward large migration flows to Peru's cities.[12] This epic movement of people from country to city changed the face not only of Peru's capital Lima, but of the nation itself.

While the scale of Andean mobility has certainly changed in today's global world, the larger history of travel, migration, infrastructure, and circulation described here is crucial to consider when attempting to understand the value and aspirational worth that people of the Mantaro Valley ascribe to migration to foreign destinations today. The more recent proliferation of communications technology, tourism, a renovated airport outside Jauja, and multiple daily bus routes to Lima and the lowlands on the eastern slopes of the Andes have only accentuated this history of travel and circulation. Women like Inés and Domitila who decide to leave their homes and families in the valley to search for work and opportunities in Lima or abroad embody this history and it shapes their subjectivities in profound and powerful ways.

The Central Highway and the Promise of Mobility

"Why would you want to live there?" Inés asked me, astounded. She could not fathom the possibility that anyone would voluntarily consider living so far away from the main road. We were standing in her mother Doña Rosa's sparsely equipped grocery shop in the town of Matahuasi. The shop is located at the roadside of the *Carretera Central*—the national highway connecting the Mantaro Valley with the nearby mining areas of Morococha and La Oroya and with the capital Lima on the coast. I was looking for a place to live for a longer stint of fieldwork in the valley and was considering Barrio Ferrocarril in Matahuasi where I had lived during a prior period of fieldwork a few years earlier, next door to a family with transnational ties to New York City. I liked that part of Matahuasi because it was a quiet area on the outskirts of town surrounded by artichoke fields, tall eucalyptus, *níspero*, and *guinda* trees, and lush green pastures toward the banks of the Mantaro River. Inés didn't like that part of town at all. "It is more convenient for you to stay up here," she said persuasively, and by "up here" she meant her mother's house right next to the highway. "Here, you are closer to Huancayo, you can get to Jauja in fifteen minutes and the bus to Lima stops right outside our doorstep." The literal physical access to geographical mobility was a key consideration for Inés. As she spoke, clouds of dust rose up in the air as miniature tornadoes outside the shop each time a bus, truck, or car drove by, evoking immediate images of movement, connectivity, and speed.

The Carretera Central, which connected the valley with Lima, with La Merced and Satipo in the lowlands, and with the southern highlands of Ayacucho and Huancavelica, had been the center of Inés's life since childhood. For generations, it had been a vital resource not just for the family's survival but also for their prosperity. It injected continuous lifeblood into a prolific family enterprise that included a gas station, a roadside restaurant, a productive dairy farm, and Doña Rosa's grocery shop. As a child Inés had learned to respect the Carretera and be careful when crossing it or playing next to it. Later, she and her two sisters had followed its curves toward the coast when they, as hopeful provincial youth coming of age in the tumultuous and politically unstable 1980s, sought to improve themselves through education and better paid jobs in the capital. The Carretera encoded the dreams and fantasies of Inés and her fellow provincial youth and made them feel real and full of possibility.

The road also evoked bittersweet memories of loss and deception. It was this road that in 1972 took Inés's father away for good when he followed the path of his three brothers-in-law and abandoned Doña Rosa with four young children as he headed toward a new life in Miami and never looked back. What was once a prosperous and complex family enterprise with a gas station, a restaurant, a productive dairy farm, and the grocery shop was now a random collection of decaying infrastructure

Figure 1.4. La Carretera Central in Matahuasi, 2013. (Photo by Author)

in a changing social landscape. Doña Rosa and Inés's uncle Willy were the only two family members left on the farm. The rest of the extended family had moved to either Huancayo, Lima, or the United States and the older generation had passed away. The gas station was now closed, the restaurant once buzzing with activity was empty and displayed deep cracks on both inner and outer walls, and while the pastures on the property were still lush and green, none of the milk cows for which Matahuasi had earned its name as the Cattle Capital of the Mantaro Valley were in sight. Several of the neighboring farmhouses also stood empty and locked up. Their former inhabitants, Inés told me, had left for Lima and those with more luck, she emphasized, had migrated abroad.

"Seriously," Inés repeated. "You will be much more comfortable here." Inés clearly did not share my romantic, urban fantasy of pastoral life as an ideal context for my temporary fieldwork accommodation. The truth is that there probably wasn't much, if anything, idyllic about rural life under the socioeconomic conditions which dominated the region at the time. Agriculture was halting as a result of the deregulation of markets and small-scale farmers struggled to produce to the demands of the market and compete with foreign food imports, often priced below the cost of agricultural production in Peru (cf. Mayer 2002). The Mantaro River running behind Barrio Ferrocarril was so seriously contaminated by residuals from the area's extractive industries that it was inappropriate for human use.[13] "You will also be isolated down there," Inés insisted. In her worldview, the Carretera was not only the symbol of connectivity but also of a particular form of sociality.

Scholars have shown that infrastructures—particularly roads and railroads—are not just technical or physical objects but they operate at the level of desire, encoding the dreams of individuals and societies by representing the possibility of being modern and having a future (Dalakoglou and Harvey 2012; Kernaghan 2012; Larkin 2013; Sneath et al. 2009). Harvey and Knox (2012), for example, analyze roads in Peru as technologies for delivering progress and development and explore affective dimensions that allow roads to retain the strong yet generic social promise they hold in Peruvian society. These scholars suggest that roads evoke at least three promises of emancipatory modernity: the promise of speed and connectivity, the promise of political freedom, and the promise of economic prosperity (2012:523). They argue that "it is not in spite of unruly processes that infrastructures emerge as a form of social promise, but rather . . . through the experiences of life within and alongside unstable forces that infrastructures gain their capacity to enchant" (2012:525).

Inés was evidently captivated by the Carretera's promise of connectivity, mobility, progress, and freedom. Her daily struggles to get ahead were deeply entangled with the animated force of the Carretera as desire and promise. Its mere presence unleashed a powerful, visceral sense of possibility in Inés even if she was fully aware of its dangers. Kathleen Stewart has noted how mobilizations of affect, here understood as desires or emotions that shape social action, are always either "promising or threatening to amount to something" (2010:340).[14] This "something," the never-ending sense that there *had* to be something ahead, something better and more exciting, is the condition of modernity itself.

But despite the Carretera's capacity to enchant it did not always fully deliver on its promises of a prosperous mobile future. Or at least its deliveries were unpredictable. The morning after our conversation about housing opportunities and closeness to the Carretera I returned from

Huancayo to Matahuasi and found Inés's son Angel playing outside Doña Rosa's shop. "I thought you had left for Lima already!" I said, visibly surprised. "We are leaving today," Angel responded. I found Inés in the kitchen preparing lunch to the sound of Rossy War on the radio, a popular *cumbia* singer in Peru in the late 1990s. Doña Rosa was outside cutting grass for her guinea pigs. Inés was in a good mood that morning and immediately told me excitedly: "My aunt in Jauja has told me about a person who has contacts in Argentina for work." "Oh really?" I said. "I thought you wanted to go to the United States." "Yes, I do," Inés replied. "But you also know I want to leave here as soon as I can, right? Today I am here, but tonight I'll be on the road once again, and tomorrow who knows . . ."

Later that afternoon we accompanied Doña Rosa during a ritual cleansing with a healer (*curandera*) from the nearby town of Apata. Doña Rosa had been suffering from a facial rash and no ointments could help her get rid of it. As the healer swiped the guinea pig (*cuy*) over Doña Rosa's body amidst clouds of tobacco smoke and splashes of pure alcohol (*caña*)—a ritual called *jubeo*—she told us that this treatment served many purposes: It could diagnose an illness, it could extract evil from an afflicted person's body, and it could restore health and balance (see Rimachi 2003 for a discussion). The *jubeo* could also prepare a person for future challenges. I noticed how Inés's attention sharpened; she was listening carefully now. I later learned that *jubeos* are commonly used among aspiring migrants to prepare their bodies for departure and to enhance good luck for an upcoming journey, but when I asked Inés if she was considering it she wasn't sure. It would leave a strong odor of pure alcohol and cigarette smoke on her hair and skin and she didn't want others to look at her on the bus since the *curandera* strictly advised against showering until at least a week after the ritual. The *jubeo* made the human body sensitive to shifts in temperature and other factors and thus precautions had to be taken. Inés finally decided to do it. When I asked her what made her change her mind, she answered: "You never know when the opportunity to travel will arise and when it does you must be prepared."

When we hugged each other goodbye outside Doña Rosa's shop before Inés and Angel boarded the midnight bus to Lima, I could still smell the alcohol in Inés's hair despite attempts to reduce the odor by using an old cologne from her mother's bathroom. As I watched the bus speed into the darkness and finally disappear, I imagined how a few hours later it would descend slowly upon Lima in the emerging daylight with Inés and Angel sleeping in its belly. In Lima, the Carretera always lost parts of its glamor. But in the highlands, just as the railroad had done before it, the Carretera stood as symbol for a journey—not the well-known journey to Lima on the overnight bus, but the much bigger journey ahead which the guinea pig was preparing the traveler for. Yet it was no secret that the realization of transnational migration as an aspirational project of mobility required hard work. First and foremost it required a visa.

Salir Adelante as Aspirational Force: Inés's Visa Story

The intensity and passion with which so many Peruvians pursued their dreams of aspirational mobility never ceased to strike me. Why were people like Inés and others so eager to leave their home country and travel to foreign and faraway lands where life is also hard, inconclusive, and unpredictable? How to explain the determination, and the affective force from where it emerges, with which aspiring migrants like Inés so vividly imagined and so carefully devised their plans for a mobile future?

As long as I had known Inés and her family she had been talking about her plans to leave. When I occasionally stayed with her or even when I visited her for just a few hours in Lima or at her mother's in Matahuasi, I witnessed her tireless work on this aspirational travel project. She spent most of her free time in Huancayo or Lima's many Internet cafés looking for travel opportunities and she organized her everyday life around that goal. She was also impressively consistent in caring for the networks she already had abroad. Occasionally she would ask me, her anthropologist friend, if I knew someone who might be able to help her out:

> Ullita, I take this opportunity to ask you if you somehow can help my brother and me to travel to another country; if you know someone who can lend a hand, you know, through a letter of invitation or an employment contract. I am sorry to ask you this, if it bothers you just forget about it, but let's keep talking, ok? Some friends of my godmother are coming from the U.S. this week [and] that is why I'm on email almost every other day, so write me when you can.[15]

Inés was not the only person who asked me if I had any contacts that could help them migrate or if I could assist them at least with the visa application process. While nobody ever mistook me as an insider to the U.S. consulate's visa section or as a specialist in the U.S. visa system, many actively sought to engage me in conversation about it. Nor was Inés alone within her own family in her fixation on migration to a foreign destination as the way out of a truncated social existence in Peru. Her sisters Amparo and Mercedes were also trying to leave and her brother Gabriel once called me to see if I could offer any ideas, contacts, or travel advice, although he never followed the path of his sisters abroad. All three sisters had attempted to reconnect with their long estranged father in Miami to have him petition them for family reunification, but without much luck. After several failed attempts at communication, Inés and Amparo each applied for tourist visas which they planned to overstay. "We would stay as illegals," Inés said self-consciously and quickly added: "But I think it's worth it . . ."

Amparo was the first of the three sisters to receive her tourist visa. She made plans to leave by herself and send for her husband and two sons at a later date. Inés, by contrast, was not that lucky. As she waited for a decision on her own visa, she pondered alternative strategies for how to "salir adelante" in Lima. On one occasion she told me: "I started working about a week ago and it's going very well. I am getting to know a lot of people who are important in Lima and in politics. I hope it will help me somehow in the future. I'm still trying to locate my father with the help of some friends in the U.S.; hopefully it's worthwhile."

Inés's striving to "get ahead" was not just a string of rational calculations about how to increase her earnings or help her family. Her efforts were as much an aspirational project of class mobility which required embodying the right marks of belonging. Her new office job in a medium-sized company required her to "dress well" and engage in various forms of self-care and stylization of her body and she had already learned how to move around in a convincing way for the urban office work environment. Inés happily spent money on facial creams, power suits, and high-heeled shoes and she embodied the white-collar identity with utmost seriousness and grace. But even after landing in what she and others considered a good office job in the capital, Inés soon resumed work on her overseas travel plans.

She did so for a variety of reasons. The first was that her new boss had become infatuated with her and started harassing her at work. Secretarial jobs of the kind Inés aspired to frequently came at a high price in a sexist and discriminatory urban environment where male bosses and supervisors claimed an almost inherent right to their front office female staff. At the end of the day, gender and racial barriers often truncated the possibilities of upward social mobility in this sector, as Inés herself experienced. But there was also another reason, a more profound yet also more diffuse one that had to do with the conditions of modern life itself. Scholars of modernity have pondered how, as a form of life, modernity makes itself possible by setting a difficult if not impossible task. Zygmunt Bauman argues: "It is precisely the endemic inconclusivity of effort that makes the life of continuous restlessness both feasible and inescapable, and effectively precludes the possibility that the effort may ever come to rest" (1991:10). Even when they were not being harassed, a white-collar office or professional job was not necessarily enough to satisfy the aspirational force that drove these provincial women's strivings for self-improvement and modern, urban lives in the capital. Inés thus soon quit her job in Lima and went back to dedicate herself full-time to her travel preparations. In March 2001, she went to the U.S. embassy in Lima to "research a few things." I didn't hear much from her over the summer that year but then suddenly the day after 9/11 I got an email from her. Seemingly unaffected or at least very far away from world events, Inés was overcome by a visceral sense of joy and excitement:

> *Flaca* [skinny, her nickname for me], you have no idea how much joy it gave me to receive news from you. From what I can judge these last few days have been wonderful for me. THANK GOD! I just got out of the U.S. Embassy and you know what??. . . guess what?. . . now we can meet there in the U.S., *flaca*, they gave me the VI . . . SASASASASA . . . I am so happy. Chances are that I will travel with my mom at the end of October or in the first days of November. We'll keep you posted, soul sister, I'm dancing on one leg.[16]

Inés's ultimate dream, the dream of traveling to the United States, was about to be materialized. Despite the fact that she repeatedly expressed her desire to travel as a way to "do something for all the family members who are still here," I always saw her migration plans more as a project of individual self-improvement. Domitila was different. She too was an aspiring migrant who at the time of my long-term fieldwork in 2004–05 was preparing to leave the town of Urcumarca for the United States. Her family had tapped into a U.S.-bound migration flow initiated by her much older aunt Asunción Torres. Asunción, who was the first Urcumarquina to travel to the United States, had since the 1990s helped many other family members travel. Indeed, she had made a promise to herself: "I wanted to take advantage of the contacts I had and so I promised myself to bring at least one son or daughter from each of my eight siblings [to the United States] so that they, in turn, could help their families." A second-degree niece in this tightly knit family network, Domitila's migration when her turn came around therefore seemed less of an aspirational project of individual self-improvement and more of a moral obligation to help her entire family get ahead.

Salir Adelante as Moral Obligation: Domitila's Migration Story

As the oldest of eight siblings, Asunción herself had left Urcumarca at a young age in the early 1950s. Her absence from the family household meant one less mouth to feed daily and her migration earnings constituted an important economic contribution to the family in Urcumarca. Asunción first found work in the nearby city of Jauja doing household chores in the home of a well-off family. Later, she tried her luck with various kinds of informal commercial activities and she also did factory work in Lima. Her most stable position in which she remained for many years was as a domestic worker in the house of a wealthy upper-class Limeño family. Her employers (*patrones*) were members of Peru's political class and were often sent abroad on diplomatic missions. In 1972, they invited Asunción to join them because, as they had told her, "she was like family" (cf. Romero 1992). Asunción became the first Urcumarquina to travel to the United States.

The Andean women who "made it" to the United States in these early years mostly worked as domestics in Lima and left Peru on labor contracts signed with their Peruvian or American employers. These contracts were required to process a domestic worker visa but many employers didn't honor them once in the United States. Few women objected to this because they didn't want to lose the opportunity of migrating legally with an employment visa and therefore ended up working for much less than what their contracts stated. Some returned to Peru with their patrons upon completion of their diplomatic missions while others stayed abroad and consequently became undocumented when their employment visas expired. Some also "deserted" the patrones before their contracts expired because of exploitative working conditions that included sexual and physical abuse.

The women who opted to stay in the United States frequently sent for close family members, including children. Those who could apply for their relatives to come legally via family reunification did so, but those who lacked papers arranged for their relatives to travel via unauthorized routes. The unstable economic and political situation in Peru in the late 1980s made it unattractive for Asunción to return to Peru when her contract expired. She had saved up some money and when her youngest son Paulino, a police officer in Peru, was sent to an area of the southern highlands of Peru that was controlled by the Shining Path (*Sendero Luminoso*), Asunción decided that it was time for him to migrate. Through the brokerage of a "contact" in Lima, Paulino traveled to the United States in December 1989. He arrived in Maryland in January 1990 after twenty-seven days of travel through several transit countries as he was passed from one local smuggler to the next. Asunción then paid back a total of U.S. $4,500 for this "travel package."

Soon after his arrival Paulino became instrumental in helping his mother fulfill her promise to help other family members "salir adelante" through migration. Over the next decade, the Urcumarquino collectivity in the Washington, D.C.-Maryland area grew exponentially, reflecting a pattern similar to what has been described in the migration literature as network-based migration: A pioneer migrant opens the path for subsequent migration of other closely related family members, extended kin, and later coethnics (*paisanos*) (Boyd 1989; Menjívar 2000; Paerregaard 2008). When I first met the family in 2004, they had already facilitated the migration of at least thirty-nine family members and *paisanos* from Urcumarca to Maryland, of which twenty-two were Asunción's direct nephews and nieces.

Asunción's original impetus to facilitate the migration of other family members was not a selfless act of altruism. She was looking to comply with social obligations of reciprocity to extended kin, who had been looking after her children and her land, and helped her fulfill responsibilities to ritual kin (*compadres* and *ahijados*) and through fiesta sponsorship to the patron saint and the community at large during her years of absence from Urcumarca. Furthermore, the "access" to migration that she and her son now facilitated for other relatives firmly positioned not only her family at the top of the local social order in the community and among migrants abroad, but it also increased the reputation of the town as a prosperous community with a large migrant constituency abroad. Paulino himself embodied the ideology of "salir adelante" like nobody else and he expected others to strive equally to overcome poverty through dedicated efforts of self-improvement. He cited lifelong hardships as a key motivation not just to work to get ahead in the United States, but also to help others out:

> Because I had a mind-set to overcome, from the beatings that I have received in life, and from living in poverty, I had strength, I had a vision. I tend to see the future of the person. Crying isn't worth anything; it doesn't get you anywhere. So I said to myself when I arrived [in the United States]: Either I grind to a halt here or I live well here. But I was never a conformist. I have always been forward-looking. So one has to move on.

This belief colored Paulino's disposition to help those who displayed a similar desire and effort to "salir adelante." Domitila's sister Anita was one of these relatives. A second-degree niece of Asunción, Anita had witnessed the U.S.-bound migration of several of her cousins and friends and was determined to leave the community, because, as she said: "There is no future here." Her parents first approached Paulino to solicit his help and Paulino agreed to help them by sponsoring Anita's migration. Once in the United States, Anita immediately started to work toward bringing another sibling. She saved all the money she could from her cleaning, babysitting, and housekeeping jobs to help her younger sister Martina migrate and join her in the United States, because as the common mantra went, "there is no future for her in Peru." This reflects the general expectation that when a member of a family migrates successfully this person will pull (*jalar*) other family members or close kin, including godparents or godchildren.

Since her arrival in Maryland, Anita had strengthened her position within Paulino's family and had become the godmother (*madrina*) of Paulino's U.S.-born daughter. As a result of this "kinwork," Paulino helped Anita prepare for Martina's travel by lending her money and brokering the travel arrangements with a "travel agent" in Lima. But Anita's plan for Martina's mobile future took an unexpected turn. A few weeks before the trip was supposed to take place, Martina disappeared from Urcumarca with her boyfriend. Rumors started circulating in town that Martina was pregnant and didn't want to leave. Her refusal to embody the mobile project her family had planned for her is an important reminder that even in an economy of mobility where travel and migration are largely constructed as something to be desired, individual people may differ from the norm and attempt to assert their own agenda. At the last minute, Anita's oldest sister Domitila, who was a single mother living in Jauja, had to dutifully take the younger sister's place in this family-planned migration project. The travel documents were modified by a migration broker in Lima and with just a few weeks' notice Domitila left for the United States.

Migration scholars have argued that the decision of who gets to migrate next in the context of specific networks is seldom a discrete decision by individual actors, but rather a collective one closely linked to other social and economic processes at the household, family, community, and regional levels (Boyd 1989:642). Domitila had not been an obvious next candidate in the first place both because she had a young child herself, but also because, in spite of economic and emotional hardships after having been abandoned by her child's father, she was doing fairly well in Peru. She had a university degree and had managed to create a livelihood for herself and her son in Jauja working as an administrative assistant in her son's school. The suggestion that Domitila should join Anita and the large extended family in Maryland therefore came as a major surprise to Domitila. Unprepared for this life change at such short notice, the prospect of leaving her six-year-old boy behind with his grandparents in Urcumarca caused Domitila great suffering. While she did see migration to the United States as "an opportunity to progress," she didn't feel, as did her sister Anita, that it was the *only* opportunity she had. She also felt that leaving her son behind could be a step in the wrong direction for the future she envisioned for him. She worried that leaving him with his grandparents meant that he would have to go back to the village school, which, according to Domitila, provided only a precarious education compared to the city school he attended in Jauja. Swept up by events she couldn't control and tied up in multiple and contradictory social and moral obligations, Domitila was heart-broken, but understood she had to go.[17]

As the oldest female sibling Domitila knew she was not in a position to decline the travel opportunity. That would have been an act of defiance of the values of reciprocity and sociality that defined life and governed social relations in Urcumarca. To say no to a gift, here the gift of migration, as Marcel Mauss ([1925] 1967) reminds us, is to deny the relationship that it implies. Reflecting on her tumultuous departure from Urcumarca, she later said: "All the arrangements had already been made and almost paid for. How could we possibly lose this opportunity? We never knew if we would get such an opportunity again." Domitila here evokes a collective "we," toward which she felt a strong moral obligation.

Yet she doubted until the last minute. On the evening of her departure, her mind was made up but her body was feeling heavy, the future weighing her down. Her son refused to come out in the courtyard to say goodbye. By nature a quiet boy, Alejandro was more quiet than usual. He didn't cry but opted to shelter himself from his mother's departure by doing his homework inside the house by the flickering light of an old petroleum lamp. Before disappearing into the darkness of the night, Domitila dwelled for a moment by the window looking at him through a crack in the broken glass. Why was she doing this? Why? As she stood there about to lose him to the mercy of time, she told herself that she was doing it for him. She was leaving him there, at six years old, doing homework by himself at the poorly illuminated table for the sake of his future. She did it so that he could get ahead. But as she walked into the darkness to catch the night bus to Lima at the roadside outside Jauja, this future no longer seemed to make sense.

Getting By or Getting Ahead?

It was 3 a.m. on a weeknight in October and Inés was sitting outside on the stairs of her uncle's home in Miami weighing her options. She was in a bad mood that night. It had been more than a month since she had arrived in Miami and she had still not been able to stabilize her situation. She was staying at her uncle's together with Amparo and her family who had been there a while already. The arrangement was far from ideal. The space was crammed and the atmosphere in the house tense. Amparo was working with their uncle in his construction company, but Inés had no work yet and was starting to feel anxious about it. She made herself useful here and there and the uncle gave her a little money for her efforts, but it wasn't amounting to anything close to a salary. She was also feeling uncomfortable in the house and in her darkest moments she contemplated returning to Peru. "My uncle doesn't want us to go out, he doesn't want us to cook in the house, so what can we do?" said Inés angrily. "He doesn't want us to talk to other Latinos, and when we receive phone calls he gets angry and says: 'I am not a receptionist to be getting calls from all these people.' It is really dreadful," she concluded.

A lawyer at a community center told Inés to get an individual taxpayer identification number (ITIN) to be able to get paid and purchase things, but he would charge her a $65 fee to help her get it. Amparo had looked into purchasing a social security number from a third party for her, but this too was expensive. Someone had offered Inés "a crocket one," as she said, but she didn't fancy the idea of walking around with a deceased person's ID. She also considered the option of marrying someone for papers to be able to work legally, but didn't want to take any chances with someone she didn't already know; and her cousin who was a U.S. citizen didn't seem to be interested in helping her either. Inés had also considered moving up north to Orlando, where her ex-husband's father and uncle lived, but dropped the idea after her sister-in-law warned her against it. "She tells me they are equally after you about anything, all day long. They don't want you to use the phone, they don't want you to use the kitchen; they don't want you to do anything!"

Domitilia, by contrast, had inserted herself quickly upon her arrival in 2005 in the local labor market niche that Peruvian women in suburban Maryland had created for themselves as housekeepers and cleaning personnel. Her network of fellow Urcumarquinos helped her "get ahead" in economic terms, but her relative success in finding a job and sending her first and subsequent remittances back home didn't help Domitila to flourish. Other migrants commented that she seemed "withdrawn" and some even insinuated that she was arrogant because she never participated in the social activities of the community. Domitila defended herself by responding that she was there to work and preferred to relax in her room when not doing so. The sense of her migration being a moral obligation to her family in Urcumarca, not something she had done for herself, continued years after her arrival.

Migrants' immediate affective and visceral responses to the initial hardship and emotional costs of migration depended on many factors, including opportunities in the destination context and whether or not the person had left family behind. In her analysis of affective and bodily responses to urban poverty and social inequality exacerbated by neoliberal restructuring in Nicaragua, Elysée Nouvet (2014) questions the difference between two survival strategies among a mother and her daughter in an urban shantytown: the strategy of "carrying on" and that of "curling up in bed." The first alludes to the kind of bootstrap performativity discussed earlier in this chapter whereas the second strategy represents a refusal to engage with it, which, Nouvet reflects, might itself be a form of agency. Nouvet seeks to increase our understanding of "how the body pushed to its limits may mold the social by contributing to a sense of what feels doable or impossible, right or wrong, in need of transformation or not" (2014:86). She demonstrates that while her two female interlocutors had distinct corporealized ways of experiencing their relentless poverty—that is, "carrying on" versus "curling up in bed"—which may represent seemingly contradictory engagements with social and everyday life under precarious conditions, they both "animate[d] a sense of the present's painful inadequacy, which may be socially transformative" (2014:98).

Similarly, Domitila's self-imposed isolation and Inés's frustration over her *im*mobility upon arrival are examples of different affective responses to the realization that migration is not a dance on roses and that migrants' premigration dreams and expectations for what would be possible via migration to foreign destinations soon prove unrealistic for the kind of life ultimately available to them in these destinations (cf. Chu 2010; Mahler 1995; Menjívar 2000; Sabogal 2005; Vigh 2009). The things migrants had imagined possible before leaving Peru, all the signs of migration-driven "progress" that they had perceived in their hometowns in the valley or urban neighborhood in Huancayo and Lima—the brick and cement homes built with migration earnings, visiting return migrants' conspicuous spending during patron saint festivals, and the cool new outfits and state-of-the art technological gadgets which members of transnational households sported to attract the attention of others— all this suddenly seemed very far away as the daily worries over how to get papers and a decently paid job started to settle in. Aurelio, another migrant from Urcumarca who arrived in Maryland in the early 2000s, leaving behind his wife and two children in Lima, reflected upon the disjuncture between the actual experience of everyday life in the United States and what he and others had imagined before leaving Peru:

> The American Dream is the dream of many, that's why we want to be here. . . . But when one arrives here it's different, living here one realizes that it's different. I would like people over there [in Peru] . . . I don't know, let them know that it's very different than what we think when we leave. That vision we have when we come. It's very difficult here; it's very hard to begin. You don't know how to behave. You don't know how to do things. It's so hard. . . . Maybe for some it's different, but for most of us it's very hard. Here you are nobody.

The transition from a well-known home to a new social environment and from being somebody to "becoming a nobody," in Aurelio's words, placed many recent migrants in a state of limbo. The language barrier, for example, curbed the self-fashioning strategies of most provincial Peruvians upon arrival and marked them racially, socially, and culturally as foreign in the United States. Indeed, scholars working at the intersection of language and racialization practices have argued that white public space is itself constructed through an intense monitoring of language use and speech patterns of racialized populations, including Latinos and African Americans (Hill 1998; Urciuoli 1996).[18] Several of my informants explained how they in many instances had been made to feel dumb or reduced to the status of children, because they could not communicate "correctly" and also had few or no opportunities to learn or improve their English. Some managed to take free "English as a Second Language" classes, or ESL for short, offered at night by churches, community centers, or immigrant aid organizations, but most were so burdened with travel debt and remittance responsibilities that they invested all their time in income-generating activities.

Such signs of "linguistic disorder" (Hill 1998) were not the only ones which marked recent migrants as not belonging in the specific contexts of Miami or suburban Maryland. Knowing and speaking a language is one way of claiming belonging; learning to display the right corporeal marks of belonging in particular settings, as noted by Shamus Khan (2011), is quite another. "Corporeal knowledge," Khan says, drawing on Bourdieu, "is hard to embody or mimic because it relies on experience" (2011:121). Aurelio's indication that in the context of the larger U.S. political and racial economy he and his fellow Peruvians "don't know how to behave" or that they "don't know how to do things" when they arrive is telling for how the ability to succeed in "getting ahead"—now in a new transnational and racial context—is predicated not just upon cognitive knowledge about how to get a construction, cleaning, or babysitting job or where to buy prepaid mobile phone cards, but also more importantly on how successfully a person can discipline his or her body into knowing how to act within particular relationships and social environments. Learning how to inhabit social relationships, navigate new situations, and move one's body through space in appropriate and context-specific ways is part of human interaction anywhere, but the successful mastery of particular embodied forms of knowledge and claims to belonging become ever more crucial in contexts of migration and racialization.

Amparo's arrival scene illustrates this point. When she arrived in Miami her uncle, El Tío, picked her up at the airport. She had not seen him for over a decade because he had returned to Peru only twice since he left for the United States. Amparo noticed that he had changed and it made her feel uneasy. Not only had he legally changed his original Peruvian name to an Anglo American one in order, in his own words, to avoid racism and discrimination for "being Hispanic," but, well aware of the racialization processes affecting Latin American migrants daily in many of their interactions with Anglos and other Latinos, El Tío had consistently since he arrived in the 1970s worked to modify his demeanor, speech, and bodily conduct to move around Miami's suburban landscapes and dealing with Anglo clients without calling too much attention to himself. It was undeniable that he had embodied if not the privilege of whiteness then a complete denial of his Peruvian origins. As they exited the baggage claim area, Amparo chatted loudly and in lively tones in Spanish, offering news about family members in Peru, but El

Tío quickly asked her to stop and not to look at anybody because, as he instructed her, "people are going to look at you" (*la gente te va mirar*). He also requested her not to speak in Spanish with him in public.

The airport incident was not all Amparo had to stomach within the first few hours of her arrival. El Tío was working on a construction site nearby and decided to go there directly from the airport. When they got there Amparo tried to help him measure up a plot of land, but wasn't being successful in completing the task in her high heels and dress pants (*pantalones de vestir*), an outfit that she had chosen specifically for her trip to avoid being singled out and questioned by immigration officers. She lamented not having changed her clothes at the airport and she was angry at her uncle for putting her in this situation. She felt it had curtailed her chances for making a good first impression as a reliable and industrious woman. "I didn't want him to think that I was unable or unwilling to work, because I have always worked to make a living and live a respectable life. Always. I was never afraid of getting my hands dirty," she said firmly, but quickly added: "But I also didn't want to ruin the only pair of nice shoes I had brought with me."

The impetus of a growing number of Peruvians from the Mantaro Valley to migrate to foreign destinations as discussed in this chapter is continuous with long-standing practices of migration and circulation in this region of Peru. For centuries, valley residents have traveled and moved between their rural communities and urban centers to avoid abuses of various kinds, take advantage of opportunities, and to access urban lifestyles and education for their children. For most of the twentieth century, migration to Lima or to the provincial capitals of the Andes was the most feasible strategy for those who hoped that formal education and the acquisition of urban competence would allow them to shed the stigma of rural backwardness and redeem themselves as "gente decente" in the city. At the turn of the new millennium, foreign destinations have increasingly become the imagined and idealized sites for the realization of such modern, urban, and cosmopolitan aspirations.

But mobility within an international system of nation-states does not occur in a political vacuum and few Peruvians have unrestricted access to the much sought-after foreign destinations. The majority are indeed still required, and increasingly so, to seek authorization to move over greater distances and their efforts are both facilitated and constrained by emerging infrastructures, institutions, and technologies—what I refer to as the "migration industry" in the next chapter. This migration industry increasingly works to facilitate the migration of lower class Peruvians of all regional and class backgrounds to a variety of foreign destinations, but it does so at great cost and risk for the individual migrant. Its experts offer not only actual travel arrangements but also careful advice to aspiring migrants of provincial, lower class backgrounds about how to successfully embody the effortlessness by which a frequent traveler moves through foreign embassies, airports, and immigration checkpoints. Like its predecessors—the railroad and highways—the migration industry too operates at the level of desire and fuels lower-class Peruvians sense of possibility by extending the promise of mobility and emancipatory modernity via migration to new ranks and scales.

2

Paper Fixes

The Making of Mobile Subjects in Peru's Migration Industry

When I first met Agapito in June 2004, his wife Asunta had been living in the United States for almost four years. Agapito had hoped to join her ever since she had left Huancayo in 2000 sick of cancer and in need of advanced medical care. But lack of sufficient funds and the need to care for their three children in Peru during Asunta's absence had impeded him from making any travel plans. Yet Agapito spent significant time and money traveling between the highland city of Huancayo and the capital Lima to assemble an extensive file of documents and paperwork that he had paid a migration broker to submit on his behalf to the U.S. embassy in Lima. It was his hope that when the time was ripe, this pile of documents would materialize in a visa that could unite him with his wife Asunta abroad.[1]

Many people in the Mantaro Valley I spoke to during fieldwork, just like Inés and Domitila, wanted to migrate internationally should the opportunity arise, yet few were able to do so by authorized means and routes. In the current global economy of migration, only a limited number of Peruvians of provincial background have access to a legally obtained U.S. visa. The rise of the global security state after 9/11, the general expansion of immigration and border control, and the long-lived forms of institutionalized racism in both Peru and the United States which continue to reproduce racialized boundaries—in short, the governmentality of immigration (Fassin 2011)—has also impacted the categories of "risk" against which visa applicants are evaluated.[2] Within this post-9/11 political and racial economy, it is virtually impossible for low-income, racialized Peruvians from the Andean provinces or from Lima's many shantytowns to obtain a foreign visa via official means.

The difficulty in accessing official visas from the U.S. embassy in Lima moved many migrants of provincial and lower-class backgrounds aspiring to migrate to the United States to work hard to extend themselves through objects, technologies, and embodied skills that they hoped and indeed believed would give them access to transnational migration and mobility. Many turned to "document fixers" (*tramitadores*) or what I here call migration brokers to get their mobile projects off the ground. Whereas the *tramitador* who shuffles, files, and alters documents is a classic figure in urban Peru—and elsewhere in the world (cf. Caplan and Torpey 2001)—the migration broker specializes in connecting aspiring migrants with global labor markets abroad. I draw on Rubén Hernández-León's (2008) definition of the migration industry as I define migration brokers as intermediaries who—motivated by the pursuit of significant financial gain—offer a range of services that facilitate and sustain international migration from labor-exporting countries like Peru to global labor markets. These often highly specialized services include the production and alteration of particular documents such as passports, visas, and other ID documents needed for international travel or complete "package solutions," which include financing, transportation, visas, and passports, and sometimes even job placement in the desired destination country.

My ethnographic insights about these complex brokerage arrangements are unavoidably partial: They are patched together from informants' descriptions; informal conversations with brokers in Azángaro—the infamous street in Lima publicly known as Peru's falsification Mecca—and with staff at the Jorge Chávez International Airport in Lima; formal interviews with government officials; and from exterior and interior observations made in the offices of the Migration and Naturalization Services (DIGEMIN) and at the U.S. embassy in Lima. Most of this material was generated by following my informants who frequently traveled in person between the Mantaro Valley and Lima to complete the various procedures indicated by their brokers in preparation for an upcoming trip.

Agapito and I frequently talked about both the economic and emotional cost of migration, but I specifically recall one afternoon behind the counter in his hardware store in Huancayo when he first told me about his experience applying for a U.S. visa. At one point in our conversation he disappeared into the modest back room where he lived with his three children and returned a moment later with a large manila envelope with worn edges. With an almost ritualized seriousness, he revealed its contents: His passport, his DNI (the Peruvian national identity document), copies of his U.S. visa application, additional passport photos, his military service document (*libreta militar*), his voting card (*libreta electoral*), and a range of other documents supposedly needed for the visa application process. As I flipped through the file, I noticed that the name on several of the documents was Adrian, not Agapito. When I inquired, visibly puzzled, Agapito said: "*Hay que ser moderno, sino no viajas!*" (You have to be modern. Otherwise you won't travel!).

Why did Agapito's ambition of mobility—and the actualization of it—hinge upon changing the rural and indigenous-sounding name on his passport to a more modern-sounding one, as his broker insisted? Was Adrian a more "modern" name because it is more common in cities, whereas the name Agapito in Peru connotes an almost exclusively indigenous or rural identity?[3] And what did "being modern" even mean in Agapito's worldview and why was it seemingly so central to the prospects of traveling internationally?

This chapter examines these questions by looking at the multiple ways in which aspiring migrants prepare for travel through legal documentation and by embodying the modern social identities that such documentation is imagined to represent. Drawing on anthropological approaches to the legal production of persons through the materiality of documents and the bodily performances that authenticate them, I explore how aspiring migrants navigate the world of document fixers, loan sharks, travel agents, lawyers, notaries, and state bureaucrats, including consular staff and U.S. immigration officials, and how they mobilize, circulate, and embody particular forms of knowledge necessary for international travel. As I detail these interactions and relationships, I also provide accounts of the institutions, technologies, social and cultural forms, and relationships that shape and constrain migrants' efforts.

While legal documentation is only one aspect of travel preparation, the fixation on documents among participants in my study and the trust they bestow on their brokers in Lima to produce, acquire, or fix their documents for them must be seen within a global historical context in which bureaucratic documents and sociotechnical regimes more generally have been central to the production and disciplining of populations; indeed, they are a staple of modern statehood (Caplan and Torpey 2001;

Fassin 2011; Mitchell 2002; Scott 1998). A growing anthropological literature shows that documents are more than just instruments of representation within bureaucratic institutions, and that their aesthetic and
affective materiality goes beyond representation and is constitutive of
ideologies, knowledge, practices, and subjectivities (Hull 2012). Moreover, the specific coupling of a perceived "requirement" to be modern
and shed any signs of indigeneity and rural backwardness, including
one's given name, is also linked to what legal documents mean in the
Peruvian context specifically—and what they have meant historically—
especially to less privileged Peruvians of rural and indigenous background (Lund 2001; Poole 2004; Salomon and Niño-Murcia 2011). In
the colonial period, the Spanish Crown created the Law of the Indies
as a legal instrument to divide Indians from Spaniards into separate republics and legal spheres and scholars have suggested that the ambivalence of Peru's elite toward its indigenous populations, as illustrated by
the fact that they were only partially included in the national project
after independence, reflects this colonial legacy (Thurner 1997; Walker
1999). More recently, Poole argues, a lack of documents was the most
common reason for unjustified detentions especially during the violent
conflict, and documents often were purposefully misread at government
checkpoints by abusive authorities. She states: "a personal identity card
was simultaneously a peasant's only guarantee and his source of greatest
vulnerability to the arbitrary power of the state" (2004:36). Similarly,
but focusing on how the state defines the indigenous people of Cuzco as
they move through the urban landscape to obtain legal documentation
from a number of public offices, Lund (2001:3) shows how valid identity
documents, as material and mediating objects, are experienced in everyday life by marginalized Peruvians as central not just to their access
to certain rights and entitlements, but also as their only real protection
against false accusations. In short, documents are one of the important
techniques by which people come to embody the state.

When it comes to mobility beyond the boundaries of the nation-
state, the freedom of movement for men and women gets even more
constrained as it becomes entangled with the policing of physical borders and with the production of racialized boundaries (Inda 2006; Fassin 2011). Here the Peruvian case is different from that of other Latin

American and Caribbean migrations as described in the existing literature. Unlike undocumented Mexican and Central American migrants who typically cross the Mexico-U.S. border without documentation to emerge paperless on the other side, most Peruvians along with other South Americans who traveled to the United States in the 2000s generally came by air. They therefore rarely lacked travel documents; indeed, they often had an excess of them at their disposal—sometimes obtaining them fraudulently.[4] Many Peruvians saw the assemblage of an extensive paper file in preparation for migration as the central activity that could facilitate international travel although they knew that these documents couldn't stand alone but had to be embodied to produce the intended effect of allowing them to "pass" as legitimate mobile subjects in the eyes of government officials.

Preparing for international travel—whether intended as migration or not—therefore centrally involves a process of becoming an appropriately documented subject. Aspiring migrants from the Andes didn't always have the contacts or knowledge to go through this complex process on their own. Lured by the stories told by family and friends who had successfully migrated to the United States, many turned to migration brokers to actualize their mobile projects. Over the process of working with a migration broker, many prospective migrants came to see their broker as possessing almost magical powers to produce mobility through legal documentation and travel arrangements, for which migrants paid large sums of money, and with good reason. As nation-states in the post-9/11 era deploy ever more sophisticated documentation and screening technologies to establish people's identity and subsequently authorize or disqualify a particular population's quest for mobility, brokers in the migration industry also benefit from the rapidly expanding markets for international migration and its cutting edge technologies. As a result, the state no longer holds the *de facto* monopoly and exclusive authority to issue the documentation needed for international travel and migration. With the emergence and proliferation of migration industries, marginalized populations have asserted their share of global mobility and in so doing they have challenged the previous exclusivity of the state not just to document populations but also to authorize their mobility.

78 | PAPER FIXES

Peru's Migration Industry

Migration scholars have long recognized the central role of migration entrepreneurs in initiating and facilitating migration flows (Harney 1977; Salt and Stein 1997; Kyle and Koslowski 2001). Whereas earlier studies focused primarily on informal and illicit activities that were seen to exist apart from and in opposition to the state apparatus, recent work calls for more complex analysis of the total social infrastructure that connects particular migrant circuits with governments, employers, NGOs, and the migrants' own networks. Rubén Hernández-León proposes a new definition of what he calls the migration industry, as "the ensemble of entrepreneurs who, motivated by the pursuit of financial gain, provide a variety of services facilitating human mobility across international borders" (2008:154). Recently, Ninna Nyberg-Sørensen and Thomas Gammeltoft (2013) have expanded Hernández-León's concept of the migration industry to also include what they call the "control industry," that is, those entities that work in close coordination with states to expand markets for the management and control of migration. These "control providers" include multinational corporations and their private subcontractors, international humanitarian organizations, and NGOs of various kinds who compete for contracts offered by governments and supranational institutions for the design and implementation of migration management and immigration control policies worldwide. Such an expanded approach to the migration industry, Nyberg-Sørensen and Gammeltoft argue, helps us better understand how global migration has become steadily commercialized and how the distinction between state and market with regards to migration governance in the contemporary world is being increasingly blurred.

The migration industry plays a key role in producing and facilitating new global migration flows, not just in Latin America but across the globe. The scope of the services offered by this industry has augmented and proliferated worldwide since the 1990s and is integral to what Trouillot (2001:129) calls "fragmented globality"—that is, the increased but selective flexibility of capital along with a deepened differentiation of global labor markets within and across national boundaries. While overlapping in some aspects with the legal definitions of "human trafficking" and the "smuggling of migrants" as defined by the UN in two distinct protocols supplementing the UN Convention against Transnational Organized Crime,[5] the migration industry is not to be confused with them. Indeed, critics of the trafficking paradigm have argued that a focus on certain forms of migration as trafficking reflects receiving states' interests and efforts to control undocumented immigration (Brennan 2008; Hernández-León 2008). By focusing instead of the myriad of practices that produce, facilitate, and control mobility as an industry, scholars have been able to move beyond the limitations of normative legal approaches to global migration governance and question the validity of binary oppositions such as legal/illegal, formal/informal, and documented/undocumented in the production of particular migration flows and in migrants' experiences. In my study, the concept usefully allows me to approach the issue of unauthorized migration of Andean Peruvians from the perspective of the different actors involved in its production and examine ethnographically how competing forms of moral reasoning and concepts of il/legality come into play.

The recent expansion of the migration industry in Peru exemplifies not that globalization is rendering the state irrelevant to the alignment of populations and territories, as assumed by early globalization studies, but rather that state power today is organized differently, often under the auspices of private companies and suprastate entities (Trouillot 2001; see also Thomas and Clarke 2013). Migration industries exist and thrive in intimate relation to immigration policies, migration management procedures, and enhanced border control, precisely because states and nonstate actors alike operate within the same global markets for migration control, facilitation, and management, as Nyberg-Sørensen and Gammeltoft Hansen (2013) suggest. When considering the increasingly restrictive immigration policies and heightened immigration control adopted by the United States in the post-9/11 era, it is hard to imagine that the migration industry will be out of business anytime soon in most of the world's migrant-sending regions.

Paper Fixes

John Torpey (2000) has powerfully argued that a central defining element of the modern state has been its claim to monopoly over the right to authorize and regulate the movement of people. He argues that passports and other identity papers historically have figured centrally in this process of monopolization. Passports are a central part of national governments' technology of codification and surveillance and visa systems are a supplementary means by which a country may screen potential travelers before they arrive at the border (Salter 2004:73). The process of becoming appropriately documented is therefore central to the preparation for international travel.

Any Peruvian can—at least in theory—acquire a Peruvian passport by applying to the Dirección General de Migraciones y Naturalización (DIGEMIN) in Lima or any of its provincial branches, and paying the appropriate fee.[6] DIGEMIN opened a branch in Huancayo in 2003 as part of President Toledo's larger decentralization initiative.[7] This branch was authorized to carry out most of DIGEMIN's central service areas. Between October 2003, when the office was inaugurated, and November 2004 when I interviewed the staff there, DIGEMIN in Huancayo had issued more than 1,600 new passports and the number was steadily increasing, with approximately 250 to 300 new passports every month (this number did not include the large number of renewals of old passports). Moreover, many Huancaínos continued to travel to Lima either to apply officially for travel documents with DIGEMIN's central office in Lima or to "fix their papers" (*tramitar sus papeles*) with a migration broker.

If passports are easy to get, acquiring a visa at the U.S. embassy in Lima by contrast is a more complicated and daunting task. Aspiring migrants complained that it had become increasingly difficult to obtain U.S. visas—and they were right. After 9/11, under President Bush's "War on Terror" policies, the U.S. government became more aggressive in its attempts to secure the U.S. borders and channeled billions of dollars every year into border enforcement and increased scrutiny of travelers at U.S. embassies abroad. Scholars have referred to this strategy as the "delocalization of the border" (Salter 2004:80) and have argued that it represents an expansion of border regimes and immigration control into sending countries—a form of policing at a distance (Bigo and Guild 2005)—which in turn has created a growing market for irregular migration in the world's migrant-sending regions.

The range of actors involved in Peru's migration industry varies, as do the services and products it offers. Some brokers offer "all-inclusive" travel packages that include travel documents, transportation to the foreign destination, accommodation during transit, allocation of jobs in foreign labor markets, bribes to airport police, and other unforeseeable costs. Such packages are assembled on the basis of a particular broker's contacts, but they were also affected by structures of opportunity that opened up in the process. These all-inclusive packages seldom have a fixed price because of such fluctuations, which, one must assume, leaves a considerable profit margin for the broker and his or her subcontractors. During my fieldwork, aspiring migrants in Huancayo and migrants in the United States reported travel costs ranging from U.S. $4,500 to $12,000 for travel to the United States between 1990 and 2004. Other brokers offered small-scale or partial services such as filling out a visa application or falsifying one or two documents, and charged more modest fees.

Any Peruvian who needs to buy counterfeit documents or alter an already existing document, whether it concerns his or her legal identity, educational credentials, documentation of livelihood assets, or travel documentation for an unaccompanied minor, can go to Jirón Azángaro in the center of Lima. This street is home to hundreds of small print workshops and notary offices that offer state-of-the-art technology to produce any imaginable document. Used by people of all class backgrounds, the popularity of Azángaro and its "document industry" must be understood in the context of a society in which sociotechnical regimes and a bureaucratic culture that demands documentation for every minor transaction with the state is a key way to socialize citizens to its omnipresence (Lund 2001; Skrabut 2014), but where informality, corruption, and weak governance structures also are key factors shaping contemporary publics (Berg and Tamagno 2013; Mujica 2011).

Occasionally, the National Police's special unit on document fraud searches the businesses in Azángaro in police raids and confiscates their machines and raw materials. But somehow these operations always manage to get back in business in a matter of days or hours, often with the silent acknowledgment of local police officers who have been bribed in the process. I witnessed several of these police raids on the national evening news during my fieldwork; the most extensive one occurred on June 30, 2005, and affected more than fifty of Azángaro's print shops.[8] Despite these crackdowns, which have caused some of the more com-

Figure 2.1. Azángaro Antifalsification Campaign. (Courtesy of the Colegio de Notarios de Lima)

plex operations involving larger machines to move out of the area, Azángaro's businesses continue to thrive.

Most of the migrants in my study hailed from provincial and working-class backgrounds and few of them had been able to get a visa on their own via official channels. Some were occasionally lured into using the services of *tramitadores* they met on the street despite public warnings by various state agencies, the U.S. embassy, and several NGOs not to use such services. However, most of them obtained recommendations for brokers from family members or friends already abroad who themselves had migrated successfully.

Jenny was one of these aspiring migrants. In her quest to migrate internationally, this working-class woman from Huancayo in her mid-twenties had contacted an old school friend, Fabiola, who lived and worked in Washington, D.C., seeking a recommendation for "someone who could help." Fabiola was quick to offer a recommendation and Jenny called the broker immediately to ask for an appointment. Jenny exchanged very little information with the broker during this first phone call. Most brokers demanded discretion and didn't give out much or any information over the phone to people they had not yet met. But the broker did ask Jenny to appear in her office in Lima within the week if she really was serious about travelling.

A First Encounter with a Broker

The travel agency was located in the middle-class neighborhood of Miraflores and Jenny arrived early to her appointment. She had asked me to accompany her, and given that this was also my first direct encounter with a broker, I approached the occasion with trepidation. Someone buzzed us inside a tall metal fence and we entered the building, both of us intimidated despite our very different stakes in what we were about to experience. We asked a young woman inside for Señora Pilar and she directed us to an office and told us to take a seat. A few minutes later, a middle-aged Limeña probably in her early fifties passed by and looked at us with a penetrating gaze. We guessed she must be Señora Pilar, the owner of the agency.

The woman disappeared into the next-door office. From our seats in the front office we could see her talking to a client through a thick glass wall, but no sound penetrated through it. Airline commercials, maps, and tourist posters from Morocco, Tunis, and Mexico adorned the walls of the agency, making it look like any other travel agency in the capital. The only indication that something migration-related was taking place in this office was a large silver and copper image of the Virgin of Guadalupe in a corner. The patron saint of Mexico and also the most popular religious and cultural image among undocumented Mexican migrants in the United States (Gálvez 2009), this Virgin is not commonly venerated in Peru. A bouquet of red and white flowers—the colors of the Peruvian flag—was placed next to the Virgin. I wondered who had offered the flowers—perhaps Señora Pilar herself or one of her clients in anticipation of a successful journey?

When Señora Pilar finally returned to the front office, she asked Jenny who had sent us. Jenny answered quickly that it was Julia Quispe from Huancayo, Fabiola's mother. "Oh!" Señora Pilar said in recognition. "Please, come on in, *pase niña*! What can I do for you?" I was not sure if the invitation was extended to both of us, but I took a chance and followed Jenny. "So what can I do for you?" Señora Pilar repeated, and asked us to take a seat in her office while scrutinizing us both. Jenny was visibly nervous and murmured something about wanting to go to the United States and that her friend Fabiola had told her about this agency and how it helped people to leave. Then Señora Pilar looked directly at me and asked: "And you, what brings you here?" I froze. While in retrospect her question could have been easily anticipated, I felt unprepared to answer it. After a moment of silence that seemed eternal, I said that I was just accompanying my friend. I couldn't think of a better response. The conversation continued between Jenny and Señora Pilar, who purposefully proceeded to completely ignore me.

"So where would you like to go, *niña?*" Señora Pilar asked Jenny. "To the United States," Jenny said. "I'd like to join Fabiola there; she's my best friend," she added quickly. Perhaps she hoped that referencing her close relationship with a former client would improve her chances of the broker agreeing to help her. After grilling Jenny for a long time about her background, her family, their economic situation, and Jenny's travel objectives, Señora Pilar concluded:

> I can help you, but you have to get your passport and open a savings account in a major bank. Then you come back and talk to me. But next time you must come by yourself. If you decide to travel you must come back by yourself and I will inform you of all the details. I will charge you a fee of $2,000 dollars to guide you through the process. You pay me $1,000 up front and when you get the visa you pay me the additional $1,000. I can give you a receipt of this as a service fee, if you like. But you have to get the visa yourself. I can coach you, but you have to get the visa. How much have you saved already?

Jenny responded that she had saved U.S. $3,500 already, which I knew wasn't true (she had saved much less, yet she was confident that if a travel opportunity opened up her family and friends would feel obliged to help her pay for it). Señora Pilar immediately exclaimed that Jenny needed *much* more than that if she *really* wanted to travel, but she refrained from giving a total price or any explanation of why much more money was needed. With that remark Señora Pilar got up from her chair. The consultation was over. As I went to the rest room I heard her tell Jenny in a friendly and motherly tone: "Don't worry, *hijita.* I will get you out of here in whatever possible way (*yo te voy a sacar como sea*). Don't worry. You will be traveling (*tu sí vas a viajar*)."[9]

I waited for almost fifteen minutes before Jenny finally came out of Señora Pilar's office. We thanked the receptionist and left quickly. Once outside Jenny told me that while I was in the restroom Señora Pilar had scolded her for bringing me to the appointment. Jenny imitated her broker's penetrating voice as she parodied her: "Why did you bring her—are you crazy, she could be someone from the consulate, she is *Americana*, can you imagine if she were to look for something, then I am screwed (*me fregue*). I can't tell everyone how I do business." Never mind that I had no U.S. citizenship or even permanent residency in my possession, but in Señora Pilar's eyes I was an "Americana," not someone who needed a broker to get a visa, but someone who was probably out to nail people like her who benefited from connecting local labor with global labor markets.

Most migrants were well aware that dealing with migration brokers involved the risk of getting scammed; indeed, there was an abundance of such stories in both the local and national news media. Consequently, migrants looked to establish a relationship of trust with their broker as a way to minimize this risk. The brokers I had the opportunity of interacting with all took pride in building their reputation and growing their business. They knew that just like in any business satisfied customers could lead to a potentially larger client base through word-of-mouth recommendations. Brokers were interested in earning a good reputation and reassured concerned clients about the quality for their work:

> This is Azángaro and there are many liars (*mentirosos*) around here who seek to rob their customers. For example that guy [points to someone at the end of an alley], he says he is a *jalador*, but what he really does is cheat and steal from his clients. He got into the habit and apparently he earns more this way than by doing the regular work. He takes advantage of people's distress and they fall into his trap. But I'm known here and I offer you a good job.

In fact, scamming incidents did happen frequently and when they occurred there was no consumer protection. Aspiring migrants were always at risk of losing their hard-earned or borrowed money.[10] Yet the fear of being scammed was never as pronounced as the fear of being interrupted en route. This was especially true of the migration of unaccompanied minors who were being brought to join their migrant parents abroad, a topic I discuss when addressing the separation of families in chapter 3.[11]

But while most informants either knew or had heard of someone who had been *estafados* (scammed) by a broker or even had experienced it themselves, many more had stories to share about how they had been abused in encounters with state officials more than once in their lives. This helps explain why people were so open to dealing with migration brokers and why they preferred to pay for such services rather than dealing with official bureaucracies on their own. Whereas aspiring migrants rarely saw state officials as representing their interests, in contrast they viewed the broker as a reliable guarantor of international travel through a variety of travel modalities and to virtually any desired destination.

Hierarchies of Destinations and Travel Modalities

The travel options and price range of "travel products" offered by migration brokers have changed over time in accordance with shifting immigration policies, labor market demands in destination countries, and new technologies simultaneously used to control and facilitate migration. While Spain, Italy, and Japan had already emerged as major destinations for Peruvians since the late 1980s and Argentina and Chile in the second half of the 1990s (Escrivá et al. 2010; Paerregaard 2008; Stefoni 2005; Takenaka et al. 2010; Tamagno 2003), the United States has remained a major destination for Peruvians overall. Those Peruvians who migrated in the 1980s and 1990s and who didn't obtain an official visa or had family members already in the United States who could petition them often took the long route north through Central America or Mexico. Once in the United States they tried to regularize their status using various strategies. Many applied for political asylum upon arrival but only a small portion of applicants received it. The majority had their requests denied but appealed their cases numerous times, and some were eventually deported (Berg 2010).

By 2004, few people in the Mantaro Valley regarded the paperless route out of Peru through Mexico that had dominated international migration flows to the United States in the 1990s as a desirable option. Crossing the U.S.-Mexico border as *mojados* (wetbacks) or smuggled as human cargo was seen as simply too dangerous and not worth the risk, especially for women. As a result most aspiring migrants who wanted to leave the valley in this period "traveled by plane" (*viajar por avión*). Traveling by air covered a range of travel options at different price levels organized along a hierarchy of desirability, with the officially issued visa as the most sought-after option. Peruvians were also still eligible at the time to participate in the yearly congressionally mandated Diversity Immigrant Visa Program offered by the U.S. State Department to persons from countries with low rates of immigration to the United States who met certain eligibility requirements. This changed after 2007 because too many Peruvians (over 50,000) had become legal permanent residents in the United States over the previous five-year period. Consequently, Peruvians no longer qualified for the visa lottery. If an official visa was not granted, an aspiring migrant could opt for a legitimately issued visa obtained on the basis of fraudulent documents and a fabricated narrative and personal file (this would still enable the person to travel "legally" by air). Finally, if such options failed the last option was to travel to Mexico and then enter the United States via the U.S.-Mexican border without documents, often after a long and complex travel itinerary involving multiple intermediate countries. This latter option through Mexico ranked lowest in the hierarchy of travel options and was often seen as a means of last resort when all other options had failed.

Migration brokers evaluated particular clients for how well they seemed to fit into particular visa categories and some went to great lengths to prepare their clients to embody the right identity for a given visa category. This involved complex processes of stylization and modification of the body through clothing and hairstyles and the adjustment of linguistic and other markers through which aspiring migrants learned to carry themselves and embody the privilege of mobility in the appropriate manner. In this way, brokers hoped to circumvent the heightened scrutiny reserved for racialized populations in process of admission to the United States.

Fitting into Visa Categories

On its website the U.S. embassy in Lima announces that its consular section grants visas to most of the visa applicants who are interviewed there daily, and that it has granted visas to "Peruvians from every region and from a wide variety of backgrounds."[12] Yet I continuously heard of rejected visa applications, mainly from working-class Peruvians from the Andean provinces.

The visas granted by the U.S. embassy in Lima follow the standard U.S. visa system, which encompasses well over thirty different visa categories referred to by letters and numbers. For example, an A-3 visa is for domestic employees accompanying a diplomat or foreign government official; a J-1 visa is for exchange visitors, including intern programs for university students and au-pair programs; an R-1 is for religious workers, and so on. But brokers don't use these numerical categories when speaking to clients. Instead they use categories that are emic to the migration industry, such as traveling "like an artist" (*viajar como artista*), "like a nun" (*viajar como monja*), or "like a businessperson" (*viajar como empresario*).

The politics of race, class, and gender at work in the brokers' recommendation of visa categories to their clients was nothing short of striking. I was told that when Japan was a popular migration destination for Peruvians in the early 1990s, brokers offered to help Peruvians of non-Japanese descent to travel "like a Japanese" (*viajar como Japonés*). This travel modality occurred in the context of a period of increased Nikkei "return migration" (Nikkei is the term used to designate Japanese migrants and their descendants), because the Japanese government offered visas to Japan to Peruvians of Japanese (Takenaka 1999).[13] Traveling "like a Japanese" involved purchasing expensive false Japanese ID papers (*kosegi*) certifying the traveler's entitlement to a Japanese last name, but it also required racial and bodily mimesis to successfully pass as Japanese. In the early 1990s, several clinics in Lima were known to offer eye surgery to "stretch the eyes" (*jalar los ojos*), making them phenotypically Asian. This particular service catered to a niche market of Peruvians of non-Japanese descent who were looking to migrate to Japan by taking advantage of the liberalization in Japanese immigration law for descendants of Peruvian Nikkei. In 1991, stories about these "false Nikkei" first started to appear in the national newspapers in Peru.[14] Later that same year the Japanese government began to require tourist visas for all Peruvians entering Japan (Takenaka 2004).[15] While the case of Japan represents an extreme case of embodiment because of the surgical modification of the racialized body to fit a visa category, it illustrates how far aspiring migrants are willing to go to realize their dreams of migration.

Sometimes a broker would offer a client the opportunity to travel with an altogether different nationality; thus, several of my informants had entered the United States with nationalities other than Peruvian. Aurelio, a construction worker from Urcumarca living in Maryland, had left Peru in 2000 "as an Argentine" (*como Argentino*). With loans from his brothers already in the United States and an extra small loan (*hipoteca*) against the value of his home in the popular neighborhood of Los Olivos, he had purchased an Argentinean passport, Argentinean ID papers, and a marriage certificate issued in Buenos Aires, and used these documents to travel to the United States from Buenos Aires at a time when Argentineans could still do so under the U.S. Visa Waiver Program. Argentina's participation in this program was terminated in 2002 in light of the country's financial crisis, which was assumed to cause more Argentineans to migrate and seek unauthorized employment in the United States. Similarly, Tamagno (2003) has discussed how Peruvian migrants at the beginning of the 2000s entered Italy with Venezuelan passports and residence papers at a time when Venezuelans did not require visas to enter Italy.

The fact that it was deemed advantageous to leave Peru with a different nationality has to do with the way Peru was perceived internationally in the 1980s and early 1990s. Terrorism, the drug trade, corruption, and the cholera epidemic of 1991 all contributed to "bad press," which consequently constructed Peruvians as dangerous criminals, terrorists, or as contagion to the host country. This image persisted for a long time, making it unlikely that a foreign embassy would grant a tourist visa to a Peruvian citizen without extensive scrutiny. Several of my interviewees who migrated with visas in the 1990s reported that they had been subject to greater scrutiny at border checkpoints and ports of entry than travelers of other nationalities. In the eyes of an INS official in the 1990s, any Peruvian could be a drug mule or a terrorist and therefore a potential risk to U.S. society. This changed in the early 2000s after

Peru's economic restructuring and through new political alliances in Washington.[16]

Light skinned and urban Huancaínos would typically be advised to apply either for a tourist visa based on their potential to embody urban middle-class social identities; a student visa based on claims to already existing educational credentials and the promise of future individual achievement; or a special business visa which capitalized on the production and circulation of a new type of citizen—the entrepreneur—much touted by neoliberal developers and policy makers (Cánepa Koch 2013; see also Tapia 1998). Migrants from rural areas or those from provincial cities who had not mastered the skill to act "urban" and "cosmopolitan" to a degree that would convince an immigration officer could be advised to travel on a religious visa, for example. When Jenny returned to Señora Pilar's agency, Señora Pilar had suggested that Jenny travel as a nun (*viajar como monja*) on a special visa for religious missions. According to Señora Pilar, traveling as a nun was the most feasible strategy at that particular moment for someone with Jenny's profile: young, single, and of humble (*humilde*) demeanor. "Humble" in this context is a racially coded term associated with people of lower-class Andean origins. *Buena apariencia*, which literally translates as "good appearance," but in Peru connotes a "nonindigenous" appearance, was another term I frequently heard in these contexts. In contrast, characteristics deemed undesirable were indicated by terms such as *achorado*, which in Peru means an individual with a defiant character, often a member of a nonwhite, urban, and lower social class.

Several Peruvians I interviewed in the United States had "traveled as artists," which almost always meant as a member of a folklore ensemble invited to perform in Peruvian-owned restaurants and at cultural venues abroad. This visa category put into play a potentially ambivalent relationship to the concept of an ethnic and cultural background. It required not only the ability to dance a variety of folkloric dances from various regions of Peru (including *huaylash* from the Mantaro Valley), but also an extensive portfolio with photo albums and printed posters and flyers announcing performances in various Peruvian cities to establish a credible history of a person's membership in a particular group, band, or dance ensemble. Traveling "as an artist" was not so much about erasing indigeneity as it was about producing and objectifying it—much like the folklore performances I will discuss in chapter 5—in ways that translated a rural background into positive cultural capital.

Each visa category thus required detailed preparation and rehearsals of the social identities they indexed in order to appear credible. Brokers warned aspiring migrants that their chances of getting a visa would stand and fall on the basis of their performance during the visa interview. This allowed brokers to displace any responsibility for a rejected visa application onto the client. Some brokers asked migrants to rehearse their new bodily identities to perfection but no matter how hard the migrants worked or how convincing they appeared in the eyes of the broker, it was always the consular official who had the last word on the matter.

The Visa Interview

The mere sight of the U.S. embassy is enough to understand why so many aspiring migrants not only feared the visa interview but found it daunting just to enter the embassy. Located in the upscale residential neighborhood of La Molina, the embassy had been rebuilt in the mid-1990 to protect itself from attacks by Sendero Luminoso and MRTA and it was meant to look and feel like a fortress. Everything about this space was alienating: the architecture, the heavy security checks at the entrance, the double glass doors, the impeccable but cold marble floors, the intense air conditioning, the "group system" invented to handle the large numbers of people entering the premises every day herded as they were by armed guards at every step of the process.[17] The staff inside were cordial and friendly and most spoke Spanish, yet the cultural difference informing the "bureaucratic styles" of U.S. versus Peruvian state officials made it difficult for aspiring migrants to gauge the reactions of the consular staff to their paper files.

The appointment at the embassy for the visa interview—along with the actual entry at a U.S. airport—is one of the key instances in the migration process where the legitimacy of a person's claim to mobility can be destabilized, questioned, and come under siege within a matter of minutes. Scholars have described how state officials read affective and bodily expressions such as anxiety and fear as reasons to warrant further questioning, detention, and deportation (Gilboy 1991; Salter 2008).

Figure 2.2. The U.S. embassy in Lima. (Photo by OtakuCrazy of Wikimedia Commons)

Salter (2008), for example, argues that decisions made at the border, or what he call "border examinations," are specially meant to alienate each and every traveler crossing the frontier, not just migrants or refugees. In the case of Fuzhounese migration to the United States, Julie Chu describes how "the work in paperwork" becomes most important (2010:126) when migrants encounter foreign state officials and institutions. Unlike encounters with local bureaucracies, where people tend to mobilize personal contacts or look for culturally shared connections to establish communication, in the face-to-face encounters at foreign embassies or at overseas ports of entry it is the documents themselves that serve as the central point of mediation between the visa applicant and the state official. Yngvesson and Coutin have also described the heightened "tension between papers (which should authenticate a self that preexists its documentation) and the de facto experience of a self that exceeds its documentation" (2006:179) during these moments of border crossing.

Brokers and more experienced family members or acquaintances therefore carefully instructed aspiring migrants to be calm and display no emotion so as not to evoke any suspicion of a possible mismatch between the paperwork and the embodied self before the state official. Self-control was a central element in the display of tacit embodied belonging that made up a successful performance. The idea was to act as "entitled" as possible and display a natural ease in inhabiting both elite urban spaces and what Marc Augé (1995) has called "non-places," that is, the self-contained spaces such as airports in which individuals appear to be connected in a uniform manner as they transit through space, but where no organic social life is possible.[18] Chu refers to the specific embodied skills required to transit in these spaces as "airport habitus" (2010:148). Airport habitus is a way of comporting the body to pass smoothly through departure and arrival checks, without giving anything away at the most basic level of bodily affect and communicative gestures which could compromise the travelers' claim to free and unquestioned mobility.

When a migration broker coaches an aspiring migrant to travel using a particular visa category, he or she assesses the prospective migrant's ability to convincingly carry the relationship between the written description of the travel document and its personal embodiment. Whereas external cognitive knowledge can be memorized and faked, embodied knowledge cannot. Either you have and feel it or you don't. Aspiring migrants' ability to carry themselves in particular ways is so crucial because it is on this basis that consular staff and immigration officials will either disqualify or embrace their claim to mobility and movement across national borders. The question, as Lund (2001:22) puts it, becomes about whether "the accumulated documents describing the body being presented stand up to scrutiny."

Provided that a visa is granted in Lima, another big hurdle still lies ahead: the encounter with the immigration officer at the U.S. port of entry. In preparation for this last step, migrants were sometimes offered additional advice or "pre-flight briefings" (Tamagno 2003) that included final advice on clothing styles, hairstyles, and what kind of suitcases to bring. The latter followed the general rule of reducing the quantity and increasing the quality of luggage and carry-on bags. This point about suitcases as an indication of a particular migrant identity was also brought to my attention by Leonora, a middle-class Limeña, who prior to her permanent relocation to Miami worked as a flight attendant out of Jorge Chávez International Airport in Lima. Talking about her experience working at the airport counter, Leonora said: "We could always tell who the migrants were. The lower-class Peruvians with a lot of luggage were going to Paterson. When they were approaching the check-in area some of my colleagues at the counter would joke about them and say 'Here come the Patersonians.'"

Airlines have long been mandated by international law to carry out migration control functions such as preventing people who they suspect are traveling on counterfeit documents from boarding an aircraft (Feller 1989; Nyberg Sørensen and Gammeltoft-Hansen 2013). If they fail to carry out these functions the carriers could face economic sanctions. Flight attendants and airport ground staff thus become central actors in the "control industry" and aspiring migrants must continue to carefully monitor their behavior throughout check-in, departure, and entry to the destination country. A moment of absentmindedness or neglect (*descuido*) even in the check-in area in one's own country can compromise the aspiring migrant's mobile future. Only in the comfort of a relative's living room or dormitory in the U.S. city of destination can the migrant traveler fully relax—at least temporarily—and consider the travel part of the migration journey completed.

Luck, Papers, and the Biometric Body

In 2002, the U.S. Congress passed the Enhanced Border Security and Visa Entry Reform Act, which mandated the use of biometrics in U.S. visas. The new law required that after October 2004 U.S. embassies and consulates abroad could only issue machine-readable, tamper-resistant visas and other travel and entry documents that use biometric identifiers. It also required foreign countries that wished to remain in the U.S. Visa Waiver Program to use only machine-readable, tamper-resistant passports that incorporated biometric and authentication identifiers.[19] The standard biometric screening for visa applicants in the United States is established to be a digital photo and ten fingerprints scans, which are collected at the visa interview and stored in a database. When the successful visa applicant enters the United States, passport scans, new fingerprints, and a recent photograph are held against this database for comparison, making it more difficult to travel on altered travel documents.

The question of biometric data storage and management and the introduction of biometrics as the border technology par excellence have spurred much debate among scholars and policy makers alike. Scholars have shown that biometric technologies as applied in different contexts and regions are central to the remaking of borders, of bodies, and of identities in today's world (Dijstelbloem et al. 2011; Magnet 2011; Van der Ploeg and Sprenkels 2011). Critics of biometric identification have problematized the ways in which bodies become related to identity under this regime and what the political ramifications of this coupling might be (Van der Ploeg 1999). Biometric technology generates what Irma van der Ploeg calls "a readable body." This technology, she argues, "transforms the body's surfaces and characteristics into digital codes and ciphers to be 'read' by a machine" (1999:295). Yet, the meaning of the biometric body is always contingent upon the contexts in which it will be read and how it is tied to identity within the context of the social and political institutions that control the international movement of people. Magnet (2011) has argued that biometrics at the border and in other realms of society offers "new visualization technologies to definitely identify bodies and sort them according to risk—a classification process fueled by xenophobic anxieties and intimately connected to the capitalist enterprise" (Magnet 2011:125). It is likely, as also suggested by Salter (2006:185), that the burden of surveillance will continue to fall disproportionately on the poor and marginal.

Before the implementation of biometric screening systems at USCIS checkpoints, it was still possible and relatively easy to travel on someone else's passport. For example, two brothers in my study traveled to the United States in the 1990s using the same passport twice. Once in the United States, the older brother mailed his passport back to his younger brother in Peru, who used it to travel the following year and successfully argued that he had lost his entry card and that his passport did not get stamped when he reentered Peru. When I inquired how that could have been possible, one of them said, "We look like each other . . . and they [i.e. the immigration authorities] can't tell the difference anyway. To the *gringos* all cholos look the same." But in the biometric era, not all cholos "read" the same. When equipment for biometric screenings started to be established at the major U.S. ports of entry after 2002, some migrants ended up getting entangled in the documentary traces left during their own previous migration attempts—or in traces left by others in their name.

The heavier reliance on biometric identification also puts more weight on the visa interview and less on a portfolio of supporting documents. In fact, the website of the U.S. embassy in Lima now explicitly states that "the U.S. visa application is interview-based rather than document-based and the Consular Officers typically do not review additional documentation that is provided."[20] This website also informs the reader that the average visa interview lasts 3 to 5 minutes, which raises all sorts of questions about the arbitrariness by which visa decisions are made. Gilboy (1991), for example, has shown how inspectors from the now defunct INS informally shared experiences that supported official "risk profiles" with racialized national stereotypes and more recent research confirms this finding (Magnet 2011).

When a visa application is denied, the most common reason given is that the applicant did not demonstrate strong enough ties—whether social, familial, or economic—to their country of origin to convince the officer that they have no intentions of migration but that they will return to their country before the visa expires. Indeed, section 214(b) of the U. S. Immigration and Nationality Act requires the interviewing consular officer to assume that the applicant intends to immigrate and if s/he is not convinced otherwise a visa is denied. Migrants interpret the outcome of such decisions either as a product of their own failure to perform convincingly, or simply as sheer bad luck in a larger economy of things beyond their control. When Inés, whose story was analyzed in the last chapter, was denied a visa in her first attempt to obtain a visa legally, she proclaimed: "I am sick of my bad luck (*estoy harta de mi suerte de perro*)." Yet in her case, bad luck was not a reason to give up on her project of mobility: less than a year later Inés was living in Miami.

Claiming to be out of luck might also reflect migrants' visceral response to the injustices of discrimination and racial profiling, here understood as the targeting of particular individuals by law enforcement agents based on visible personal characteristics that may also include markers of difference other than race, including ethnicity, national origin, language, and religion. Critical race theorists have used the concepts of microaggressions to characterize the racial affront that minorities encounter in many situations in everyday life (Romero 2008), but perhaps nowhere is the risk of becoming a target of racial profiling so imminent as at the immigration checkpoint. When it occurs the consequences for migrants and their families can be devastating.

Rosita's Impasse: When Documents Fail

Now and then migrants arrive at an impasse. In *Cruel Optimism*, Lauren Berlant defines an impasse as a "time of dithering from which someone or some situation cannot move forward" (2011:4). When an aspiring migrant fails to perform at a visa interview; when a broker disappears unexpectedly with years' worth of savings of an entire extended family; when border guards single migrants out for further questioning on the basis of racial profiling and "risk categories"; or when a deportation order is issued or executed and migrants are forcibly exiled; then the fantasies and aspirations of a mobile future that was supposed to offer the migrant labor stability, education for his or her children, existential tranquility, and perhaps even a brick house of his or her own in the hometown, starts to crumble.

When Rosita first told me her story in Lima it was just a few months after her detention and involuntary return from Atlanta. Rosita had been on her way back to Chicago after a trip to Peru and had to change flights in Atlanta. When attempting to board the plane in Atlanta she was held back in a random security check and an immigration inspector asked Rosita to accompany him to a separate room for additional interrogation. A light-skinned, middle-class Huancaína and not the typical candidate for a racially profiled security check, Rosita always traveled with her pile of documents certifying her good legal standing and her family's properties in Peru, just to play it safe, as she said. She had recently applied in Chicago for an extension of her tourist visa , because she had been unable to return to Peru after the usual ninety days, and had already received the USCIS notification confirming that the extension had been granted. She was confident of her own lawfulness and didn't think much of what she perceived at first to be a routine security check. She saw the situation as an inconvenience that she had to deal with, a temporary stalling of sorts, which would soon *arreglarse* (get fixed) so that she could continue her trip and be reunited with her husband and children in Chicago.

In Chicago, Rosita was a housewife and did not work outside the home. The family lived off her husband's salary. Her husband and children had overstayed their visas, but Rosita prided herself on still using the same multiple entry tourist visa that she had used when she had first arrived. She always made sure she was in good legal standing and was proud of never having overstayed her visa. The flexibility of her dedication to the home allowed her to return to Peru every three months to take care of the family's pending affairs or to visit other family members and extended kin in Huancayo and Lima. Unfortunately for Rosita, the USCIS officer had no time for her attempts to explain the full circumstances of her frequent travels in her very limited and broken English. Her accent immediately placed her in the category of a suspect traveler. Rosita was taken to another room and was told to admit to having worked in the United States without authorization. She was also accused of tax evasion on money that she presumably had been paid in cash while "working illegally" in America. Rosita didn't understand all the details of the accusations, but was outraged. How was it possible that she, who had her paperwork in order, was being subjected to this kind of treatment? "They treated me like a simple chola," she said, visibly upset when reflecting on the incident in retrospect. Her use of a Peruvian racial category to explain how she had felt denigrated and discriminated against is telling. She was assuming that this kind of treatment was normal toward a "chola" (cf. Weismantel 2001), but clearly didn't conceive of herself as one. Singled out as a potential "illegal alien," an immigrant worker who had worked without authorization in the United States, her very presence at Atlanta airport was highly questionable in the eyes of the USCIS officials. A Spanish-speaking USCIS officer told Rosita that she could not leave the room before she signed some paperwork. It was getting late and Rosita was desperate to make her connecting flight to Chicago, so she consented to sign. When she boarded a plane many hours later her destination was Lima, not Chicago.

Back in Peru without her husband and children, Rosita was desperate to return to the United States as soon as possible. She eventually ended up in Señora Pilar's daughter Elva and her son-in-law's office in Lima by way of Jenny, to seek help in appealing her case. For a $50 fee, Elva's husband, a lawyer, agreed to request Rosita's file from the USCIS and evaluate it. But Elva also warned her that it could take up to three months for the file to arrive and only then would they be able to offer Rosita an answer about the possibilities of appealing the case, for which they would charge additional and much larger fees. Rosita protested and said that she couldn't wait that long. She had already been in Peru for five months and she wanted to move beyond the impasse of her present situation. Despite her frequent email, Skype, and phone conversations with her husband and children in Chicago, which offered her some solace by allowing her to "mother" her children from a distance—the subject of the next chapter—her present situation had become both unsustainable and unbearable. Rosita's husband and children were also unable to travel because they were undocumented. "But why don't they all come back here?" I pressed one afternoon over tea in my apartment. After all Rosita and her husband still had some family properties in Huancayo and they owned a house in a middle-class neighborhood in Lima. It didn't seem like such a bad option to me to have the whole family return to Peru. But Rosita was firm. She didn't want them to return permanently to Peru for her sake, because as she insisted: "I don't want to jeopardize the children's future."

I knew Rosita was talking to different people and trying to get a recommendation for a migration broker, but I didn't know the details about the travel options she was considering. Then one day she was gone. I learned from her cousin in Huancayo that she had bought a "package solution" from a broker that included a new passport and a complex travel itinerary involving a week on a cruise ship in the Gulf of Mexico. She had been instructed to bring a slick suitcase with several evening gowns for the cruise. The cruise was "for real," her cousin said, but Rosita would later get off the ship and cross the U.S.-Mexico border in Arizona. Risking not only a fine and imprisonment for "illegal reentry" to the United States, but also her life in the process, Rosita was determined to be reunited with her family at all costs. Stuck and immobile back in Peru, she embarked on a risky journey and eventually emerged paperless in the Arizona desert with no documentary traces of her preborder crossing self. Previously a lawful visitor to the United States, Rosita had now been transformed into a criminal alien by virtue of reentering upon removal from U.S. soil—a necessary transformation to be able to reunite with her children in Chicago.

The migration trajectories discussed in this chapter demonstrate the twofold challenge faced by Andean Peruvians who attempt to access transnational mobility in today's world. On the one hand, the rise of the global security state has resulted in new surveillance apparatuses at international borders and within national territories along with new regimes of exception that have led to disproportional detentions and deportations of unauthorized migrants (Inda 2006; Peutz and De Genova 2010; Fassin 2011). These logics shape the experiences of contemporary migrants as well as the logics of the bureaucracies that they must navigate throughout the migration process. On the other hand, migrants must also navigate new racialized boundaries that have emerged both within source and destination countries. Just as migrants carry documents that have to be validated by state agents, so too must the racialized identities that migrants either claim or try to avoid at all costs be ratified by others or else they will get "treated like a chola," as in Rosita's case.

Despite the endurance of certain racial projects, there is also arbitrariness at work here. Unlike Agapito in the opening vignette whose indigenous looks and embodied "rural habitus" gave away at the most basic level his lack of urban and cosmopolitan competency and eventually forced him to give up his migration plans, Rosita's lighter skin, demeanor, urban competency, and middle-class lifestyle initially made her a candidate for a U.S. visa, yet none of these embodied qualities prevented her from being targeted as an "illegal alien" within a broader racial economy. However, despite the fact that she actually possessed the appropriate permit to reenter the United States legally, Rosita's personhood was read against a broader discourse of immigrant illegality and the persistent practices of racialization of Latin American migrants and U.S. Latinos overall in which all travelers from Latin America are assumed to be potential visa overstayers unless in the blink of an eye they can prove otherwise. Rosita's failure to communicate successfully with the USCIS officers to deter them from identifying her social identity as a "migrant," put her on a plane back to Lima.

The unauthorized migration resulting from the "paper fixes" discussed in this chapter ultimately puts migrants on an almost unavoidable path to "illegality" that has deep and enduring consequences for the unfolding of their lives once in the United States. When an overstayed visa makes travel back home an impossibility, migrants turn to mediated forms of long-distance communication to stay in contact with relatives, mother children from a distance, participate in life in the hometown, and express and edit their own feelings as they learn to enact, embody, and experience familial and social relations across time and space in new ways. These mediated practices and processes are the subjects of Part II of the book.

Transnational Socialities

3

Remote Sensing

Structures of Feeling in Long-Distance Communication

"When I first arrived I felt awful about leaving *mis bebes* in Lima," Amparo confessed as she sipped her clove and cinnamon tea after our lunch in one of Miami's Peruvian restaurants. Like most Peruvian women of provincial origin who migrate internationally she had left behind her husband and two sons aged seven and fifteen when migrating to the United States in 2000. "At first, I called them every day, sometimes more than once a day," she said. "As I wasn't there with them I tried to find out how they were doing, if they were eating, if they behaved with their father, and how they were feeling. I was used to be around them all the time." Amparo, who had migrated from Matahuasi in the 1990s, had set up a small grocery shop after arriving in Lima where she settled with her husband in the working-class neighborhood of La Victoria. The shop allowed her to be around the house all day and she prided herself in knowing everything that was happening in her children's lives. "With the shop," she said, "I could supervise my children. I cooked for them and made sure they did their homework. I could be on their case all day long." In Amparo's perception of appropriate parenting, being on her sons' case all day long (*estar encima de ellos*) was equivalent to being a good mother, but she soon faced great challenges sustaining this set of values.

When Amparo's husband José was laid off from his job as a driver for a government agency in 1999, life had changed for the family. They needed to act quickly to diversify their household earnings and minimize the risks to their already vulnerable household economy. It was the last year of the Fujimori regime and for working-class Peruvians the future looked bleak. When they discussed their options, migration was instantly on the table. Amparo had previously worked as a live-in nanny in Chile's capital Santiago, but didn't want to go back there. "Chileans don't treat people well," she said categorically, referencing the widespread discrimination of Peruvians in Santiago that she had experienced firsthand.[1] Instead Amparo and her sister Inés decided to contact their long-lost father and a maternal uncle in the United States. The following year Amparo left for Miami and the year after that Inés followed suit. Both left their children behind in the care of husbands and extended family.

Recent scholarship has established that the separation of families is one of the hidden social costs of globalization (Abrego 2014; Dreby 2010; Hondagneu-Sotelo and Avila 1997; Isaksen et al. 2008; Parreñas 2001). While the separation of families for purposes of work is nothing new (e.g., Thomas and Znaniecki 1996), recent case studies from Latin America, Asia, and Africa indicates that the transnational family resulting from the global division of labor is becoming an increasingly common family form across the globe (Abrego 2014; Baldassar et al. 2007; Baldassar and Merla 2013; Núñez Carrasco 2010; Parreñas 2001).[2] As migrant parents, especially mothers, depart for overseas labor markets—like Amparo in the opening vignette, and Inés and Domitila whose stories were discussed in chapter 1—they leave their own children to be cared for by unpaid relatives in the home country. This reorganization and reconstitution of motherhood to accommodate the spatial and temporal separations produced by migration was first documented by Hondagneu-Sotelo and Avila (1997), who concluded that among the Mexican and Central American working-class migrant women they studied in Los Angeles, this practice of "transnational mothering" is an increasingly common result of the feminization of global migration and of the expansion of motherhood beyond the realm of social reproduction to include breadwinning.[3] These entanglements between different women across the world based on relations of paid and unpaid labor are now commonly referred to in the literature as "global care chains" (Hochschild 2000:131) or as an "international division of reproductive labor" (Parreñas 2000). They result in numerous social and emotional contradictions for the domestic workers and their children and other dependants in the home country. These more vulnerable members of transnational families experience a "care deficit" or a "care crisis" because of the massive export of their mothers and caregivers (Hochschild 2000; Isaksen et al. 2008; Parreñas 2001, 2002, 2005b).

Peruvian transnational migration, like other migrations, is gendered in particular ways and has characteristics that merit attention in a comparative discussion of transnational families and long-distance kinwork accomplished through transnational communication. Following initial feminized flows of migrants, Peruvian migration generally displays a high degree of gender equity (Durand 2010).[4] Contrary to other cases where it is common for one parent to migrate while the other stays behind, it is not uncommon in the Peruvian case for both members of a couple to migrate or for both a child's parents to migrate, given Peruvian migration's general rootedness in family reunifications (Leinaweaver 2010). But perhaps most importantly, to a great extent Andean transnational families are socially organized according to principles characteristic of what Leinaweaver (2008, 2010) calls "child circulation," that is, the moving of children between households within Peru as an important part of local family-making efforts and social mobility among poor indigenous Peruvians. Especially in contexts of rural-to-urban migration, it is not uncommon for internal migrants to leave their children with grandparents or other relatives in Andean villages or in provincial cities. Take, for example, Nelly who migrated to the United States in 1989 to work as a domestic worker for a Peruvian diplomat's family in Washington, D.C. Nelly was originally from Urcumarca, but was brought to Lima by her mother when she was two years old. At age eleven, she was sent back to Urcumarca to live with an aunt and go to school in the village because her mother couldn't support her schooling in Lima. When Nelly was fourteen she returned to Lima to live with her mother and to study and work in the capital. This is a fairly typical example of child circulation. These long-standing forms of social organization characteristic of the Peruvian Andes must be kept in mind as the immediate precursor to the separation involved in the transnational circulation of migrants across the U.S.-Peruvian divide.

Women like Inés, Amparo, and Domitila who had no choice but to leave their children behind to work beyond Peru's borders continued to reproduce kinship ties and social relations more broadly from abroad. As transnational families and the practice of transnational parenting is becoming more common globally it is also changing as a result of new technology, legal regimes, and multidirectional exchanges across generations and between genders (Baldassar 2007; Baldassar and Merla 2013;

Mahler 2001). Some scholars suggest that transnational motherhood has been revolutionized by the emergence and use of new media environments through which migrant parents can participate in the daily lives of their children and other relatives in the home country in ways that achieve degrees of copresence that simulate "face-to-face" social interactions (Madianou and Miller 2012). Yet as I show in this chapter, the availability of new technologies did not always materialize in seamless and close relationships now mediated in new ways.

The initial optimism of studies that privileged attention to the empowering effects of new media to bolster the bonds of kinship and sociality within global settings and help migrants negotiate their absence from home more effectively is now giving way to a growing body of literature which documents the multiple and often contradictory role that new communication technology plays in the management of transnational family relations (Fresnoza-Flot 2009; Madianou 2012; Madianou and Miller 2012; Mahler 2001; Parreñas 2005a, 2005b; Wilding 2006).[5] While copresence and other affordances are generally assumed to be positive not just in the context of transnational family relationships but in contemporary social life more generally (Urry 2003), the technologies that offer these affordances are increasingly demonstrated to be both "a blessing and a burden" (Horst 2006). While giving the appearance of free and unrestricted communication, new technology also produces new forms of surveillance, intrusion, and control, and contributes to altering basic power asymmetries—for better or for worse—in parent-child or husband-wife relationships.

This chapter examines the mediated relationships and transnational forms of sociability and affect constituted by long-distance communication practices in contexts of prolonged family separation. Despite the many benefits of greatly enhanced global communication in today's interconnected world, migrants often experienced what one woman referred to as "communication problems." These communication problems frequently came to stand for the difficulties of navigating social relations under the impact of global migration and prolonged family separation not only literally, because communication was too costly, impractical, or complicated, but also figuratively, because of difficulties of speaking and sharing experiences across the U.S.-Peruvian divide.

To better describe the experience and affective dimension of prolonged separation—especially between parents and children—within the context of everyday life in Andean transnational families I evoke the concept of *remote sensing*. According to the standard geographic definition, remote sensing refers to the acquisition of information about an object or a phenomenon on the earth through technological mediation, but without making physical contact with the object. Despite the concept's status as a technical term which seems to suggest a unilateral gathering of information, I find that it accurately portrays migrant parents' attempts to "know something" and "sense something" about an object of desire (a child) from afar. This communicative and sensory practice reflects the contradictions set in motion by the migration process, which are often aggravated by prolonged physical separation.

Sustaining the right kind, form, and frequency of connections is important for migrants' sense of themselves as good mothers or parents, dutiful daughters, and faithful wives according to predominant notions of Andean personhood, motherhood, and childhood. Both migrants, their children, and other relatives in Peru rely on the partial truths produced through practices of communication that attempts to unleash, contain, or embargo certain emotions from transnational circulation. These practices must therefore be situated within a larger affective economy in which long-distance communication is embedded, appraised, and valued.

Long-distance communication, I argue, is key to the ongoing production of transnational social relationships, but it requires hard work and complex exercises of emotional management in order to connect and communicate effectively across borders. As a set of mediated communicative practices, long-distance communication is contingent on reception and circulation, not simply on the intentions of the producer or sender. By focusing on the experiences and meaning of copresence, absence, connection, forgetting, and loss that migration and prolonged separation engenders, I seek to illuminate the affective dimensions of everyday life among Peruvian labor migrants and what matters to such people in flux—but also what matters *between* people who forge mediated global connections that are both discursive and profoundly embodied.

Mediated Relationships

When people migrate they seldom do so alone. People migrate as parents, children of elderly parents, couples, members of transnational families, and local communities. Migrants are socially situated subjects, but they are endlessly constituted anew over the course of the migration process and within the context of particular relationships.[6]

A major concern among transnational families is to follow the welfare of children, spouses, other family members, friends, and *paisanos* back home. I often found recently arrived migrants constantly preoccupied with upholding the social bonds of kinship with their families in Peru. This long-distance social reproduction of kinship ties is never automatic and requires hard work, resources, energy, and attention that often drain resources from other endeavors in order not to lose its social meaning (cf. Di Leonardo 1987). Most migrants engage extensively in long-distance communication; they remit small amounts of money from their meager earnings; send gifts, and circulate a variety of material and media objects. Because the majority of Peruvians in my study eventually became undocumented in the United States once their initial visas had expired, they could not return to visit and relied to a greater extent on electronically mediated forms of communication through which they tried to assert some degree of presence in the lives of the ones they had left behind in Peru.

Anthropologists have long asserted that relationships—whether in "face-to-face" situations or otherwise (Goffman 1959)—are intrinsically a mediated social form. Indeed, most will concur that there is no stage to a relationship prior to its objectification through social interaction (Madianou and Miller 2012:142). Daniel Miller (2007) has argued that most social relationships are constituted by the dialectical relation between idealized notions of particular kin categories reflected in social norms and the actual persons who inhabit these categories in more or less successful or compliant ways. Transnational relationships and the communications that constitute them are no different in this respect. They not only reveal actual category-appropriate behaviors (i.e., the mother or the child), but also discrepancies between the actual and the normative (Madianou and Miller 2012:141). What complicates the dynamics of social relationships in contexts of global migration is the prolonged separation of family members due to legal and political barriers. Yet scholars have argued that new media environments have the potential to make people "tangible" and copresent even if only in electronically mediated form (Madianou and Miller 2012:122).[7]

Yet while recognizing that all relationships are mediated and come to exist only as they get objectified in social interaction, it is possible to argue that particular kinds of media frame and mediate relationships differently. Take, for example, the written documents discussed in the previous chapter. While it is easy to see written documents as simply giving access to what they document, we saw how documents—as an embodied technology—mediate the relationship between migrants and immigration officials, and in Hull's words "shape the significance of the signs inscribed on them and their relations with the objects they refer to" (2012:254). Yet if prompted, state officials will most likely deny the mediating role of documents as a tactic of power and authority—what Mazzarella (2006) calls the "politics of immediation"—and will, if asked in an official capacity, take the document to give direct access to a self that preexists its documentation and thus establish a relationship between writing and truth.

Scholars who address the literacy/orality issue in Andean societies have noted that in many areas of the rural Andes, writing and the written process correspond to unresponsive and often coercive external powers where the writing itself comes to maintain authority and legitimacy. Poole (2004) has noted that since the colonial era writing and documentation, as powerful markers of social class, have been seen by many Andean Peruvians as something which had to be produced in order to deal with coercive and racializing bureaucratic or legal procedures. They clearly understood, as Salomon and Niño-Murcia (2011:180) note, the popular saying "el papelito manda" (the paper rules). Because of this historically direct relationship to power and authority, writing is therefore generally not considered among Andean Peruvians as a conversational medium to talk about social and intimate personal relationships.

"I save my letters in this box," Agapito once told me while chatting in the back room to his hardware store in Huancayo. He pulled out a shoe box from underneath his bed which contained a neat little pile of letters and cards, and started to look for a particular letter I had asked him about. Agapito liked letters, he told me, because they can be saved (*los puedes guardar*) yet he also confessed that he seldom read them more than once.[8] He just kept them. Their materiality and object status, it seemed, allowed them to be stored and used as proof of Agapito's relationship to Asunta in a situation where distance and the lack of economic resources made it uncertain whether they were ever going to be together as a couple and a family again.

While Internet communication and telephony have proliferated in more recent years and made written letters a virtually obsolete media form today, I was occasionally asked to deliver letters and *encargos* myself when traveling between Peru and the United States during fieldwork. What surprised me when people shared these letters with me were their short length and stylistic characteristics. Contrary to Eurocentric ideals (and practices) of personal letters as spaces for intimate confessions, these letters were almost always extremely short and formulaic in style (cf. Lund Skar 1997). Most of them seemed to be written with the explicit purpose of reporting no news (in Spanish, *sin novedad*), which in the context of violence and poverty meant good news. On one occasion, traveling as such a contemporary "chasqui messenger," I delivered a letter from Paulino in Silver Spring to his *compadre* Damian in Vitarte, a popular neighborhood on the outskirts of Lima next to the highway leading to the Central Highlands. A chasqui is a messenger who during the Inca Empire delivered important official messages across the imperial (and here the transnational) territory. They were part of an elaborate communication and transport infrastructure which included an extensive road system supported by institutions such as the *tambos* (inns), *collcas* (warehouses for food storage), and bridges that allowed for the flows of population, labor, products, and information, which sustained the Inca Empire. I spent the afternoon with Damian and his family talking about life in the United States, about Damian's brothers who also lived in Silver Spring, and about Paulino and his family. Damian also called Paulino on the phone while I was present to report on my visit and talk about the news I had brought him from the United States, not about the letter, which he hadn't yet opened. When I left late in the afternoon, the envelope had been looked at and scrutinized, but it was still lying on the coffee table, unopened. It was the accompanying oral message from me, the person delivering the letter, which was the most important part of this transfer of information (cf. Lund Skar

1997). At first glance this incident could easily be taken to mean that Andean cultural practices are dominated by traditions of oral delivery; indeed, this has been a common assumption in much scholarship—although these practices were never exclusively oral, as new historical work on literacy has shown (Rappaport and Cummins 2011; Salomon and Niño-Murcia 2011). Rather than assuming oral and dialogical traditions in Andean life to be inherently characteristic of Andean societies, it is perhaps more productive to talk about the particular affordances of different kinds of media practices and how in turn different technologies are evaluated to satisfy distinctive needs for particular kinds of communication.

The experiences of transnational communication that I refer to and analyze in this chapter extend over a period of more than fifteen years (late 1980s to the present). Needless to say, major technological developments have taken place over this period which have changed the global mediascapes that Peruvians inhabit, and radically altered the spatiotemporal experiences of transnational families, including their possibilities for long-distance communication. In general, however, most Peruvians in my study preferred media technologies based on oral and visual communication rather than writing.[9] For Nelly, who had migrated to the United States in 1989 as a domestic worker, letter exchanges with her two daughters who lived with their grandmother in Lima were infrequent. Nelly's mother Guillermina, who took care of the two girls, Melanie at age seven and Doris at age three, had had little formal schooling and writing wasn't her strength. "Besides," as Nelly said, "the mailman didn't come to Flor de Amancaes, even today [2004] the mailman doesn't go there." (Flor de Amancaes is a former squatter settlement in Lima; like other shantytowns, it has developed into an urbanized neighborhood adjacent to the Río Rimac.) Instead, Nelly and her family used audiocassettes—an entirely aural form of communication and the dominant transnational communicative form during the late 1980s and 1990s—that they exchanged about once a month. Guillermina sent her cassettes through a remittance agency in the middle-class neighborhood of Miraflores where she would also pick up the monetary remittances from her daughter in the United States. Nelly in turn sent hers through a Hispanic remittance agency in Potomac. When migrants like Nelly recounted their experiences or allowed me to listen to old audiocassettes, it was clear that they understood how to exploit the difference between letters and audiocassettes as distinctive kinds of early media.

Before the privatization of telecommunications in Peru in 1994, phone calls were very expensive and therefore limited and they were generally initiated in the United States because of the lower cost of international calls there (Castells et al. 2007). Furthermore, fixed phone lines in homes were rare commodities in the early 1990s in the rural towns or marginal urban neighborhoods of Peru where most of the lower-class families had lived prior to migration. Nelly's mother, Guillermina, for example, did not have a landline telephone at the time of Nelly's migration, because very little infrastructure was available in Flor de Amancaes and phone lines were very difficult and expensive to get installed. To receive Nelly's periodic phone calls from abroad, Guillermina took the children to the shop of a family friend in another section of Flor de Amancaes close to the main road at the entrance to the settlement. Guillermina and Nelly always agreed beforehand about what time Nelly should call. But despite their efforts at careful planning, the disjuncture in the flow of everyday life in two distant countries would complicate their attempts to connect. Sometimes Guillermina's friend was not there when she and the girls arrived to receive their phone call or the friend's phone service was discontinued due to lack of payment. Yet failed attempts to communicate were most frequently caused by complications during Nelly's workday, which made it difficult for her to call at a specific and agreed time. Nelly took care of a special needs child with multiple health issues and this made her work schedule unpredictable.

Phone calls became more common after the privatization of telecommunications in Peru because of their greater accessibility and lower cost. Phone calls were generally preferred to deal with practical matters which needed quick solutions, but also for the weekly check-in to see how the children were doing. In 1995, Nelly finally had a landline telephone installed in Guillermina's house, but at this point Nelly's daughters, Melanie and Doris, had already been with their mother in the United States for almost three years. But at least, as Nelly said, the landline connection facilitated communication with her mother and younger sister left in Peru: "Now at any moment we can talk." In practice this meant that Nelly could call her mother any time *her* schedule permitted and that she didn't have to wait for Guillermina to arrive at her friend's store.

Nonmigrant relatives usually get the short end of the stick when it comes to initiating long-distance communication.

Without a doubt, wireless telephony represents the future of communication in both rural and urban areas in most Latin American countries and elsewhere in the developing world (Castells et al. 2007). The construction of cell phone towers and the installation of satellite systems has in the past decades enabled wireless telephony in many parts of rural Peru and resulted in the rapid adoption of mobile technologies in places where landline telephones were never installed.[10] Abroad, cell phones are indispensable tools for migrant workers in order to contact employers, leave a callback number, coordinate transportation needs in suburban settings, and communicate with family members back home. Many migrants also equip their elderly *campesino* parents or children left in custody of grandparents in highland Peru with cell phones (cf. Tamagno 2005).[11] While Peruvian migrants in the United States generally have regular cell phone subscriptions, their family members in Peru for the most part have prepaid subscriptions commonly purchased by their migrant relatives.[12] This enables migrants not only to avoid credit checks and fixed contracts when purchasing a phone in Peru, but also to control expenditures and call volume. Even when using a prepaid phone card, it is still relatively expensive to make long-distance calls from a cell phone in Peru and consequently members of transnational families in Peru still use these almost exclusively to recieve calls. During my fieldwork villagers from Urcumarca, even those who possessed cell phones, used prepaid phone cards to call from the only functioning public phone located in one of only two shops on the central plaza of Urcumarca. On Sunday afternoons, villagers with family abroad would come to Doña Fabiana's shop to receive their weekly phone calls from abroad.

Despite the overwhelming benefits of global mobile communications, we must not forget that deficient or nonexistent basic infrastructure in many rural communities in Latin America, including stable sources of electricity, makes it very difficult to charge a cell phone even if an area is globally connected through a satellite communication network. During my fieldwork I observed that rather than high-tech and expensive technology and electronic devices, it was the proliferation of low-tech and relatively cheap communication technologies including prepaid satellite phone cards used on landline phones, prepaid mobile phones, and publicly accessible Internet cafés (*cabinas públicas*), which enabled most U.S.-based Peruvian migrants and their family members in Peru to communicate frequently across borders. They thus bore witness to the truth of Vertovec's claim that cheap telephone calls are "the social glue connecting small-scale social formations across the globe" (2004:222).

Besides wireless telephony, Internet access through public Internet cafés—the so-called *cabinas públicas* that were invented in Peru in the mid-1990s—was a popular and inexpensive access point to technology both in the capital Lima and in the provinces.[13] Often located in a storefront with ten to twenty computers, the *cabinas públicas* are frequented not only by noisy teenagers playing the latest online video games, but by Peruvians of all ages—including older adults accompanied by children in their custody—trying to reach migrant relatives abroad through *videollamadas* (video calls) via Skype, or other kinds of VOIP technologies.[14] I observed and listened in on numerous conversations by members of transnational families in *cabinas públicas* in Huancayo, Jauja, and Lima about everything from coordinating the use of remittances and making decisions about the care of children to attempts to resolve long-distance marital conflicts over the Internet. Agapito, for example, whose desire to migrate I analyzed in chapter 2, took his three children to a *cabina pública* next door to his home in Huancayo every Sunday to "talk to their mother on the computer," as he said. Yet the lack of privacy in the *cabinas públicas* made Internet-mediated communication less ideal for someone like Agapito who didn't feel comfortable discussing what he considered private matters in a public space.

Unlike Agapito, his children were in frequent email contact with their mother. Asunta, who was literate, had access to email in her brother's house in Los Angeles and she had learned to use it from her brother's U.S.-born adolescent children. Agapito never saw the emails and didn't seem to quite understand the concept: "They leave messages with their mother via a kind of postal system in the computer, I am not sure how it works, but they come home and say: 'There was a message from mama.'" The children never printed out the emails from their mother to show Agapito, but reported selectively on these communications to their father. They also at times used this uncensored channel to complain to their mother about Agapito when they felt he was being too strict or didn't allow them to do certain things. Asunta would then try to mediate the conflict between the children and their father in private phone conversations with her husband.

According to Madianou and Miller (2012), the way many transnational families today maintain long-distance relationships has been transformed by the emergence of what they call "polymedia": an emerging communicative environment of various new media technologies that together offers new affordances for the enactment and experience of social relations across time and space. Polymedia environments, these scholars argue, contribute to making the absent other tangible and therefore come to constitute the other person and hence the relationship itself. They also note that digital media cannot in and of itself resolve the emotional difficulties around separation experienced by this "new type" of connected transnational family (2012:87–90, 130–31). But while Madianou and Miller offer the disclaimer that not all global migrants operate in these environments, their conclusions are mostly applicable to highly urban and globally connected migration systems such as the Manila-London circuit they studied, which has relatively unproblematic access to media of all sorts.

The increasing availability and access to global communication technologies created the expectation of frequent communication among transnational families and in social relationships. These expectations were often difficult for Peruvian labor migrants abroad to meet, because of complicated work schedules, long workdays, and little free time at their disposal. New technologies could alter people's feelings by momentarily collapsing distance and institute forms of copresence, but at the end of the day most migrant mothers in the United States mourned their prolonged separation from their children and other relatives. Feelings such as pain, loss, suffering over separation and distance, longing, sadness, and nostalgia or the more positive emotions of love, compassion, intimacy, and belonging continued to animate the lives of migrants in affective and material ways despite the changing technologies used to produce these social and intersubjective relationships through long-distance communication.

The Politics of Connecting

When Amparo first arrived in Miami she immediately started to work with her uncle El Tío who had lived in Miami since the 1970s. At first, she called her sons from her uncle's home or office every other day using cheap prepaid calling cards that she purchased from a local Latino-owned grocery store (cell phones were very expensive at the time). She would ask the boys about their homework, about what they had done during the day, if they had washed their clothes, eaten lunch and dinner, and if they had obeyed their father. Connecting with her children through frequent phone calls and being able to "mother" them from a distance and reassure herself that they were getting proper nourishment, *cariño* (care), help with homework, and parental moral guidance and support gave her a sense of satisfaction which helped dissipate the sadness she felt about being thousands of miles away from her family.

El Tío quickly noticed that Amparo was calling her children in Lima often. In the beginning, he didn't say much about it, but as the days passed he started to complain that Amparo spent too many hours on the phone. He questioned her disposition to work and help in his home office and house, and even her intentions in coming to the United States. "Why come here if you are going to be on the phone all day nagging them back in Peru?" he said to her one day, obviously irritated. Not usually shy about defending herself, Amparo was first devastated over El Tío's accusations, but her desire to connect with her kids and her husband back in Lima was greater than her fear of being reprimanded by El Tío. To minimize the tension she started calling only when he was out of the house or late at night when he was asleep.

Complaints like El Tío's were a common source of tension in relationships between established migrants and their recently arrived relatives who attempted to navigate the rocky terrain of transnational communication. Celestina, a migrant in her early forties from the highland community of Llamapsillion, had just brought her goddaughter (*ahijada*) Alejandra from Huancayo to Silver Spring, Maryland, in 2005. Celestina placed the teenage girl temporarily with her mother-in-law, Asunción, who—when not hosting recently arrived relatives from Urcumarca—lived by herself in a small suburban home. "This way Asunción has company," Celestina said, reflecting the Andean cultural and moral ideal that elderly people should not live alone, even if they were physically and mentally capable of doing so.[15] Yet the arrangement didn't turn out quite as Celestina had hoped. Asunción soon started complaining to Celestina and her husband Paulino that Alejandra "lived glued to the phone" (*vive pegada al teléfono*).

Alejandra, who had just turned nineteen before arriving in the United States, had left her boyfriend in Peru and suffered from severe homesickness. She arrived with no savings, indebted to Celestina who had helped her migrate, and when I first met her she had not yet managed to get a cell phone of her own. Consequently, she had to make her phone calls from Asunción's landline using satellite calling cards that she bought with the little pocket money she earned by helping Celestina with her cleaning jobs in a Hispanic minimarket in one of Silver Spring's many strip malls. Asunción could not blame Alejandra for using the phone without paying because she bought her own calling cards, but Asunción was still irritated that the girl was monopolizing the house phone and, even more so, that she was spending valuable time on the phone when she could be doing "something useful" (*algo útil*) in the house instead.

To defuse the tense situation with her mother-in-law, Celestina decided to place Alejandra as a live-in nanny (*cama adentro*) with a Korean American family in an upper middle-class section of Washington, D.C. Celestina knew this family well because she had cleaned their house once a week for several years. She knew they were looking for a new nanny and her ability to successfully recommend someone qualified increased Celestina's symbolic capital vis-à-vis her former employer and within her own community. The last thing Celestina said to Alejandra the evening we dropped her off at the front porch of her new workplace was: "Don't stay glued to the phone, *hija*. They won't like that. Don't call anymore. Forget this boy. Now that you are here you have to give priority to work and saving money."

Celestina's advice to Alejandra, as well as El Tío's appeal to Amparo, illustrates the predicament of migrant workers who have to compromise their own emotional lives in order to be read as economically productive in the United States. Sometimes these demands came in the form of well-intentioned advice (*consejos*) by more seasoned relatives or *paisanos* who had figured out the ways and preferred modalities of work life in the United States. But it was not only fellow migrants who would advise, encourage, or demand that novice migrants under their tutelage communicate less with their home country in order to make the transition to a new life easier. Long-distance communication—too much of it or at the wrong time—could also put migrants at odds with their employers.

Migrants' work situation commonly impacted their availability to engage transnationally with family and kin in the home country. In Washington, D.C., and in suburban Maryland, most Peruvians who migrated in the 1990s ended up in various kinds of low-income entry-level jobs. Male migrants typically labored in the construction sector or in gardening and landscaping if they lived in suburban areas, and women worked mostly in care and personal services as domestic workers, nannies, baby sitters, cleaning personnel, or in low-end retail.

Live-in nannies felt the pressure to be constantly available to the employer most intensely and this affected their communication with family members in Peru. Long work hours and the lack of easy access to communication technology in the early 1990s confined them to the familial space of their employer's homes and simultaneously cut them off from their own familial and transnational intimate lives. Live-in nannies like Nelly had very little disposable income to spend on costly phone calls. Furthermore, her Peruvian employers controlled the number of calls she could make per week based on what they deemed she could afford, and they deducted the cost of the phone calls from her already meager weekly salary by checking the numbers on their phone bill. They told her that they wanted to help her ensure she could pay for her own long-distance phone calls. Nelly never dared to complain to her employers, because she feared that they would send her back to Peru if she started to "create trouble" (*crear problemas*), as she said. When she started to work a second job cleaning other homes in the neighborhood, she gained more autonomy, and was increasingly able to make long-distance calls to her daughters in Peru at her own discretion. This coincided with the arrival of more Peruvians and other Latin Americans in the neighborhood and an increase in the number of agencies, calling centers, and shops selling satellite phone cards and offering greater access to long-distance calls.

When cell phones became more common, employers' control over migrants' communications diminished in some ways. But while carrying one's own cell phone and being able to use it freely in public spaces such as playgrounds and parks give migrant women some freedom, it also creates the need for new forms of self-regulation. Rosario's story illustrates this point. Rosario worked as a live-in nanny in a wealthy section of Washington, D.C. She told me that her *patrona* (female employer) was very strict with phone conversations during work hours and didn't want her to be "glued to the phone." Rosario respected her employer very much and didn't want to disappoint her. Although she had not left any children behind, she had caretaking responsibilities for her aging mother back in highland Peru. She struggled to reconcile her mother's need for attention with her U.S. employer's demand for her undivided attention to the children she was paid to look after.

One day Rosario's mother fell ill and Rosario had to call her during work hours. Rosario's mother lived far away from the main plaza where the town's two public pay phones were located. Typically, Rosario called once, the shop owner Isabel would send someone to alert her mother, and then Rosario called an hour or so later. On this particular day Rosario's mother was already waiting for her phone call in the shop. It was late in the afternoon in Washington, D.C., but not yet time for Rosario's employer to come home. But, as Rosario said: "I must have had bad luck (*mala suerte*) that day, because suddenly she walked in. Since I was on the phone with my mother I did not hear her enter the house. When she saw me on the phone she got very upset and started yelling at me . . . the little one started crying and it was all very chaotic." Rosario hung up with her mother immediately. "I was so embarrassed," she said visibly uncomfortable by the act of remembering. "I wanted to disappear and never come back here."

Rosario's visceral reaction to the employer's angry outburst was intensified by her vulnerability and status as a subordinate, and as disposable labor. An underpaid domestic worker in a strained economy, she had everything to lose should her employer decide to fire her because of this incident. Mary Romero (1992, 2012) has famously argued how it often can be difficult to identify subordinate work conditions among domestic workers because employer-domestic worker relationships are always already entangled in complex webs of affect (see also Young 1987). Ironically, while feelings and emotional attunement are the most valuable commodities produced by workers in the care industries—from childcare and elder care to sex work—they are also seen as distractions that prevent them from performing as compliant and docile workers. For months after the incident Rosario feared losing her job and she avoided phone calls from anyone but her employer during work hours in case the employer would walk in on her again while she was taking to relatives in Peru.

Rosario's story illustrates how employers' expectations of exclusive availability and dedication to the affective labor they pay the domestic worker to undertake in the social reproduction of their own households and families coerces migrant women into compartmentalizing their affective engagements into a "here" and a "there," where one is legitimate and desirable and the other illegitimate and problematic. These constraints on affective displays were inherently racial and gendered and worked to curb migrant workers' ability to socially reproduce their own families from afar. In general, the necessary and complex navigation between a "here" and a "there" (cf. Boehm 2012)—itself a result of migration, "illegality" and the inability to return, and the prolonged separation of families—were experienced by many migrants as daily balancing acts between work demands in the United States and caregiver responsibilities toward children and other dependent family members in Peru. When asked directly about this process in the context of ethnographic interviews, many women stated in pragmatic terms that leaving their children in the care of relatives back in Peru was the price they had to pay in order to be able to provide them with food on the table and a good education. But this initial matter-of-factness would often crumble as they continued to narrate the painful separation that was at the heart of their experiences of migration and manifested itself through forms and processes of transnational communication.

"Remote Sensing" and Partial Truths

Few migrants had anticipated the "emotional punch" (*golpe emocional*) that prolonged family separation turned out to be, nor had they foreseen the painstaking emotional work that went into communicating with their children from abroad and deciphering—from relatives' partial reports, the children's own stories, and their own gut feelings—how their children were *really* doing and if it was all worth the effort. Despite their efforts to be in frequent touch, transnational communication between migrants in the United States and their children or other family members in Peru was far from seamless.

Several studies that highlight the emotional costs of transnational families have noted that transnational communication has several overlapping purposes (Carling et al. 2012:203). The first is to exchange information and engage emotionally with each other through inquiries about daily activities such as progress with schoolwork and well-being and to offer advice, provide comfort or consolation, or discipline from afar (Alicea 1997). The second purpose is to confirm the relationship itself and ensure its survival by continuous affirmation through kinwork including long-distance communication. These overlapping purposes are enmeshed in moral and affective economies that structure both practical behaviors and moral judgment in transnational parenting. Within this complex moral and social terrain mothers, children, and their caregivers expected one another to abide by dominant "feeling rules" (Hochschild 1979), but also to perform the appropriate emotion management work in order to cope with the painful challenges of separation.[16] This involved expressing one's emotions in the socially and culturally appropriate way.

When Nelly communicated with her daughters during the three years they were separated before her children joined her in the United States, she used the occasion to check in on their schoolwork and well-being and in between calls or audiocassettes she responded to their requests by sending them gifts as a way of compensating for her absence—a compensation strategy scholars have called "commodifying love" (Parreñas 2001). Recounting her experience of communicating via audiocassette in those years of separation, Nelly said:

> The girls would read their book to show how far they were getting [in school] and they would say they were doing ok and that they liked the things I sent them. I sent them clothes, I sent them dolls. Everything I could I tried to send, no, like that, little by little, but I sent them stuff . . . then they were happy and they said they missed me.[17]

The children in turn were socialized by their caregivers in Peru into what they considered appropriate emotional responses to their absent migrant mother.[18] But there were also limits to what they could say, according to Nelly:

They couldn't say much of what they really felt because my mother was there and my sister, they would tell them not to say certain things because "Your mother is going to suffer or she's going to cry," so they tried not to say, but it's there in their voices when they are about to cry, you know. The same with me, each time I talked with them or when I listened to the tapes I felt like I was going to cry, just from hearing their voices. When I called them, the same . . . [her voice breaks] . . . that sadness would creep in, of not seeing them, but that was how we communicated.

Guillermina and sometimes Nelly's sister Paola closely monitored both phone calls and recordings of audiocassettes, and attempted to socialize Nelly's daughters in the culturally appropriate "feeling rules." These two caregivers ensured as far as possible that the children wouldn't say anything that could hurt their mother or make her cry. But affect as embodied and visceral experience is slippery and doesn't always align with dominant "feeling rules" (cf. Stewart 2007). Children are not just passive recipients of emotional experiences, as suggested by Heather Rae-Espinoza (2011); they actively engage in representing the affective ties to their parents abroad and the relatives who provide substitute care, and they do so in ways that "hid[e] problematic effects and represent . . . acceptable ties to their émigré mothers and to their grandmothers who provide . . . substitute care" (2011:129).

Despite Guillermina's efforts to discipline the affective interactions between her daughter and grandchildren, Nelly claimed that she could still "hear in the children's voices when they were about to cry." Nelly's affective attunement to her children, her "remote sensing" of the trembling in her daughters' voices, resonates with anthropologist Michelle Rosaldo's claim that what distinguishes thought and affect is fundamentally a sense of engagement of the actor's self.[19] In her attempt to highlight the simultaneously felt and cognized aspects of emotions and challenge the assumed Carthesian duality of mind and body, Rosaldo coined the term "embodied thought," which she defined as follows:

Emotions are thoughts somehow "felt" in flushes, pulses, "movements" of our livers, minds, hearts, stomachs, skin. They are embodied thoughts, thoughts seeped with the apprehension that "I am involved." Thought/ affect thus bespeaks the difference between a mere hearing of a child's cry and a hearing *felt*—as when one realizes that danger is involved and that the child is one's own. (1984:143)

Nelly repeatedly sensed—and also claimed to know—how the children's voices started changing when they were about to cry. She felt it in her body and her bodily response was immediate and visceral.

Transnational communication, then, is as much about what is said as it is about the uncertainty left by that which is unspoken but still felt in often very immediate and visceral ways (cf. Baldassar 2007; Madianou 2012). Not "telling the truth" (*decir la verdad*) when talking with family members over the phone or exchanging letters was not considered lying (*mentir*); instead, it was understood as a strategy of masking and of concealing the truth about something or someone. Caregivers in Peru—most commonly grandmothers—would use such affect management strategies to minimize the suffering of migrant mothers abroad. Some migrants felt that such attempts by caregivers to "protect them from bad news," or from demands by their children that they could not do anything about anyway, came in the way of their practice of "remote sensing," of feeling and knowing from afar, what was going on in their children's lives. According to Nelly:

> No matter how much you talk on the phone it isn't like seeing them. Sometimes they say yes yes we are doing great, but we know that sometimes they don't tell us the truth. They say that they are doing fine so that we won't worry, therefore I always doubt because I am always thinking about whether they are really ok or not.

Statements such as this reveal a common and profound feeling of being left out of something and the frustration of not being able to console and comfort by one's sheer presence. But while concealing the truth about someone's well-being was still construed as adhering to the moral obligation to remain connected, silence or forgetting, in contrast, were not.

Olvido and Estrangement

The expectations about being connected that emerged from the increased availability of enhanced global communication technology were highly gendered and subject to moral judgments when not met. Scholars have shown that children in transnational households often reproach their mothers rather than their fathers for having left them (Dreby 2010; Menjívar and Abrego 2009). Scholars have also documented the fact that fathers are more likely to abandon their children, yet they give different reasons for it (Landolt and Da 2005; Dreby 2010). Most of all, scholars agree that men face far fewer repercussions than women if they lapse in their familial, provider, and/or caregiver responsibilities (Carling et al. 2012:194–195).

While an occasional failure to communicate might not have major repercussions for either men and women (unexpected events can always occur), the continuous evasion of communication was a violation of social norms. The lack of communication and silence in situations where both old and new technologies were available but not used, came to stand for *olvido* (forgetting) in my informants' narratives. At best they scorned it and corrected it and at worst they considered it an incorrigible immoral act. Translated as forgetting, *olvido* in the context of Peruvian transnational migration was the failure to perform what Michaela Di Leonardo (1987) calls "kinwork." Di Leonardo suggests that for many Italian Americans it is kinship *across* households as much as women's work *within* households that fulfills cultural expectations of a satisfying family life in the United States. But in the context of transnational families between Peru and the United States, the threshold of what a satisfying family life might mean was different. In situations where migrant women had outsourced housework and child care to relatives in Peru to take up work in the United States, the work of kinship—here in the form of letters, phone calls, presents, cards, remittances, and other communications—became a crucial realm of practice to keep transnational families afloat. The mediation of relationships facilitated by the circulation of both objects and technologies allowed participants at all ends to continue to believe that such a thing as "a family" still existed and could be continuously reiterated as a meaningful form. While this kind of kinwork was generally seen as women's work, men were also increasingly held accountable for transnational communication (cf. Abrego 2014). When migrant men failed to engage in transnational obligations they could also become targets for blame, as did men who stayed behind and were disconnected, but generally the social consequences were less severe than for women.

Olvido, or forgetting, was often evoked in these transnational contexts and was interpreted as lack of love, compassion, devotion, or care. When brought up by nonmigrant relatives in Peru *olvido* came to stand for an undesirable adoption of "egoistic attitudes" or "American values," the two being virtually synonymous in the minds of many of my interlocutors. Relatives in Peru used the term to describe noncommunicative or evasive behavior by migrant relatives abroad who had cut off all or some channels of communication with their families back home. As the anthropologist—a quintessential mediating figure in transnational research—I was also frequently asked to "not forget" when I left a research setting after a visit and I was also periodically accused of *olvido* even if in a humorous manner if I didn't answer phone calls or emails over a period of time. Inés, for example, frequently said: "Ingrata, te has olvidado de los pobres!" (translatable as "you have forgotten about us, the poor") when I failed at times to stay sufficiently connected.

Ben Orlove has noted that the idea of "being forgotten" has multiple meanings in Andean societies. When Orlove was getting ready to depart his field site in Puno after a year of fieldwork by the Lake Titicaca, locals often approached him with the request not to be forgotten, which caused him to wonder about the meaning of "not forgetting" (2002). Searching for an answer Orlove turned to popular Andean music and found that forgetting is frequently tied to notions of betrayal and abandonment, for example in the case of a departed lover. But what Orlove found most surprising was that forgetting is not an individual act or something that happens to a person, but a social act that at worst could be deliberate and intentional (2002:5–8). The lover or the persons who forget are therefore accused of violating the social bond—they may be called ungrateful (*ingratos*) because they negate what has been given to them, or pretentious because they deny social equality by failing to care for or renew the social relationship.

This social aspect of forgetting is present not just in love or spousal relationships (and in representations of them in popular culture), but also in relationships between parents and children and between citizens and their government. For example, scholars have noted that it is common for people in more remote rural areas of the Andes to refer to their towns or themselves as *pueblos olvidados* by the state (Orlove 2002; Stepputat 2004, 2005). Racial and class inequalities operating in Peru since at least the colonial period had indeed rendered the small towns in the Andes vulnerable to being overlooked and forgotten, and therefore the request to not be forgotten operates at both an interpersonal and a societal level. Yet both are intimately linked to a historical and contextual sense of vulnerability, the sense of being abandoned or forsaken by a lover or one's government. To be forgotten here comes to bear profoundly historical and contextual meaning having to do with one's value as a person or as a human being denied (Orlove 2002:12–13).

In the context of transnational migration, *olvido* operates in a similar dual way. Migrants abroad often complained that the state forgot about them as soon as they stepped on the plane and some were also critical of more recent efforts by the state to reach out to migrants abroad because they saw it as a strategy to hypocritically try to make up for a lost relationship. But most commonly, I found the expression used in the context of social relationships within transnational families. Here it is again synonymous with abandonment, problematic in its intentionality, and often interpreted as an act of defaulting on one's obligations to family and extended kin. Because this was a violation of Andean norms of reciprocity, relatedness, and appropriate sociality, it also prevented the noncommunicating or "disappeared" person from becoming or remaining a full person in the context of the relationship with the social group. If there was one thing that many migrants and their nonmigrating counterparts could agree on, it was that *olvidarse de alguién* (to forget someone) was a despicable and immoral act. When Doña Rosa's husband Raúl abandoned her after migrating to Miami in the mid-1970s. Rosa's standard comment whenever I brought up the topic in conversation was: "He forgot about us (*se olvidó de nosotros*). He never looked back, called, or sent as much as one written letter." This was enough to construct the departed ex-husband as an essentially immoral human being from a position of moral superiority.

Over the years, Rosa made some attempts to reconnect with Raúl on behalf of her children, but she was unsuccessful. A few months before leaving for Miami in 2000, Amparo got through to her father. When I asked why she thought he answered her this time, Amparo frowned and said: "He knew that I was on my way to Miami and that he'd better answer now because if he didn't, I would be standing on his doorstep any day kicking his door in." Amparo had invoked their biological relationship and asked him to sponsor her visa application in spite of the twenty-five years of silence between them. After a few weeks of back and forth and several attempts at communicating by phone and email, Raúl changed his phone number to a private one. Amparo was dismayed with her father's attitude and turned instead to her maternal uncle for help. She was less disappointed at her father's unwillingness to help her than his failure to answer and return her phone calls and emails, and his decision to change his phone number and to deliberately and intentionally cut off all contact. "Can you imagine, Ulla," she said. "A person like that doesn't have any decency." It was the unwillingness to communicate which constituted the worst default on the moral obligation to his family. This was ultimately unpardonable to Amparo. "He forgot about us," she finally stated, somewhat angry, somewhat resilient, as she reiterated her mother's exact words.

Olvido was also at play in Nelly's oldest daughter Melanie's experience of her estrangement from her father. Ever since Juan left Nelly when Melanie was only five years old, Melanie had had a strained relationship with her father. When Melanie first told me the story of her relationship with her father we were sitting on one of the guest beds in Melanie's grandfather's house in Urcumarca, taking a quick break from peeling potatoes for the communal dinner that Melanie's grandparents were offering that evening in honor of the patron saint of Urcumarca. Melanie had recently gotten her U.S. residency and this was her second time visiting Urcumarca for the patron saint's fiesta in September. As we sat there on the iron beds with woolen blankets, scarfing down chocolates that Melanie had bought at a CVS pharmacy in Washington, D.C., the day before leaving for Peru, she suddenly struck me as a very mature young woman trying to make sense of the tumultuous childhood she had recently left behind. "These memories come back to haunt me every day," she confessed. When Juan left Nelly for another woman, Nelly soon left for the United States to make a living that would allow her to provide for her two young daughters. Nelly's mother Guillermina encouraged the children to see their father periodically and they did so every other week, although these encounters,

Melanie recalls, were always brief. Melanie was afraid of visiting her father; she feared that he might take her and her younger sister Doris away from their grandmother to live with him and his new wife. When I asked whether she had ever been resentful of her mother for leaving, her answer was yes, but that her mother had stayed in touch with her and Doris. With the help of her grandmother, Melanie had been able to reframe her relationship with her mother and understand it not as abandonment but as a temporary condition. She was able to see in retrospect that her mother was making a sacrifice to support her and her little sister Doris. In contrast, Melanie was not able to reconcile her sentiments toward her father Juan—not even after she had joined her mother in the United States.

Melanie consistently referred to the estrangement she felt from her father as "communication problems," and explained:

> I felt he never took time for us, well, at least that's how I felt, no, maybe it was more frequently than what I remember, but since I was angry with him . . . I knew he had another woman, I knew he had his family and I felt that when he came [to see us] I was only getting the leftovers of what my sisters would get.

The fact that Juan had a new family was hurtful to Melanie and she always felt set aside when comparing herself to his "new children." The distance between them grew when Melanie and Doris left for the United States:

> At first things stayed almost the same. We had to call him and some-times when his line was disconnected, we couldn't communicate. There were years when we wouldn't talk for six months. . . . Then my resent-ment grew and our relationship was not very good, not even over the telephone. The more I grew up the more I realized, right, [about] the situ-ation, and the more angry I got. Sometimes he would call, but because it's expensive to call from Peru . . . and when his line was disconnected we wouldn't really expect him to call us, because there wasn't any other way to communicate with us, then sometimes my grandmother would have to go to his . . . to the place where he worked to tell him to call us. There were times when he didn't even call for my birthday!

The "communication problems" reported by Melanie resonated with similar reports from other migrants. Communication problems can here be understood both in a literal—as with costly phone calls or disconnected phone lines due to lack of payment—and a figurative sense, as with the difficulty in speaking or sharing one's feelings. Communication problems aggravated the tension in transnational relationships already caused by spatial and temporal distance. Growing into adolescence and early adulthood, Melanie was still unable to travel back to Peru because of her legal status, and her anger at her father's silence grew. Whenever he did call she would spend most of the phone call reproaching him for not communicating and for not caring about them.

Then one day something unexpected happened. Juan died tragically and unexpectedly in a car accident in Lima. Melanie had just started college in Florida and was living away from home for the first time in the eight years she had been in the United States. Her father's death impacted her deeply. "I was a mess," she recalled. She experienced an enormous amount of guilt, especially because the communication between her and her father had become increasingly negative in the months before the accident:

> During the last years of his life, I was complaining to him quite a bit. I complained that he didn't call, that he didn't care about us, that he had split up with my mother, many things that children feel . . . and then he would say that he didn't call because I would only complain. I never asked him to send me things. Always what I would say to him was: "I don't want you to send me anything. I don't want you to tell me that you're going to send me money, the only thing I want you to send me is a card saying hi, how are you, I'm alive, bye." That would make me happy, but he would say that the situation was too difficult and that I had to understand . . . the last times we spoke [on the phone] were not very nice conversations. Exactly three months before the accident we had an argument during the last call from him and that's when I said the worst things to him. I have felt incredibly guilty all those years. I felt guilty, I mean, guilty of the things that I said and sometimes even guilty for his death even though I had nothing to do with [it], it was an accident, but I felt guilty about that too. Even today, right, I feel a little bit guilty for not being able to understand and for judging unfairly.

Melanie's experience of the transnational connection with her father was marked by a deep sense of betrayal, abandonment, and loss. It was a wound that had not been able to heal for many years. Although the estrangement she felt from him did not start with migration, it became more intense when the spatial and temporal scale of their separation changed. When Melanie's and Doris's initial visas expired they could no longer return to Peru to visit their father until their green cards came through eight years later. In 2002, two years after her father's tragic death, Melanie finally received her U.S. residency and she immediately began to plan a trip to Peru on her own. She visited her father's tomb, met his family again, including her half-siblings, and was able to tell them about her feelings. Only then, she told me, did she experience some kind of relief from her grief and a sense of closure to the multiple "losses" of her father—first to divorce, then to migration, and finally to death—which had haunted her for most of her childhood and adolescence:

> I told them the truth. I complained a little because I felt that because of them my father had abandoned us, that because of them I didn't have a father, and so still right now it hurts a little when I'm saying this . . . But I met my sisters, now there are five of them and there were only two when I left for the U.S. I learned my father's story and then that feeling of guilt diminished. Maybe also because I was growing up, because when I arrived here [back in Peru], that's when I realized what his reality was here and I realized that he did love us, but that maybe it was not possible for him to be there for us, to talk as frequently as we wished, or to send us anything. Even now I feel like if he had just been able just to say hi, how are you . . . but I understand it a little more now. He had five [other] children so the situation was very difficult for him too.

Now a young woman, Melanie's narrative illustrates her embodied memories of what it felt like from a child's perspective to be left by one's father. It also illustrates how communication flows in transnational relationships especially between parents and their children is a highly gendered domain. When Nelly had first migrated, leaving her daughters with her mother in Lima, she was constantly unsettled (*pendiente*) by being away from her children and she tried to compensate for her absence by calling as frequently as she could and sending audiocassettes often. But Juan had a new life and a new family. For him maintaining the relationship with the children from his first marriage was not a priority, or at least in the day-to-day it ranked lower on his to-do list than to attend to the children who were right there with him.

While some parents managed to maintain meaningful relationships with their children in Peru from abroad and eventually send for these children after a few years, like Amparo or Nelly, others had less luck in this regard. Leisy Abrego (2014) has recently critiqued the common depiction of transnational families as unproblematic split households that are geographically spread out, but otherwise function like a regular family through long-distance communication and remittances. Such depictions, she argues, unhelpfully dismiss the painful separations and the daily realities with which members of such families in separate locations must negotiate in their everyday lives—often only tentatively—while they plan and hope for future reunification (2014:23). Abrego's characterizations of the painful experiences of separation and loneliness within Salvadoran families resonates with the experiences of most of my Peruvian interlocutors, given that Peruvian transnational families are also notable for their prolonged separations. Aurelio's story illustrates this predicament.

Growing Apart

Aurelio, a father of two, came to the United States in 2001, leaving behind his wife and two children in their modest home in one of Lima's *pueblos jóvenes* (squatter settlements). The initial idea was that Aurelio would establish himself and send for his family at a later date. But Aurelio's wife did not get her visa approval, as they had hoped, and she didn't want to run the risk of crossing the border with two young children. Like many other Peruvians who arrived via unauthorized routes, Aurelio himself had not been able to adjust his immigration status and his work situation was unstable, preventing him from sending regular remittances. Time, distance, and tension over money started to wear on their family. This was evident in the changing dynamics of Aurelio's communication with his wife and children and his relationship with his wife:

I am very frustrated because they don't want to talk to me anymore. My daughter sometimes comes to the phone, but my son mostly refuses to talk to me. I am not sure if this will change as he gets older, but right now he doesn't want to talk to me.

Scholars have shown that women often work as mediators between migrant husbands and children in the country of origin (Pribilsky 2007; see also Dreby 2010). Aurelio felt that his wife didn't do enough to make the children talk to him. "So what is going on with your wife?" I asked. Aurelio looked at me and said resentfully: "My wife, she is the real problem, I don't even know how she lives (*no se ni como vive*)." He didn't know much about her whereabouts and thought she was seeing someone else. When prompted he referred to their relationship with the popular saying, "Amor de lejos, amor de pendejos" ("Long-distance love is a fool's love"). "If you are away from your partner for too long," Aurelio said with bitterness in his voice, "she will find someone else to substitute for you. You can be sure of that."

Aurelio's story has no happy ending. Although he and his wife had originally planned to have her join him in the United States with their two children, the long wait had exhausted their relationship. Failing to fulfill all his obligations and reciprocal commitments and unable to re-turn to Peru to visit because of his unresolved legal status, Aurelio grew distanced from his family, even as he still called and sent small remit-tances whenever he could. While his wife and children still depended on his remittances to pay for school supplies and basic needs, time and dis-tance had made him otherwise marginal in their everyday lives in Lima.

To escape the loneliness and overcome his sorrows, Aurelio turned to heavy drinking. Other migrants from Urcumarca talked about him as "being depressed," but most of them immediately acknowledged with empathy that he was drinking to "forget his sorrows" (*olvidarse de sus penas*). A combination of factors led him on a downward spiral. When I last saw Aurelio during a research trip to Maryland and Washington, D.C., in June 2012, he had a pending order of deportation and was living in the shadows.

The sociality of relationships between migrants and their family members back in Peru change as a consequence of migration and the political economy of what "a productive life" in the United States should look like. This is evidenced, for example, in different conceptions of time. Dreby (2010) has noted that parents in the United States often experience time as flying by because of their busy workdays, whereas for children left behind it drags on as they wait to be sent for by their parents. In these contexts, "staying in touch" becomes ever more important (Baldassar 2007:406). But the particular notions of appropriate sociality which shape transnational relationships also apply to translocal kin networks within local migrant communities and family networks in the United States.

Nelly always expressed a strong sense of disapproval of the way her relationship with her brother and younger sister who also lived in Washington, D.C., had changed after their arrival in the United States. Even as she attributed this to their busy work schedules which made them less inclined to spend time with each other, she condemned outright what she saw as the erosion of old loyalties based on family and kinship ties. Before they used to be united, Nelly complained during an interview in Lima, but now they lived increasingly apart from each other:

> Before when we were [in Peru] I was closer to one of my sisters who lives there [in the United States], but we had problems [in the United States]. . . . It's not the same any more, you know, and since she has her own family it is also different now. I don't know why but being [in the United States] changes the way a lot of people are. Instead of bringing us closer, I think we have become more distanced, we grow more apart. This does not only happen to me, it happens to a lot of people.

Nelly's sense of people being negatively affected by the demanding work environment and the daily routines in the United States was indeed widespread and has been documented by other scholars (Mahler 1995; Menjívar 2000). In *Fragmented Ties* (2000), Menjívar shows that network instability is closely linked to the structures of opportunity that Salvadoran migrants encounter upon arrival in the United States. The same is true for the Peruvians in my study, as their work and living situations in the United States also affected the resources they had available to help friends and family in need. Several of the participants in my study frequently commented that people became more egoistical in the United States, with less empathy, and that they cared less for each other.

Many, including Nelly herself, attributed this to what she understood to be the corrupting effect of money on social relations:

> Some people fight amongst themselves, I have more than you, you know, or you this or that, I mean, they attack each other. I don't think we fight like that [in my family], each has their own life, I mean, we're not as close as we were when we were here [in Peru]. That's why I'm saying that living there [in the United States] money has changed us . . . we do talk, hi, how are you, and maybe what does mom say, or did you talk to mom, but my siblings never ask: "How are you?" or "How can I help you?" or "Do you need anything?" or "I'm coming to see you." Now everything is about money.

The distance that people's demanding and busy working lives in the United States imposed on social relations was particularly hard to cope with during an illness or when experiencing economic hardship. Nelly was not the type of person who felt comfortable about asking anyone for help, not even her close relatives. She expected them to be sufficiently attuned to each other's well-being so that they would know when someone was in need of economic or emotional support. To be there for each other was an unquestioned cultural and moral value, but it was one that many migrants had an increasingly hard time upholding in the context of work life in the United States:

> I've been ill many times, very ill, because I suffer from asthma and my family hasn't even noticed. Once I was brought to the emergency room and they didn't even know about it until I came back home and was doing ok, but before it wasn't like that, someone in the family was sick and we were all there doing our part.

Other families who relied on larger support networks were more readily available when someone felt ill, organizing turn-taking systems of care, and if the person lacked medical insurance, the family or the local community would also organize fund-raising events. But while Nelly's is perhaps an extreme example of ending up in the emergency room "without anyone noticing it," it reflects a more general sense of being on one's own while everyone else is busy being economically productive. This sometimes goes so far that they default on what most Andean Peruvians understand as basic social obligations. This tension of the entanglement of affect with larger economic projects and relations was at the heart of everyday life in transnational families.

Economies of Affect

Scholars of transnational families—mostly working on Mexican and Central American migration flows—have established that transnational families have become an increasingly common family form; that the largest volume of care work falls on women both at home and abroad; and that mothers and fathers practice (or fail to practice) parenting from abroad through monetary remittances, gifts, and long-distance communication (Boehm 2012; Dreby 2010; Hondagneau-Sotelo and Avila 1997; Parreñas 2005a). Abrego (2014) asks why some families fare better than others and concludes that both gender and immigration policies are influential factors in determining the outcome of particular family trajectories. This chapter builds on this recent literature to establish the crucial importance of communicative practices in the Peruvian case and importantly demonstrates how the difficulties of maintaining meaningful transnational lives are embedded in the very form and process of communication between migrants and their families.

Economy and affective belonging for Andean transnational labor migrants today are no longer necessarily generated in the same place—or even in the same country. Scholars have recently used the concept of affect to critique the long-held assumption that capital accumulation and economic projects are fundamentally distinct from the more intimate and affective realm of human experience, a supposition that has sustained numerous distinctions between "inner world" and social contexts, between the private and the public, and between subjectivity and political economy (Leys 2011; Richard and Rudnyckyj 2009). This chapter has attended specifically to the ways in which the affective and the social are embedded in larger economic projects through complex forms of social organization of transnational family life. Long-distance communication is a key area of social and emotional practice through which the entanglement of affect and economy is both produced and evidenced. For example, many migrant women had to compartmentalize the affective labor they did for payment and that which they did to socially reproduce their own families from afar. This was easier said than done and the demands of complicated work schedules to attend to the children of middle-class American families often compromised their relationship with their own families back in highland Peru or Lima. Fellow migrants who had been in the United States for a longer time also sometimes policed recently arrived migrants' management of affect and regarded it as their responsibility to socialize the newcomers into the discipline of getting ahead "U.S. style." This meant hard work and long hours, often working several shifts in a row and under precarious conditions with no benefits, sick days, or Sundays off. Migrants also had to learn how to manage others' expectations—whether those of particular employers or of family members on whom they depended for survival—of their availability. Navigating this complex intersection of affect and economic projects in which transnational communication is embedded, is crucial for migrants' ability not only to render themselves relevant across a range of contexts but also for their ability to manage the difficult daily task of reproducing social life via electronic mediation.

The increasing availability of new media has often led to celebratory accounts in the scholarly literature about seamless communication between people separated by migration. In contrast to such views, I have argued that while different kinds of media can frame communication in particular ways, it cannot ameliorate the painful experience of prolonged family separation, especially from one's children, despite attempts to keep relationships vital and alive, sometimes against all odds. The feelings of loss, longing, and sorrow produced by these separations were emotionally draining for most people—young and old, men and women alike. It was in these contexts that parents—but especially mothers—practiced what I here have called "remote sensing," that is, the attempt to feel and know something about an object of desire from afar, often in an intuitive, visceral, and embodied manner.

A central concern in these communications and attempts to feel from afar was the uncertainty about whether or not children and caregivers back home were "telling the truth" about their feelings in letters, audio-cassettes, emails, or over the phone. Despite the fact that all relationships are indeed mediated, as established at the beginning of this chapter, migrants often felt that the visual aspect of experience—being able to see one's loved ones—was key to feelings of connectivity and the affirmation of emotional bonds. Baldassar (2007:389), for example, has shown that the Italian migrants she studied in Australia preferred what she refers to as the "technology of travel," because traveling to visit offered migrants family members an opportunity to "see for themselves" how their relatives were doing. But for the Peruvians in my study, who had migrated without papers or with phony documents, visiting to "see" their relatives was not an option. Instead they sought to see them in a different way: by circulating videos of various kinds.

The possibility of *seeing* one's loved ones also offered the opportunity of holding others accountable to "visual evidence," in ways not allowed for by oral communication. Migrants generally assumed that it was easier to hide information in nonvisual forms; this led many to privilege visual technologies once these became more readily accessible to a broader public. However, as we will see in chapter 4, the idea of truth being embedded in such technologies also complicated the struggle for social cohesion across contexts and required migrants to intentionally circulate partial images of what they wanted to show and how they wanted to be seen. Yet the circulation of images doesn't entirely depend on the intention of the producer but also on the ways they are read, consumed, and circulated by others. The images are slippery and can potentially escape intended circuits of circulation, making their circulation within the context of transnational families, communities, and social relations an ambiguous affair.

4

Unfortunate Visibilities

The Transnational Circulation of Image-Objects

On a cold but sunny winter morning, I visited Doña Julia and Don Mariano in their home in Ocopilla—a former *Comunidad Campesina* now transformed into a marginal urban neighborhood at the outskirts of Huancayo. Like many other such *barrios*, Ocopilla's rapid growth was a consequence of the massive internal displacements that followed in the wake of the violent conflict between the Shining Path and the Peruvian state during the 1980s and early 1990s and made thousands of *desplazados* settle in highland cities like Huancayo. Doña Julia and Don Mariano's house was recently renovated with shining white tiles on the façade—a new decoration style, which many local residents fancy but can only afford if they receive remittance money from migrant relatives abroad. A brand new green metal fence was transparent enough for passersby to appreciate the house from the dusty street where it stood out among older neighboring adobe constructions, but still imposing enough to signal a new sense of private individualized space apart from the public space of the street outside.

Don Mariano welcomed me at the door. "Julia is not here," he said almost apologetically. "But look what we just got from Fabiola!" Don Mariano welcomed me into the living room and inserted a DVD in the DVD player. Images of a birthday celebration appeared on the TV screen and I soon recognized the well-known faces of Fabiola, Carlos, and Rodrigo—three of Doña Julia's and Don Mariano's five children who had left Huancayo in 2000 to live and work in Washington, D.C. Soon Fabiola appears on the screen. She tells her parents how she misses them and prays for their good health every day. She also informs them that she and her two brothers will soon send money for the university fees of their younger brother who is studying in Huancayo. Finally, almost as an afterthought, Fabiola recounts how she injured her foot at work and exhibits a swollen ankle in front of the camera. Tears well up in Don Mariano's eyes. With his gaze still fixed on the images moving across the screen he mutters: "*Ay mi pobre hija*, she has suffered so much."

Shared viewing of visual media, most commonly photographs and videos sent by relatives at home or abroad, was a common occurrence during my fieldwork.[1] More often than not, when I arrived at someone's home to pay a visit I would be invited to sit down in their living room (or crammed rented bedroom), and a stack of photos would be brought out or a video or DVD rapidly slipped into the VCR or DVD player. At first I often wondered why participants in my study were so keen on sharing their photographs and videos with me. Later I established that the transnational flows of visual media were central to migrants' efforts to pursue and maintain social relationships across borders and ensure their continued relevance and value as persons as well as their social positioning within the particular local and transnational networks and locations they occupied. During the often prolonged absences that characterize contemporary migration between the Peruvian Andes and the United States, videos and other communicative objects came in handy and mediated between social worlds, creating meaning and shaping social life.

Whereas the previous chapter focused mainly on oral communication, this chapter focuses on the role of visuality in the production of transnationally mediated social relations. I analyze how different genres of "migrant videos" are produced, circulated, viewed, signified, and talked about by members of a particular transnational migration circuit who construct their lives between Urcumarca, Jauja, Lima, and the cities of Washington, D.C., and Silver Spring and Rockville in Maryland.[2] I show how the video production, consumption, and circulation that mediated relationships not only between people in specific places in Peru and the United States but also between past and present, figure centrally in migrants' staging of their own social visibility as "worldly" and "cosmopolitan" ex-campesinos in a larger visual economy that spans social contexts and national borders. I focus particularly on three genres of "migrant videos": video letters (*video-cartas*), remittance videos, and fiesta videos. These are not emic categories but rather my own attempt to classify and analytically account for particular types of videos produced by and for migrants and their family and community members which have different intents, formulas, imagined audiences, directionality, and paths of circulation.[3]

Kin- and community-based media forms and practices are part of a broader global media environment—akin to what Arjun Appadurai (1996) has termed mediascapes—which encompasses a variety of media flows, including Peruvian-produced cable and satellite TV; local television programs not available on cable; video recordings of concerts of well-known *huayno* or *cumbia* singers now increasingly circulated on YouTube; pirate copies of recent Peruvian or foreign feature films dubbed in Spanish on DVD; and a variety of print media and photographs, among other cultural productions. Appadurai defines mediascapes as "both the distribution of the electronic capabilities to produce and disseminate information (newspapers, magazines, television stations, and film-production studios), which are now available to a growing number of private and public interests throughout the world, and to the images of the world created by these media" (1996:35). While recognizing that "migrant videos" are part of this broader scenario, I delimit the scope of the chapter to include only specific genres of kin- and community-based videos originating in contexts of migration for which I have been able to track not only the primary producers and consumers, but also the specific power relations embedded in the uneven paths of circulation as these image-objects move from one social arena to another. The videos discussed here therefore differ from diasporic media production in more institutional settings within "sites of minoritization" (Schein 2002), such as, for example, Naficy's work on Iranian television in Los Angeles (1993) and Kosnick's work on Turkish television in Germany (2007). Furthermore, the videos discussed do not account for the entire field of "migrant videos," and other migrant-produced media (or media produced by family members but with migrants abroad as intended audiences) may circulate on parallel paths between Peru and migrant collectivities abroad.

The availability of cheap digital recording technologies had already made camcorders and digital cameras an average commodity in most transnational households at the turn of the millennium. During my fieldwork most U.S.-based migrants who used video shot and circulated their own footage with only very basic in-camera edits. Both video letters and remittance videos thus resembled what Annabelle Sreberny-

Mohammadi and Ali Mohammadi (1994) have called "small media," that is, media which require "no independent processing techniques but contain within the hardware the possibility of instant production and reproduction of messages" (1994:26–27). The concept of small media, which includes low-tech technologies such as fax and political posters, was developed by Sreberny-Mohammadi and Mohammadi to study the media used to produce the Iranian Revolution of 1979, but the term has renewed relevance in the era of digital and mobile communication where immediate processing and instant sharing are the key defining characteristics of social media platforms, the use of which is also proliferating among Andean migrants.

But Andean media circulations and exchange of information over space did not start with the digital era. Scholars of indigenous literacies—alphabetic and visual—in the Andes have shown that societies in the Andes since precolonial times have used various technologies, recording devices, and native media genres to collect and record data, monitor different kinds of information, and produce images (Rappaport and Cummins 2012; Salomon 2004; Salomon and Niño-Murcia 2011). One of the most widely studied of these recording devices was the *khipu*, the ancient Andean "cord-media," which colonial documents indicate was used for record keeping and for sending messages via chaski runners throughout the Inca Empire (Salomon 2004; Urton 2003). Scholars have estimated that the khipu was used for at least half a millennium before the Spaniards arrived and that Andean subjects of the Crown continued to use the technology at least during the first colonial century (Salomon and Niño-Murcia 2011:71). Alphabetic literacy and narrative pictorial representation arrived with the Spaniards and became key tools of colonial domination (Rappaport and Cummins 2011; Burns 2010), hence the ambiguous relationship of Andean communities with official documents and documentary practices, as discussed in chapter 2. The khipu later developed into several hybrid media forms which Salomon and Niño-Murcia refer to as "cord-plus-paper solutions" (2011:77). These continued to develop and mold themselves around changing administrative needs for documentation. Contemporary migrant videos that circulate between the Andes and foreign destinations can fruitfully be seen as embedded in this longer and deeper history of media practice and circulation.

As a technology, video works on several interrelated levels, including the linguistic, the visual, the affective, the performative, and the social (the latter through shared viewing experiences). Of these, arguably the most important—or at least the one that is central for defining the technology—is the visual. It is also this dimension that leads migrants to positively evaluate the affordances of video technology and choose it over other technologies for particular communication purposes. Migrants and their family members indeed understood videos and other visual media, including photographs and webcam sessions, to offer unprecedented access to the true state of their relatives' feelings and well-being. I am particularly interested in exploring the complex relationship between vision and truth and how these videos serve as "visual evidence" and proof of the proper expenditure of migrant remittances, the fulfillment of care obligations, as well as to increase the social visibility of the U.S.-based migrant fiesta sponsor in the context of the community of origin. It was in the videos' status as evidence that visuality trumped other forms of text-based and aural media, offering what participants understood to be greater accountability in transnational communication, but also leading to new forms of surveillance (Foucault 1979) in the regulation of social life within transnational social spaces and settings.

Image-objects do not circulate in a political vacuum, but accrue value through the social processes of circulation in regimes of moral and cultural values—what Deborah Poole (1997:8) calls a "visual economy."[4] She proposes this concept over visual culture, because it better illustrates the constitutive role of images in processes of racialization and in shaping contested discourses around race, identity, and national identity. Analyzing a variety of image-objects including paintings, visiting cards, reportage, and photography, she shows how the scientific notion of race is built upon a modern visual economy spanning the period from the late eighteenth century to the 1930s, a period in which Peru went from being the object of colonial gazes to an independent and self-conscious nation. Poole distinguishes between the "use value" of an image-object, that is, the representational content of the image or the ability of a particular visual representation to reduce the distance between the image and its referent and its "exchange value," which indexes the value that images accrue through social processes of accumulation, possession, circulation, and exchange (1997:8–11).

The concept of visual economy is crucial to understanding the circulation of videos, especially with regard to the particular issues central to the production of visual narratives such as framing, editing, and encoding. Most participants—whether in their capacity as producers, consumers, or both—were highly invested in monitoring and negotiating the criteria for what visual information they considered reportable and appropriate for transnational circulation and what in turn they wanted silenced, edited, or left out to avoid tensions in the transnational family and in the larger collectivity of fellow migrants and *paisanos*. Yet in spite of migrants' attempts to exercise some control over the framing and encoding of the videos in circulation, the slippery indexicality of the image, as well as its potential for escaping intended circuits, often lead to unintended consequences which put family or community members at odds with one another.[5]

I conclude the chapter by reflecting upon my own video practice during fieldwork, which included shooting footage in several locations and at various points of my research, circulating this material, and eliciting responses from participants both in Peru and in the United States.[6] While my own research footage also circulated in the transnational social field it did so in very different ways and was ascribed different meanings than the migrants' videos. Reflecting upon the circulation of my own research footage offers important insights on broader issues of power, representation, positionality, and legitimacy in the production and transnational circulation of image-objects.

Staging Intimacy in Video Letters

"This is my bed and this is Carlos's bed," Fabiola narrates off-screen in Spanish while panning her camera across a small windowless bedroom. There is just enough space in the small room for two twin beds, a small table with a television and a stereo on top and a small closet stacked with clothes and empty boxes from kitchen appliances. A DVD recording of a show with *huayno* singer Abencia Meza—a popular singer around the time of my fieldwork—is playing loudly on the TV. The camera moves through the bedroom door out into a hallway and stops at the open door of the bedroom next door. "This is where Rodrigo sleeps," Fabiola continues. The camera does a quick pan and turns around. The off-screen voice continues: "We all live down here in this basement. This is the door to the upstairs entrance [the camera tilts following the curve up the stairs]. This is the kitchen [pans over the kitchen] . . . Carlos's lunch box . . . his beers . . . Let's see what we have in the fridge [Fabiola's hand opens the fridge; the footage is shaky] the things we use for cooking . . . [she opens a cupboard] instant soups . . . you just add water and that is what you eat . . . we only eat here at night and on weekends, but we always cook and bring our lunch to work" . . . [she walks to the bathroom, the camera runs for a while focusing on the floor, and is then turned off].

As visual narratives video letters offer rich material for ethnographic analyses of transnationally mediated social relationships and of transnationally mediated sociality more generally, as discussed in chapter 3. Video letters are personal and intimate visual accounts made by migrants abroad and/or family in Peru and are intended for viewing only by limited audiences such as close and extended family members and family friends. Video letters shot by migrants in the United States, such as the one described here, typically consist of a series of "scenes" filmed inside and outside migrants' apartments or houses over varied periods of time ranging from one day to several weeks. Their production needs are minimal as they are seldom edited beyond in-camera edits and only require access to a camcorder, which most U.S. migrants acquire at some point during their first years in the United States. The setup for a video letter evokes intimacy and closeness and the person making the video letter is likely to have strong personal, familial, and affective ties to the imagined and intended audiences. Sometimes it was a close relative or a friend who helped the migrant film the letter for their family members in Peru, but other participants filmed themselves by placing the camera on a tripod or a nearby table or shelf. The video letters analyzed here were all conducted in Spanish, even when participants were bilingual or trilingual in Quechua, Spanish, and English. Voice-over is recorded live as an off-camera commentary on the displayed images, whether it is a landscape from the window of a car in motion or the interior of a house. Rarely is much effort put into technically embellishing the aesthetics of the footage. Most video letters were made with the purpose of showing life in the United States to loved ones left behind in Peru and convey a more intimate testimony than what seemed possible when using nonvisual and/or textual media such as audiocassettes, letters, and more recently, emails and text messaging.

Fabiola, a member of one of the transnational families I worked with during my fieldwork, periodically made video letters for her family in Peru. Fabiola had been sending videocassettes to her parents and younger siblings in Huancayo on a regular basis since she first came to Washington, D.C., in 2000, showing small scenes of her everyday life and that of her two brothers in the United States. She did this, she said, to assure her parents that she and her brothers were doing well. Fabiola's video letters contained a mix of footage showing mundane situations (cooking, driving, doing laundry, or chatting with someone in her room or in her brother's car), social gatherings, and direct and intimate greetings addressed directly to her parents and sometimes to extended family members who she knew would watch the tapes together with Don Mariano and Doña Julia when visiting their home in Ocopilla. Fabiola usually shot the video letters herself, but sometimes one of her brothers or her sister-in-law did the camera work while Fabiola appeared on camera.

The most defining stylistic and narrative conventions in the video letter include "staged greetings" and complex closing sessions in which more greetings are extended to relatives and friends. "Say something," Carlos encourages Fabiola off-screen. She is sitting on her bed and is wearing a black T-shirt, sweatpants, and sneakers. The camera points right at her. "Greetings for my father, my mother . . . Mamita, I am doing well, resting after work, my stomach is better, I am taking it easy (*estoy tranquila*), greetings for el cholo, for Pedro [her younger brother], for Alicia, Mamita, when you see this video don't get sad, I am doing well, working to get ahead (*trabajando para salir adelante*), don't worry Mamita, what else can I tell you? Send my best wishes to my friends, to Emelina, to La China, to Aunt Carmencita . . . [Fabiola touches her own hair]. Ah . . . I have cut my hair, but I am doing ok.[7] It is more practical for going to work . . . I hope that when you see this video, you'll see that we are all doing well. We have celebrated Carlos's birthday—I made a cake for him . . . we'll send photos too. I am doing well, take good care, the same to my father, don't start crying when you see this video, Mamita . . . ah, and Pedro . . . mamá tells me that you are not behaving very well, you have to behave. Greetings to all the family . . ." Fabiola continues to name a long list of people, emphasizing the kinship connection. The video ends when the camera is turned off.

Sometimes migrants run out of words and must be prompted by their interlocutor to continue. In another of Fabiola's video letters, her sister-in-law María films her. After Fabiola's usual opening message with greetings to family members, she runs out of words. To break the silence María says: "Tell them a little more about what you do, what you eat, about the weather here . . ." Fabiola is still silent and then María herself declares off-camera: "Sometimes in these moments the words escape us." Later on the same tape, Fabiola and María switch roles and it is now Fabiola who interviews María. "You have to talk . . . say something," says Fabiola. "But you have to ask me first, don't you?" María responds. Fabiola then tries her best to mimic the interview style and generic accent of a Spanish-language news reporter: "Let us talk to the new *mayordoma* who will sponsor the fiesta this year . . . so to the new *mayordoma*, say something, send a message to Peru!" Fabiola announces. María responds slightly hesitantly: "Greetings to my mother, to my father, I miss you a lot. Today is Sunday and this is why we are at home. Here everything is work, we get up before the crack of dawn and we work all day long until the evening . . . Greetings to my only brother: Gustavito, you must study a lot, that is the only thing that is worth something, it will be the only heritage you leave behind, because money never lasts, but education does. If we had what you have now, the opportunities that you have, we would not have been here [in the United States]. Please take care of yourself, do everything that our mother tells you to do, don't shout at her, but behave well. Mamita, I love you very much (*te quiero muchísimo*), take care of yourself . . . what else can I tell you Mamita . . ."

The message of moral guidance that María directs at her younger brother, whose education María pays for via her monthly remittances from Washington, D.C., is central in her video letter and, as discussed in chapter 1, demonstrates the tight relationship between migration and education as intertwined aspects of an aspirational project. María knows that her parents and brother will watch the video at her in-laws' home in Huancayo and the public disciplining of her younger brother is meant to underscore the need for accountability and responsibility on his part. The education that María is offering her brother with her sweat and tears as a migrant abroad will also eventually put him in a position to take on the care responsibilities for their aging parents. Fabiola's video messages included similar instances of moral regulation directed at her younger brother who was studying in Huancayo, reminding him of the social and moral commitment to the education that was supposed to enable him to get ahead in life.

While video letters often are intended to assure family members in Peru that family members abroad are healthy and that there is no reason to worry about them, the tapes at times evoke the opposite feeling, often in the form of visceral, emotional reactions among relatives.[8] Fabiola's mother Julia was generally relieved to see that her children were living together harmoniously. She appreciated the fact that that their house looked clean and tidy and commented positively that her only daughter, Fabiola, looked healthy and *tranquila*. But watching the video letters also brought on feelings of deep sorrow, especially among U.S.-based migrants' elderly parents who, like Doña Julia and Don Mariano, felt terrible that their grown children, but nevertheless their children—and especially their daughters—might be struggling or suffering abroad in ways that were seen as inappropriate in terms of gender, culture, or age.

Although video letters were rarely addressed primarily to children left in the custody of extended family or other caregivers in Peru, the visual images certainly had some impact on the children who saw them. One day when I was visiting Doña Julia and Don Mariano, we watched a video letter from Fabiola in which her brother Carlos appeared more than usual. As we were watching and commenting on the various images on the screen, a young boy came running in from the back of the house and curled up with his grandfather in the armchair to watch. The boy was Doña Julia and Don Mariano's grandson who, along with his baby brother, had been left in the care of his paternal grandparents when his own parents left for the United States. As the images of Carlos, the boy's father, appeared on the screen Don Mariano told me that the boy almost didn't remember his father and that he and Doña Julia had become like mother and father to the boy and his younger brother. They had become so used to their grandparents, Mariano claimed, that they didn't even want to talk to their parents on the phone any more.[9] After a short while the boy lost interest in the video and ran off to play with a cardboard box in the nearby room.

Doña Julia and Don Mariano always shared the tapes with other relatives, friends, and *compadres* who visited their home in Huancayo and sometimes they also lent the videos to other relatives. They also frequently screened these videos for me when I visited them to get news about Fabiola and her brothers abroad. Recipients of video letters in Peru responded to them either by recording and sending video letters of their own or by commenting on the content of the videos through other kinds of media, including conventional letters, phone conversations, and more recently emails, although the latter was more common among the younger generation. Video letters were thus always the subject of conversations both in the local context in Peru and transnationally. As with any kind of image the producer's intentions often did not match up with the recipient's reaction. Consequently, the videos became dialogical as "audiences" and "producers" discussed, interpreted, and negotiated the meaning of the images in circulation in a variety of social contexts.

As many migrants today increasingly use webcams combined with various forms of VOIP, including Skype, to obtain the visual effect of copresence, simultaneity, and interactivity in transnational communication, video letters have ceded their place to other more contemporary technologies; indeed, they have been "remediated" (Bolter and Grusin 2005). When I returned to Peru for a follow-up visit in the summer of 2011, I reinterviewed several of my original study participants and found that many members of the older generation in Huancayo who previously had been recipients of video letters from their migrant sons and daughters abroad were now communicating via webcam from public Internet cafés (*cabinas públicas*) using a variety of VOIP. The children left in their custody—now tweens or teenagers—as well as the employees at the *cabinas públicas* assisted elderly Peruvians in accessing and using this new technology. In this sense, video letters can be seen as the predecessor for today's webcam-mediated communication in that they offered the possibility of sharing a birthday celebration or other festive occasion or allowed family members elsewhere to see particular surroundings. Yet video letters differ from today's webcam sessions in important ways. As visual documents they exist beyond the moment of transmission and can be seen by other relatives (or by a curious anthropologist) at a later time. As image-objects they can be stored, viewed again, and exchanged, and this made them valuable as objects of exchange that cemented the social relationship between the producers and the consumers of these videos. No participant in my study would attempt to save his or her video chats or Skype sessions for later viewing. And interestingly few if any migrants would upload video letter-like material to YouTube—even as by-invitation-only files—because they conceived of this platform as a public space not suitable for the intimate narratives about migration and migrant life that video letters represented.

Remittance Videos and the Evidence of Giving

In the early morning hours of September 15, 2004, the plaza of Urcumarca was still empty and displayed few signs of the previous evening's grand celebration: the *víspera* of the patron saint fiesta honoring the Virgin of the Nativity, which also coincided with the anniversary of the district of Urcumarca. This yearly celebration—also referred to simply as the *fiesta de alféreces* by villagers—is the most important occasion for migrant visits to their hometown in the Peruvian highlands.[10] I was on my way to Melanie's grandfather's house located on one of the dusty streets adjacent to the village plaza. As I walked through the old wooden door, with traces of green paint peeling off under the impact of the highland sun, and into the inner courtyard, Melanie greeted me enthusiastically. She was fixing her tripod as I walked in. I offered to help set up the camera and while Melanie calculated the camera's position according to where the "action" would take place, we went over the expected script of what was going to happen that morning.

The second genre of video examined—what I call remittance videos—most commonly consists of segments of raw documentary footage picturing acts of handing down collective monetary remittances or other gifts to local authorities or institutions in the hometown. Remittance videos were sometimes also accompanied by sets of photographs which also served the purpose of documenting progress on migrant-funded community projects. Videotaping the process of donating money or gifts has become a standard practice in many migrant-initiated development projects in transnational settings (see R. C. Smith 1998), yet little scholarly attention has been given to the electronic mediation of the ritualized action through which these transactions take place or to the relationships they mediate and maintain by these actions. Shot either by visiting

U.S.-based migrants like Melanie or by local municipal authorities or members of local institutions in the village, remittance videos have at least two goals. One goal is to create visual evidence that documents the proper delivery (*entrega*) and expenditure of collective remittances. While migrants in the United States use videos during visits to their hometown to document and prove to members of their organizations in the United States that a given donation was delivered in an appropriate manner, local authorities in Urcumarca also use videos (although perhaps less rigorously so) to document that a specific migrant-supported project (*obra*) was progressing in a timely manner in order to ensure continued support from migrants abroad. Both forms of recording and circulation of video footage pointed to the goal of achieving transparency and accountability through documentation and regulation, thus avoiding misuse and the disappearance of funds and gifts in the process of transfer. A key characteristic here concerns the directionality of the flow of remittance videos. Contrary to video letters, which flow in both directions within a transnational social field, remittance videos flow unidirectionally from Peru to the United States and are directly related to the transfer of money or goods.

A second goal, while more diffuse, was at the heart of the ongoing relationality produced by the circulation of collective remittances between highland Peru and migrant communities in the United States. Marcel Mauss ([1925] 1967) has famously argued that there is no such thing as a "free gift" and that the act of gift giving and the social or economic debts that arise from this act bind the giver and the recipient together in ongoing social relations which are at the core of the sociality of exchange. In gift economies, Mauss argued, the gift is more than a simple commodity; it is a "system of total services," which creates indebtedness, redistributes resources and wealth, fosters social relations, and engages issues of power and political authority.[11] In contrast to commodity economies where ownership rights are supposedly fully transferred to the new owner once an object is sold, the object in the gift economy is never alienated from its original owner. In fact, the contrary is frequently the case: the object is inalienated from the giver; that is, it is "loaned rather than sold and ceded" and compels the recipient to reciprocate (Weiner 1992).[12] This is at the core of what produces social relations. The gift thus entails a series of obligations: the obligation to give, which is the

necessary initial step for the creation and maintenance of social relationships and also the act through which one shows oneself as generous
and as deserving of respect; the obligation to receive, which is how one
shows respect to the giver, accepts the social bond between giver and
recipient, and simultaneously proves one's own generosity; and finally,
the obligation to return, which demonstrates that one's honor is at least
equivalent to that of the original giver (Mauss [1925] 1967:39–42).

The ongoing terms of indebtedness for recipients of collective
remittances—whether of money or goods—folded local residents into
ongoing relationships with their migrant donors abroad which in turn
bolstered the reciprocal commitments between the hometown and "the
sons and daughters" of the town living elsewhere (e.g., *los hijos ausentes
de Urcumarca*). Migrants in turn mobilized these relationships to boost
their fiesta sponsorships or to create political alliances.

In 2004, the Club Urcumarca—a regional association uniting migrants from Urcumarca who live and work in Maryland and Washington, D.C.—had decided to donate soccer uniforms for the local soccer
league in Urcumarca to commemorate the anniversary of the district in
September of that same year.[13] The money was collected through common fund-raising activities among U.S.-based migrants most commonly
referred to as *polladas*. A *pollada* comes from the Spanish word *pollo*
(chicken) and refers to a fund-raiser where money is made by selling
plates of cooked, roasted, or broiled chicken. The fund-raising capacity
of a pollada depends on the organizer's ability to draw on already existing
social networks (family, neighbors, and community members) to successfully sell as many tickets as possible in advance, referred to as *colo-
car las tarjetas* (place the tickets), and thus create a commitment among
possible supporters to show up for the actual event. Usually, the Club
Urcumarca collected between U.S. $800 and U.S. $2,000 on a regular
pollada attended by Urqumarquino migrants in the area. Since members
donated the food and beer they later paid to consume, money is easily
raised this way. It took just one pollada to secure the soccer uniforms for
the entire soccer league of Urcumarca. The uniforms were purchased in
the United States and later brought to Peru by club members who were
returning to Urcumarca for the patron saint fiesta in September.

Nelly's daughter Melanie was the Secretary of Sports in the Club Urcumarca when I did my fieldwork in Maryland and Washington, D.C.[14]

This position made her responsible for the donation of the football uniforms. Having received her green card in 2002, Melanie was among the few Urcumarquinos who could travel unhindered back to Peru (most other Urcumarquinos were still in the process of adjusting their status) and in September 2004, at age twenty-one, for the first time since she had come to the United States she traveled to participate in the yearly patron saint fiesta in Urcumarca along with her younger sister Doris and her mother Nelly, who was the treasurer of Club Urcumarca. Melanie had never lived in Urcumarca herself; however, the club was her mother's main social environment in Washington, D.C., and Melanie and her sister Doris had been going to the meetings and social gatherings since they first came to the United States as small children.

Around 9 a.m., just as Melanie and I finished setting up the camera for the documentation of the ceremony, the district mayor and some other local authorities arrived. Three players from the local soccer league accompanied them, carrying two boxes of beer to show their appreciation and to reciprocate and bolster the friendship with members of Club Urcumarca and more generally with *los residentes en los Estados Unidos*, which was the term most Urqumarquino villagers used to refer to the migrants abroad. Melanie's mother Nelly received the village authorities with a tray of soda, candy, and cookies—the latter items from a Duane Reade store in Washington, D.C., purchased just a few days before leaving for Peru. We chatted informally for a few minutes until Melanie confirmed that the setup was ready, the camera rolling, and Nelly gave the cue for the ceremony to start. First, the uniforms were spread out on a blanket on the ground and counted. Nelly then officially offered the donation to the district mayor on behalf of Club Urcumarca and all its members who had participated in the fund-raising drive and whose names she read from a list. They shook hands and the municipal secretary wrote up a handwritten memo in the municipal *libro de actas*, which everybody present, including the anthropologist, had to sign as witnesses to the *entrega*. The document was also signed and stamped by the mayor. In the meantime, the soccer players had dressed in the uniforms to appear in front of the camera where they offered their words of thanks and handed over the two boxes of beer to Nelly and Melanie to show their appreciation for the donation. The mayor, who was an able politician, took the opportunity to mention other local needs and later approached me, the foreign anthropologist, directly, about donating a First Aid Kit for the soccer league at the following year's District Anniversary. My consent to this request also appears on the video. Photographs were taken and the ceremony ended as Melanie turned off the video.

The ceremony had an air of solemnity, propriety, and authority, which is typical of public events in the Andes involving local political authorities. Its documentation involved all the usual technologies (memo, signatures, and stamps) through which the state asserts its authority and legitimacy through the authentication of actions involving local elected officials. Migrants' video documentation worked as an extension of such "traditional" forms of documentation in municipal record keeping. Yet because of the particular nature of this kind of visual technology, it was seen as an enhanced form of evidence. This has to do with the way people more generally attribute value to mechanically and electronically reproduced visual images. People tend to assume that the link between the information that the image displays and the event it refers to is a direct and transparent one. This is reminiscent of the notion of "photographic truth," which assumes that visual images are objective and truthful in and of themselves and that there is only one possible interpretation of the "facts" displayed. The notion or myth of "photographic truth" hinges on the idea that the camera is an objective device for capturing reality and that the images it produces therefore are unmediated copies of that reality, stripped of intentionality, and of the subjective vision of the photographer. Yet, as scholars of visual culture have argued, photographic images are highly subjective and cultural artifacts shaped by a range of beliefs, biases, stylistic influences, and intentions (Sturken and Cartwright 2001:280).

Furthermore, whereas a municipality's *libro de acta* exists only as one original handwritten record kept in the municipal offices, and there was no photocopy machine in the district at the time, video came in handy for the transnational circulation of images of the collective remittance transaction to a wider audience of stakeholders in local affairs. While remittance videos were mostly valued because of their "use value" (Poole 1997)—the value attributed to them as documentary and visual evidence—their "exchange value," that is, the positive relationships that they produced, displayed, and made available for circulation in a larger transnational social field that included both villagers and local authorities in Urcumarca and Urcumarquino migrants abroad, also played a role. As such the remittance video was a central element in a particular form of transnational sociality and exchange that sustained present and future relationships between migrants and their villages.

Back in Maryland, Melanie's footage was screened at the next board meeting of Club Urcumarca in the home of one of the Urcumarquinos in Rockville where club members who had traveled to Urcumarca shared their impressions of the fiesta. Remittance videos were seldom screened more than once or twice, usually in the context of the first association or club meetings immediately after the return from Peru of the U.S. club member in charge of the donation. In this sense their materiality resembled that of the physical letters discussed in chapter 3, which Agapito said that he would look at but then stored as objects. Contrary to video letters and fiesta videos, remittance videos were also rarely exchanged or lent out to relatives who were not members of the club. After the mandatory screening which often served as a visual background to a club member's oral report of the delivery of a particular collective remittance, the videos would be archived and kept with the rest of the club or organization's institutional records which included their *libro de actas* and requests for support from institutions and groups in the hometown. In this sense, the receipt was a valuable visual "document" because in the Maussian sense it confirmed that by receiving a gift the municipality was showing respect to the migrant community as giver, and simultaneously proved its own generosity, because the receipt of a gift also produces the obligation to return the gift and thereby demonstrate that one's honor is at least equivalent to that of the original giver ([1925] 1967:41–42). Furthermore, as Mauss suggested, to not reciprocate means to lose honor and status or spiritual power.

When Melanie screened her footage club members commented on the soccer players dressed in their new uniforms and on the importance of sports not just for the moral and bodily alignment of the players, but for the town's ability to compete successfully with the teams in neighboring towns, which was also a way to bring regional visibility to the locality. They applauded the visual evidence of the successful delivery of the collective remittance and moved on to other agenda items which included the many new requests of support they had received from local groups and individuals in the village—of everything from computers for the municipal office to school supplies for one of the local primary schools. In this light, rather than the circulation and the repeated consumption of remittance videos, it was the act of the recording itself and the ways in which the presence of the camera during the delivery of collective remittances rendered the ceremony more "official" and solemn, that constituted the most important aspect of their production. Yet the social knowledge about the act of giving that the remittance videos had evidenced continued to live on and circulate beyond the visual evidence generated by technology.

Framing Social Visibility in Fiesta Videos

Most remittance videos were shot in the context of migrants' return visits to their hometowns in the Peruvian Andes or remitted by municipal authorities, yet in spite of the visual emphasis on acts of giving, these videos were not the most important visual documentation of migrant returns due to their limited circulation. More important were the fiesta videos, which like the remittance videos also tended to be one-way only but with a broader circulation at the receiving end. These videos played a central role not only in the transnational fiesta economy, but also in the social valuation of persons that accrued through transnational circulation of migrant bodies, money, religious objects, and other substances across regimes of moral and cultural values. These videos typically chronicle local patron saint festivals and other ritualized celebrations, which mark the calendar year of both rural and urban communities in the Andes. They are important to members of transnational households and communities not only as entertainment but as a central and significant form of mediation of migrants' own status and social visibility in the context of their home communities in Peru, and in the migrant collectivities abroad that extend prior kinds of agency, self-making, and community building characteristic of Andean life.

Fiesta videos were the most elaborate of the many kinds of videos discussed here and were seldom produced by transnational family members themselves. Instead a local image industry with skilled videographers and state-of-the-art equipment consistently catered to the local and regional fiesta circuit in highland Peru and produced the videos des-

Figure 4.1. Migrant fiesta video sold in the market in Jauja, 2013. (Photo by Author)

tined for transnational circulation. Far from being rendered obsolete by the fact that most transnational households possessed camcorders, local fiesta videographers had expanded their market to include ever more sophisticated and customarily made fiesta videos destined for transnational circulation between the Peruvian highlands and migrant communities abroad. One of the main objectives of these videos was to cast the migrant fiesta sponsor in a favorable and positive light and expand the sponsor's social visibility through transnational circulation. The centrality of fiestas and festive performances in social life in this region of Peru also made the fiesta videos objects of general interest and they were often sold as entertainment at local markets in Huancayo and Jauja.

Patron saint fiestas and other key religious festivals are central events in the social and cultural reproduction of local communities all over the Andes, yet they are also sites of important contestations over power, membership, and belonging. Religious festivals structure not only the productive agricultural cycle in the case of rural communities, but they also mediate the social life of a community more generally.[15] In contexts of rural-urban migration, Latin Americanist scholars have documented extensively the ways in which fiestas and other ritual events celebrated in the context of village-based migrant associations in cities are central to migrants' efforts to insert themselves in new social environments and create meaningful communities in the urban context.[16] This also holds true in contexts of transnational migration. Andeanist scholars have shown—in writing and film—how fiestas themselves are important driving forces in migrants' transnational engagements (Gelles 2005; Paerregaard 2010). For example, in Paul Gelles and Nelson Martínez's now classic ethnographic film *Transnational Fiesta* (1993), transnational migrants from Cabanaconde in Washington, D.C., have become so central to the participation, organization, and funding of fiestas in their hometown of Cabanaconde that the event itself has become "transnational."[17]

Most U.S.-based migrants of provincial origin in my study who had been able to adjust their legal status and thus could return to Peru, would schedule their return trips around the festive-religious calendar of their hometowns. Indeed, sponsorship of the patron saint fiesta of the hometown was an important rite of passage for transnational migrants, marking their transition from undocumented, temporary workers in the United States to permanent residents. Several migrants had also taken vows of reciprocity before leaving their communities of origin whether for Lima or for the United States, promising devotion and dedication to their patron saint in exchange for safe travel in good health, rapid insertion in the labor market abroad, and successful legalization. While they would continue to venerate their saint's image abroad, returning to sponsor the fiesta honoring the image was often considered the ultimate offering to show appreciation and gratitude. Upon adjustments of their legal status many Urcumarquinos traveled to participate in the patron saint fiestas either because they themselves had assumed roles as fiesta sponsors (*alferez* or *mayordomos*) or because close kin or other members of transnational migrant networks were sponsoring the fiesta. These festive occasions were also a good time to visit the village because other relatives and friends who had left the village to work in the mining towns or migrated to Lima or other countries were likely to visit during this period.

While several of the visiting families bring their own video cameras to Urcumarca and record parts of the fiesta for their own private consumption, fiesta sponsors usually contract a local for-hire videographer to make the elaborate visual narratives that I here refer to as fiesta videos. In contrast to other genres of videos discussed here, videos of fiestas are exchanged for money. They are sold not only to the fiesta sponsor's family members, but also to Urcumarquinos in Jauja, Lima, Washington, D.C., and Maryland. Indeed, videos of the most prominent of the fiestas in the Mantaro Valley's fiesta circuit are also available at local stores in Jauja and Huancayo and marketed to tourists passing through the region as part of a "cultural heritage series." Many U.S.-based migrants—especially those who cannot travel because of their lack of legal status or because an application to adjust status has not yet been approved—have extensive video libraries of fiesta videos, which are circulated widely between transnational migrant households in Washington, D.C., Maryland, Virginia, Lima, and Urcumarca itself.

As a result of the growing consumption of fiesta videos among migrants abroad and in Lima, a local image industry of video makers and photographers has emerged in Urcumarca and other towns in the Mantaro region. Most return migrants from Washington, D.C., and Maryland who took up fiesta sponsorship in the village hired the same person—a videographer who called himself "El Yanamarquino" in reference to the valley of Yanamarca where the town of Urcumarca is located—to videotape the fiesta for them. El Yanamarquino, a videographer and a native of the neighboring town, had been filming videos of the fiestas in Urcumarca and the rest of the Yanamarca and Mantaro valleys for a number of years. He was self-taught and had no specialized training in film and video production when he first started out in the 1990s, but got access to a video camera through a relative and envisioned this loan as a business opportunity. In the beginning he filmed fiestas all over the valley and then offered them to fiesta sponsors afterwards, but in recent years he has increasingly been hired in advance by migrant fiesta sponsors to document their participation in the various festivals of their home community. El Yanamarquino was satisfied with his deal working for the returning migrants. He made a lot more money recording fiestas for U.S.-based migrants than for any other fiesta or life cycle event, including weddings, baptisms, and quinceañeras in the area.[18] Over the course of a three- to five-day fiesta, he would record ten to fifteen hours of footage, which would then be edited and cut down in length according to the requests of the fiesta sponsor.[19]

The fiesta videos typically chronicle the unfolding of the fiesta by presenting its various parts in chronologically ordered sequences (víspera, día central, etc.). These "observational segments" consist of images from all the important "minievents" that make up the fiesta and figure in the fiesta program, including the burning of huge and elaborate fireworks on the evening of the víspera at the town's central square, the mass and procession on the central day of the fiesta, the multiple meals offered to the musicians that animate the fiesta and to the community at large, the impressive performances of regional or local dances, and finally the traditional *corta monte* dance where participants dress up in characteristic Jaujina clothing used on such festive occasions. These observational segments sometimes have a voiceover track where the videographer identifies the people appearing on the tape or comments on and "translates" the local customs for the imagined audience of both migrants and non-locals. The observational segments are most commonly interwoven with interviews with the *alferez* or *mayordomo*, members of his or her family, supporters (*priostes, brazos*), and invited special guests.[20] Some videographers insert landscape images from the village and the surrounding areas into the visual narrative of the fiesta either at the beginning or throughout the video, especially images of local tourist attractions such as any nearby archeological sites or colorful local markets. Many videographers also offer to make customized versions of the fiesta videos focusing on a particular day or activity for extra pay.

In September 2004, Paulino was the *alferez* of the fiesta honoring the Virgin of the Nativity in Urcumarca. Having only recently adjusted his immigration status to that of permanent residency in the United States, this was his first time sponsoring the fiesta. In anticipation of the fiesta, Paulino made two trips to Peru to coordinate logistics, donations from family and community members, and other practical matters. He made arrangements with the musicians (both *banda* and *orquestra típica*) and on one of the trips he also hired El Yanamarquino to tape the fiesta.[21]

A few days before the fiesta in September, Paulino met with El Yanamarquino and carefully instructed him on what to record and from whom to solicit comments. One of Paulino's conditions was to avoid filming people who had got too drunk and to edit out this footage in case it occurred. "I don't want people abroad to see that aspect of the fiesta," Paulino explained to me in Urcumarca. "I never get drunk in public. The alferez is supposed to run the fiesta and make sure that everything is ready and done on schedule. If you are too drunk, how are you supposed to accomplish that?" It was clear that the stakes were high for Paulino having lived outside his hometown for the better part of two decades, first as a police officer in *la zona roja* (the areas of the central and southern highlands mostly affected by the political violence of the 1980s) and later as a migrant to the United States. The fiesta video would eventually become the means by which the grand narrative of his generosity and commitment to his *pueblo* (in Spanish meaning both the people and the town) would circulate transnationally and cement his reputation as an honorable citizen and *hijo del publo* (son of the town), and therefore also his social status and that of his entire extended family in the village and abroad.

Paulino not only instructed El Yanamarquino about who to film and in what capacity, but also whom *not* to film, especially villagers who were not on good terms with his family. He did not want any spontaneous criticism from anyone taking advantage of the opportunity to air unfavorable opinions about his family or their sponsorship on his video. Paulino wanted to make sure that he retained a sense of control over the visual narrative so that when it circulated transnationally it could both extend and amplify the social valuation of his person. Yet, as scholars of cultural consumption have argued, the process of interpreting and giving meaning to cultural products according to assumed shared cultural codes—what Stuart Hall (1980) refers to as "decoding" in his famous encoding/decoding model—seldom matches the preferred meaning of those who have "encoded" the media text.[22] Hence migrants' attempts to control the consumption and circulation of their own mediated narratives are not always successful.

One evening during the fiesta in 2004 during a dinner offered by one of Paulino's relatives, a teacher from the local kindergarten began complaining about the fact that so much money had been lavished on beer and alcohol during the fiesta while none had been donated to the local kindergarten as part of the grand spending scheme of the fiesta sponsor. Obviously irritated by this attack, Paulino first politely explained to her that if she wished to receive any donation for her school she could present a written request to him or to the Club Urcumarca in Washington, which could then consider her request along with the many other written requests they received. The tone of the conversation escalated into a critique of migrants as selfish and as only thinking about having a good time during the fiesta but not really helping the community with what the teacher identified as its "real needs." This rather heated discussion, which appeared on El Yanamarquino's original footage, was later censored and edited out from the DVD intended for circulation.

Back in the United States, the fiesta videos are circulated, exchanged, and sometimes copied among relatives and paisanos, but often a first screening is organized at the house of the fiesta sponsor. Paulino had brought back a box of Peruvian beer for the occasion and on the evening of the "first screening" the women were busy cooking up a storm. On numerous occasions when I visited the Urcumarquinos in their Maryland or D.C. homes they would almost immediately invite me to sit down in their living room in front of the TV as they popped the latest fiesta video in the VCR or DVD player. The viewing of the videos would often alternate with conversation or doing chores around the house. Viewing was also often combined with other domestic activities such as cooking, knitting, making phone calls, or helping younger children with their homework.

Figure 4.2. Manuel and his family watching fiesta videos in Silver Spring, 2004. (Photo by Author)

The fiesta images always worked as a trigger for immediate conversation about the village and its inhabitants, and I was always content with these video-viewing moments as an opportunity to elicit information or stories about particular individuals, families, or topics. When Paulino's mother, Asunción, who had not been back in Urcumarca for many years because of her legal status, saw a well-known face on the screen or someone making a statement about the fiesta, she would get into long explanations about that person's family, what their fate had been during the years of political violence in the area, or what she thought about them more generally. In this sense, viewing videos with migrants proved to be very useful ethnographic encounters.[23]

While fiesta videos had increased news value in the first weeks or months after the fiesta, most fiesta videos have long lifespans in terms of continued interest to U.S.-based migrants. Paulino's fiesta video had already been in circulation for several months when I first visited him and his family in Silver Spring in early 2005. Nevertheless, the videos were still frequently played not only for me, the ethnographer, but also for other visitors. In fact, on one of my first visits to Silver Spring, several of the Urcumarquinos mentioned when I was introduced to them that they had seen me in the video dancing with their father or uncle on the plaza of Urcumarca or talking to their aunt during the víspera. This facilitated my research and allowed me to gain entry and establish rapport with the Urcumarquino migrant collectivity in Maryland and D.C.

Images as Evidence: Unintended Consequences and Unfortunate Visibilities

Visual technologies and the images they produce multiply the possibilities of self-presentation across a transnational social field, but they also complicate and in their own way expose inherent tensions and contradictions of fundamental aspects of the migrant/transnational condition—now deemed visible by virtue of the technology itself. Images do not have value in and of themselves but accrue different kinds of value—social, political, monetary, or otherwise—in particular cultural contexts and through social processes of circulation. As a kind of symbolic, two-way remittance, video images can thus simultaneously facilitate the social and affective ties and commitments between migrants and their family members in Peru and create conflict and distance. Tracking the circulation of videos across these various contexts proved useful in order to understand the various dimensions of cross-border exchange and sociality which followed from the transnationalization of affective and economic ties within and across migrant households. As Louisa Schein (2002:230) has argued, the way that transnational and diasporic peoples understand "who they are and how they belong is never anterior to, indeed is inseparable from, the kinds of media they produce." In this way, media practices like the videos discussed here produce both subjectivities and communities.

Consequently, both migrants and their family members in Peru were highly invested in monitoring the selection and editing of information which they considered appropriate for transnational circulation and what was better kept off the record to avoid tensions in the family and in the larger community. While gossip and rumors about U.S.-based migrants and their spouses, children, or other relatives in Peru were frequently exchanged in phone conversations between Peru and the United

States, video mediation added complexity to these exchanges. The visuality of the medium required heightened awareness not only of the positive but also of the negative consequences of its circulating images. When Sarah Mahler, for example, asked a Salvadoran migrant on Long Island what he thought about the idea of videotaping immigrants and having the videos played to relatives back home, his answer was: "That will never work because no one wants their relatives to see how they *really* live in the United States." (Mahler 1995:88. emphasis in original) The fact that particular video images or clips were taken largely as unquestionable evidence of an underlying truth—this in spite of the fact that they were extracted and completely stripped from a larger social context—sometimes produced unintended consequences which could instigate a crisis or even undermine the affective and social ties which they were meant to sustain and strengthen.

A few years after she left for Washington, D.C., Fabiola bought a little camcorder for her parents that she sent to Huancayo with a distant relative who was traveling to Peru. Her idea was that her parents could use it to record video letters and footage of fiestas both in Huancayo and in their hometown of Llamapsillion for their U.S.-based children. For a while the camcorder was the center of attention in the family. It was kept as a treasure, mostly looked at and talked about, but not used. In spite of the interest in the camera, it took Fabiola's parents and brothers several months before they got a tape together which they shipped off to Washington, D.C. Most of the footage was shot in the "official" living room in the front of the house and some in an additional living room that Fabiola had ordered constructed at the back of the house for everyday use. Fabiola's brother Constantino had tried to film the various home improvements that Fabiola had sent them remittances to undertake. To build a house of one's own is a central aspirational goal of many Andean families—one that is often sought to be realized through transnational migration (Colloredo-Mansfeld 1994; Leinaweaver 2009)—and family members went to great lengths to document the home improvement projects that migrants had ordered done from abroad. When the camcorder was finally put to use, Doña Julia and Don Mariano were rebuilding the façade of the house, enlarging the front living room and the entrance area. To disguise the construction while videotaping, especially a large hole in the wall, they had covered the entire wall of the living room facing the street with a blue plastic blanket—the kind used in the market to arrange produce or other sales items on the ground. Pedro, Fabiola's younger brother, was doing the videotaping. At one point Fabiola's aunt, who was visiting that day, sat on the sofa and Pedro invited her to send a greeting to Fabiola and her brothers in the United States. The blue plastic cover appeared as an intense blue backdrop in the background of the frame of the aunt on the sofa. The tape was sent off a few days later from a remittance agency in Huancayo.

When Fabiola received the tape, she immediately criticized the blue plastic in the background wrapped over the hole in the living room wall. How was it possible that after all the money she had sent to rebuild the house, the walls were covered with cheap blue plastic of the kind used in the mercado!? Her parents later excused themselves to her, explaining that they had covered the wall precisely *because* there was a hole in it and the mason (here referred to as *maestro* or master) had not been able to come for several weeks. But this made Fabiola even angrier. "How can they be so informal?" she complained to me months later when we talked about the incident in D.C.

The "proper" use of remittances is a thorny issue in many transnational families, and family members in Peru are often eager to report back that the money they have received from relatives abroad has been used appropriately according to the expectations and instructions that accompanied the flow of U.S. dollars. Many U.S.-based migrants pay for the reconstruction of family homes in Peru or order entirely new homes built from abroad, hoping to inhabit them in the future, and most will expect videos or photographs of the progress. These kinds of requests make family members in Peru vulnerable to the documentation demands of their relatives abroad, at least if they hope the remittances will continue to flow into the transnationalized household economies.

In contrast to phone conversations, where reports on remittance expenditure can be easily manipulated and lack of progress on construction work and the like can be covered up, the visual evidence produced by video and photography creates the expectation that what appears on the photograph, videotape, or DVD is *the* truth. Consequently, tensions emerge when the evidence "exceeds" the intention of its production and gets interpreted in unintended ways. "My daughter was furious," said Doña Julia as she finished relating her version of the incident to me. "It is not good for her health. She has a bad stomach and it is not good for her to get upset. All because of the damn hole (*maldito hueco*)." Many months passed before Doña Julia and Don Mariano touched the camcorder again. The next time it was used was when a cousin filmed a family reunion at a relative's house in El Tambo upon Fabiola's request. The cousin shot the footage and later shipped the video to D.C. from a remittance agency in Lima.

Sometimes video images in circulation fit into and amplify already existing rumors or pieces of gossip which have previously circulated through other channels. Or alternatively, they may generate new bits of gossip from decontextualized images and put new rumors into circulation. Linguistic anthropologists Bauman and Briggs (1990) have argued that when pieces of discourse are torn from their interactional settings, circulated (here in electronically mediated forms), and then reincorporated and consumed in other social contexts—a process they refer to as "entextualization"—new meanings may emerge. While gossip generally is said to be information of doubtful or partial truths (Van Vleet 2003), when generated through the circulation of visual images it often gains the status of truth because of the "evidentiary" status of the image.

Gossip serves several purposes within transnational social networks. Scholars have shown that gossip may be either a source of entertainment, an informal way of obtaining and passing on information, and also a mechanism for social control by way of influencing others within the social group (Ben-Ze'ev 1994, Dreby 2009). Scholars have also noted that gossip may have both positive and negative consequences; it can be cooperative by enhancing community members' sense of solidarity or it can be divisive by critiquing those who transgress social norms (Dreby 2009: 34, 35); it may also be a tool to realign transgressive behavior and rein in the behavior of particular subjects. In all these ways rumors and gossip circulate extensively across social space and are important to structuring social life in transnational families and communities (Pribilsky 2004, Dreby 2009, Drotbohm 2009).[24] This includes the moral regulation of both migrants abroad and their relatives in the home country, regulation that may be highly gendered. Dreby (2009:49), for example, has argued that transnational gossip often causes conflicts in families, especially for mothers, who generally bear the moral burden of family separation. While rumors and gossip flow through all sorts of channels,

the visual evidence generated by video and other image technology lay-
ing high claims to truth complicates this scenario.[25]

For some time there had been rumors that Paulino had an affair with a
paisana from Urcumarca now living in Lima; however, as is typical with
gossip, no evidence or discernable source was ever revealed which could
confirm that this rumor was actually true. A year later, Paulino traveled
to Urcumarca without his wife and children to participate in the New
Year's celebrations in the village. While it was customary for couples to
go together when returning to participate in the yearly patron saint fiestas, especially if they were fiesta sponsors (it is always couples who are
sponsors, though in the case of an unmarried person, sponsorship can be
shared with a relative of the opposite sex), this year Paulino went by himself. His wife Celestina, who was from another community in the highlands above Huancayo, also had fiesta obligations to support her own
relatives and didn't want to travel to Peru on this particular occasion.

When Paulino returned to Washington ten days later he brought with
him the video from the fiesta (even if he had something to hide, it would
be impossible to return from a fiesta without the video). One evening
I saw the video of the fiesta at Paulino's mother's house while Celestina
was still at work. "You better watch this now if you want to see it," Paulino's mother Asunción said somewhat cautiously, "Celestina gets very
upset when she sees this tape. . . . I never play it when she is around."

In one scene in the video, there were images of Paulino dancing the
traditional Corta Monte dance at length with the *paisana* in question.
To my eyes there was nothing particularly romantic about the dance se-
quence on the tape. Although Paulino strenuously denied to his mother
any affective connection with the woman, the rumors, which had pre-
ceded the circulation of the tape, provided the social context for its interpretation. Asunción shook her head and ended the conversation by
saying: "He should have known that this could happen. He knows that
she [Celestina] is very jealous, so why would he even bring the tape? He
could have avoided all these problems if it wasn't for the video."

Asunción's comment points to Paulino's failure to mobilize his cross-
contextual judgment to realize that sooner or later the video would reach
his wife or other relatives in the United States and that it could have
detrimental effects on his relationship with his wife which, like all relationships, was also mediated by images.

The Visual Anthropologist at Work

Faye Ginsburg has argued that the anthropologist—just like any other cultural producer—engages in cultural productions and that these should be seen not as contradictory, but as complementary endeavors providing different kinds of insights on the same cultural object, influencing each other, and thus creating what she calls a "parallax effect." A parallax effect is the effect produced when two or more perspectives on the same cultural object render it multidimensional, thus allowing for greater depth of vision (Ginsburg 1995:65–66). I wish to conclude this chapter by discussing how my own research footage served to create such a parallax effect which served to further my understanding of the visual economy of Urqumarquino migrant videos and of Urqumarquinos' quest for spatiotemporal extension beyond their racialization as backward rural subjects in Peru's dominant racial and class hierarchy.

In March 2005, only a few months into my fieldwork with Urcumarquino migrants in Washington, D.C., and Maryland, I was invited to participate in their annual carnival celebration in Silver Spring. As in many communities of the central highlands of Peru, including Urcumarca, carnival in Maryland is celebrated with the traditional corta monte dance as its central activity. I decided to videotape the event because I knew the footage would come in handy when returning to Peru later that year. I also anticipated using this footage as a way of "giving back."[26] I shot footage of the preparations for the fiesta (making lunch, decorating the tree), the arrival of participants, the corta monte dance itself, and some minor interviews with participants. Many participants were recording the event as well and the presence of the many camcorders seemed at first to legitimize the presence of my camera and of me shooting the event.

Later in the evening, Manuel, a younger migrant of twenty-one, who was brought to the United States as a child by his parents, decided that he would introduce me to some of his relatives that I had not met yet. "Let's use your camera," he said. I enthusiastically agreed, thinking that this would be a great opportunity to get some footage of people talking directly to the camera in the interview style that local videographers in the Peruvian highlands had taught me was the true fiesta-tape form and aesthetic. The fiesta was held in the large garden of a big suburban home owned by one of the migrants. Most of the fiestas of the Urqumarquino collectivity were in fact held here because of the size of the property and the spread-out layout of the neighborhood, which offered considerable space between neighboring houses. Manuel and I started walking around in the garden with the camera to ask participants what they thought about the fiesta this year, how long they had been in the United States, and if they wanted to send greetings to family members in Peru. The latter—sending personal greetings to relatives elsewhere—was a central element in the fiesta videos recorded in Peru. Manuel, who like numerous other participants had got quite drunk, decided that he would direct the interviews. I didn't object even as I started to feel increasingly intimidated and embarrassed by his interventions. Manuel interrupted people in the middle of a dance or in the middle of a conversation. There was nothing discrete about his style of directing video interviews. Some people responded positively and just said a few polite sentences about the fiesta and self-consciously added that this event was a "typical" and "authentic" expression of "Peruvian culture."

At one point, when Manuel's cousin Juana danced by, Manuel grabbed her by the arm and pointed the camera right in her nose. I squirmed at his well-meaning efforts to help me and at his obvious lack of tact as a videographer. "Say something to the camera," he demanded. Juana started to talk willingly in English while looking at me and assuming the role of a cultural translator, who had to explain the event to a gringa outsider as a "typical Peruvian tradition." Probably thinking that I was native to the United States or in any case an outsider to Peruvian customs, she extended an invitation to all Americans who would see the tape to participate in the fiesta the following year. "No, not like that," objected Manuel. "Say something to your folks back home." He was obviously a little irritated by her response and the fact that she wasn't playing along with his attempt to conduct a fiesta video interview. "But this video will not reach my parents, so why would I say something to them?" Juana responded with a slightly offended look. More comments were exchanged between the cousins until Juana turned around and walked away. I was devastated, but Manuel didn't seem to be bothered. "Ah, she's my cousin," he said when I tried to argue against continuing the recordings.

My words had little or no effect on Manuel, who dragged me along to the next person in sight. Dino Quispe, who had come to the United

States in 2001, stopped in front of the camera. I had not yet been formally introduced to Dino or his two brothers, who were also in Maryland, but I knew his parents well from Urcumarca and his older brother Damian, who lived in Lima, was my friend. Although I had become quite friendly with the Quispe family toward the end of my fieldwork in Urcumarca, it had taken me several months to get them to speak to me about their children's migration to the United States. I later learned that the Quispes' initial reluctance to share their family migration story was because Dino had instructed his parents not to talk to anyone about him or his brothers and about when or how they had left Peru. Some people in the village still thought that the Quispe brothers lived in Lima. Most Urcumarquinos believed that publicizing one's intention to migrate too widely could lead to "bad luck" (*mala suerte*) and sure enough, several of the Quispe brothers had failed migration attempts behind them. When they finally managed to leave Peru they didn't want anyone to know until they were fully established in Maryland.

Dino's first reaction to the camera was to ask: "What is this for, who is going to see this recording?" Manuel told him that I was doing a study and that I knew his family from Urcumarca. He also told Dino that I was going back to Peru next month and would show the video to the Quispe family when I was there. Dino started questioning me about my study, asking what its purpose was and who was paying for it. While still behind the camera, I was suddenly the one being interviewed. I tried to explain as briefly and generally as I could and attend to the fact that Dino was obviously not comfortable with his image being circulated to family and community members in Peru by someone he hardly knew. After a short off-camera conversation about my project Dino decided to send greetings to his father, Alejandro Quispe, in the village, and to his wife and son in Lima who Dino hoped to bring to the United States in the near future: "Don't worry, son, very soon you will be dancing in the fiestas here," he promised in front of my camera.

This ethnographic interlude demonstrates clearly that not everyone is authorized to produce visual materials for circulation in a given transnational circuit. The ambivalence some migrants might have felt about the presence of a foreign anthropologist in their fiesta in the first place, the ways in which they understood or failed to understand the purpose of my study and my relationships with their family members back in

Peru, complicated my position not only as a participant in the fiesta, but as someone who knew and sustained social relationships with people in their community and claimed to bring the videos to Peru. Because of my outsider status and my gender, my video practice was read differently from their own recordings. Clearly, I could not pass as some female "gringa version" of El Yanamarquino. My footage had a different ontological status and its path of circulation was unknown to most migrants. Furthermore, many Urcumarquinos were undocumented and being on the wrong person's video footage in the post-9/11 surveillance era could have detrimental consequences for someone's migration project. Even if many of the people in the fiesta knew me—and knew me well— many did not and had good reasons to doubt whether my video footage would represent their mobility in favorable light. This unpredictability of mediation and circulation—of not being fully in control of one's own image—is the subject at the heart of the next chapter.

PART III

Discrepant Publics

5

Enframing Peruvianness

Folkloric Citizenship and Immigrant Personhood

The spectacle is not a collection of images; rather, it is a social relationship between people that is mediated by images.
—Guy Debord, *The Society of the Spectacle*, [1967] 1994

Nunca falta el cholo malazo que nos hace pasar vergüenza
como Peruanos, ensuciando todo y comportandose como si
estuviera en Lima. [There is always a bad cholo who embarrasses us as Peruvians, making everything dirty and behaving as if he was in Lima.]
—Journalist in Paterson, New Jersey, 2004

Every year at the end of July, thousands of Peruvians and other Latin
Americans come to Paterson from all over the Tristate area to attend
the Peruvian Parade—the yearly commemoration of the Peruvian Independence Day, *Fiestas Patrias*, organized by Peruvians in Paterson. But
the buzz starts long before one even gets to New Jersey. Behind the Port
Authority bus station on 41st St. and 8th Ave. in Manhattan, one must
have a lucky star to get a seat on one of the Peruvian-owned minibuses
(*combis*), which are always filled to capacity on these particular Sundays.
The social space of the *combi* on such an occasion is shared between people traveling with families looking to spend their day commemorating
the Patria while socializing with extended kin and friends and ambulant
street sellers hoping to make a week's salary in a day, with large bags of
flags, bracelets, baseball caps, and T-shirts bearing inscriptions such as
"Te Amo Perú" (I Love You Peru) and "Soy Peruano Carajo y Que?" (I
am Peruvian for Fuck's Sake and So What?). These inscriptions perfectly
conveyed the ambiguities surrounding national belonging among Peruvians abroad as simultaneously a nostalgic love affair and a curse.[1]

While the previous chapters have been concerned with the tension between the desires and aspirations of individuals and families for transnational mobility and the larger racial and political economy which prompts migrants to fashion themselves both vis-à-vis powerful state institutions and in the more intimate contexts of transnational communication, this chapter and the one that follows grapple with Peruvian migrants' attempt to fashion themselves collectively through public performance into subjects worthy of citizenship, recognition, and belonging in the context of larger nationalist and racial projects, in Peru and the United States respectively. This chapter examines the yearly Peruvian Parade organized by Peruvians in Paterson, New Jersey, as a key site for and register of collective self-refashioning for U.S.-based Peruvian migrants in their varied claims to citizenship and belonging. By analyzing the organization, framing, epistemology, context, and experience of the event, I explore how this large-scale public spectacle serves not only as a medium to negotiate and contest the multiple meanings of "Peruvianness" at play, but also to mediate the links between racial, classed, and gendered subjectivities and claims to national belonging in both Peru and the United States.

The parade is an important social arena in which Peruvian migrants of many different class and regional backgrounds produce themselves through embodied performance as national Peruvian subjects *and* as decent, worthy, and hardworking Latin American immigrants deserving of citizenship and recognition in the United States. This is accomplished by mobilizing and embodying visual and material properties that seek not only to redefine the categories of Peru's social imaginary, but also to alter the ethnic and migration landscape and public culture of Paterson and the United States more broadly to accommodate new Latino populations. I suggest that inversely positioned Peruvians bring different things to bear on the event through relational identifications that play out in the context of this event. For Andean Peruvians in particular, participation in the parade serves to position them as "equally Peruvian" in relation to Peruvians from Lima or the coast. Indeed, in some senses they claim to be more "authentically" Peruvian because in the context of the parade folklore claims a space for indigeneity that racially marked Peruvians—no matter their urban and "nonprimordial" identifications—can inhabit, thereby allowing them to be accommodated in U.S. public culture as "exotic" and interesting to spectating publics. Inspired by the work of Diane Nelson (1999) on competing efforts to form a "whole" national body politic in Quincentennial Guatemala and the work of Marisol de la Cadena (2000) on the social process of "de-indigenization" in Peru, I propose the concept of "folkloric citizenship" to characterize a mode of membership in a community where racially marked Peruvians can both claim Peruvian national identity vis-à-vis non-Andean Peruvians and accommodate their racial and cultural difference in an unthreatening way to American publics. I use the adjective "folkloric" here as a metacultural category that is typically employed to mark certain genres and practices within modern societies as "not modern" (Noyes 2004), but which in the context of neoliberal multiculturalism and transnational migration and mobility may also bear connotations of imagined cultural "authenticity" and spirituality that can be mobilized—in limited and specific contexts—to the benefit of the racially marked cultural Other. By "self-exoticizing," so to speak, through public performance these Peruvians are able to deploy culture and folklore to relationally "fix" their identities in ways that allow them to claim membership and belonging within larger racial and national projects.

The Peruvian Parade in Paterson celebrates *Fiestas Patrias*, Peru's Independence Day of July 28 that has been celebrated in Peru since the nineteenth century, playing an integral role in the forging of the modern nation-state. The celebration of the myth of the foundation of the republic and the proclamation of independence in 1821, the heroization of the founding fathers, the center staging of the youth and of education as the future of the nation, and the use of national symbols such as the flag and the national anthem are all key elements in such patriotic celebrations not just in Peru but all over Latin America (Beezley et al. 1994; Stepputat 2004; Wilson 2001). In Peru's capital Lima, *Fiestas Patrias* is still predominantly a military and patriotic event in which the state reaffirms its military and political power over the nation and its citizens (Degregori 2001). In the Andean provinces, by contrast, the official acts of commemoration intended to display patriotic civic consciousness are often accompanied by sporting events, bullfights, and folkloric festivals. Scholars have variously argued that local inhabitants stage and participate in such events to draw alternative connections between past, present, and future and to assert their presence within the contemporary nation-state (Harvey 1997; Stepputat 2004, 2005; Wilson 2001). For example, Penelope Harvey (1997:39) has argued that the participation in such public rituals and the continuous retelling of multiple historical layers and symbolic elements offers local residents an experiential synthesis which can not only transport past events into the present but also help organize certain futures.

In Paterson, New Jersey, the Peruvian Parade commemorating *Fiestas Patrias* has been celebrated every year since 1986 when the parade organization "Peruvian Parade Inc." was first formed. It serves as an important medium through which Peruvian migrants from Paterson and surrounding areas can draw meaningful spatial and temporal connections between here and there and between past, present, and future, and where new subjectivities that emerge from the migration process are configured. It is a way through which participants make sense of the world and of their own social positioning within it. Relatedly the parade also serves to draw important distinctions as it seeks to include some people and exclude others in the hegemonic narrative of "Peruvianness" that is produced through the event. This has implications for what aspects of Peruvianness can come to stand as a representation of "Peruvians" overall in the context of a broader U.S. public. Through their performance in a transnationalized public sphere in Paterson, Andean participants assert their historical presence and future aspirations in relation to larger nationalist and racial projects both in Peru and in the United States.

As a self-conscious staging of citizenship and claims to membership and belonging, the Peruvian parade is therefore an important site for the fashioning of the self and the collective. Migrant subjectivities, as suggested by Nicholas De Genova (2009), are indeed centrally produced in and expressed through their occupation of public space. How then are "Peruvianness" (*Peruanidad*) and "Peruvian culture" mobilized, embodied, stylized, contested, and framed for display during the Peruvian Parade in Paterson, New Jersey, and with what consequences? Which repertoires get privileged and which ones get silenced and "edited out"? What claims and counterclaims do parades express and employ and what strategies of self-fashioning do they invite? Who are the Parade's central actors and upon which sorts of contemplating or spectating publics do they depend? And finally, how do parades in the context of the U.S. public sphere work to produce both "national" and "foreign" subjects?

These questions and the epistemological and methodological issues they raise can be addressed by approaching public events as performance. Parades are sites of "articulation" in Diane Nelson's definition of this term as "a relation, a joining that creates new identifications and social formation" (1999:2). As a medium for self-definition, identification, commodification, and boundary drawing, parade performances never occur in a political vacuum, but produce a context in which social meaning is constituted and tied into a larger racial and political economy. The relational identifications between Peruvians of different class and regional backgrounds that parade performances mediate are fundamentally shaped and informed by long-term exclusionary politics of race and class, which for centuries have defined national, public life in Peru and structured intersubjective interactions and social relationships between Peruvians abroad.

Public Performance and the Production of (Trans) National Subjects

Most migrant populations and ethnic minorities in the United States organize or participate in annual parades and ethnic, religious, and cultural festivals of some sort. As immigrant communities of color have grown and diversified in the United States since 1965, these types of public events have proliferated in numbers, size, and popularity (Alba 1990:103–5). Some communities commemorate the independence of their country of origin; others honor a patron saint, and yet others participate in panethnic or pannational unity celebrations. Some are large-scale and draw in participants from a broader geographical area whereas others are smaller, perhaps even limited to particular neighborhoods.

At first glance such events seem to be about producing, clarifying, and circulating certain images of group identity for a wider public of spectators, and in so doing to be transmiting a positive image of unity. Previous scholarly work on ethnic parades in the United States has emphasized that such public events initially were invented as a staged presentation of an ethnic minority vis-à-vis a larger immigrant community and/or a national (often white) majority. In this literature the parades were seen as important moments for the staging of particular identities, displaying ethnic pride and symbolic unity across the internal political and social differences of a given minority group, and gaining cultural recognition—even when the group in question was not always in control of their own representation (Kasinitz and Freidenberg-Herbstein 1987; Lessinger 1995; Marston 2002; Schneider 1990).

But studies that focus only on the representational aspects of these parades and on the presumed preexistence of stable national identities that can be showcased miss out on the fact that such events often only partially produce what they claim to represent; that identities are inherently unstable despite attempts to "fix" relational identifications into one coherent thing.[2] Parades in this sense can be deceptive because they present an image of unity that often belies the dissonances present in collective subject and boundary formation. This is particularly salient in events organized by Latin American and Caribbean migrants or their descendants who come from societies that tend to stress national unity and deny the existence of profound racial discrimination (Oboler and Dzidzienyo 2005; Oboler 2005b).

As public performances of presumptive collective forms of membership and belonging, then, parades are ambiguous objects of analysis. They should not be taken to confirm the (pre)existence of a unified social body capable of political agency even though they may appear and indeed sometimes claim to "represent" such unified constituencies. For example, parade organizers and community leaders would often refer to their Peruvian conationals collectively as "la Comunidad Peruana" (the Peruvian Community) as if there was such a thing as an internally coherent or united Peruvian community in Paterson beyond its articulation in specific relational contexts (cf. Nelson 1999:5-7). Instead, my analysis here demonstrates that parades are public events that are not just descriptive but should be conceived of as productive sites of ongoing resignifiability.[3] Yet even as parades are fundamentally "productive," we must also ponder how they disguise differences that are otherwise inassimilable to specific politicoeconomic orders.

Anthropological studies of ritual, performance, and circulation can help us understand how migrant subjectivities and claims to both Peruvian national belonging and U.S. belonging are produced through public spectacles such as the Peruvian Parade. Anthropologists have long studied the kind of ritualized behavior present in processions, carnivals, folklore festivals, religious spectacles, parades, and other staged public events; indeed, the study of rituals has been one of the hallmarks of the discipline since its inception (cf. Tylor, Frazer, Durkheim, and Weber). Early studies of rituals were influenced by Durkheimian traditions of understanding collective representations (i.e., beliefs) and by Levi-Straussian structuralism, which relied primarily on structures of language to interpret rituals as reflections of an underlying normative and universal structure (see Handelman 1998:9–10).[4] These studies often regarded the ritual as a "redressive" mechanism to reproduce society's stability and social order (Turner 1967, 1974; Gluckman 1963).

This premise was largely dismantled in the 1970s and 1980s by post-structuralist, materialist, and practice-oriented approaches in anthropology which argued that approaches which gave myth and belief systems analytical primacy over actual practices produced ahistorical social representations and inaccurately saw ritual as a simple reproduction of a preexisting social pattern without room for social change and renewal (Bell 1992). Anthropologists instead turned to a focus on ritual as a particularly transformative realm of experience and proposed to study the transformative potential of ritual and performative action by looking at ritual effects and of rituals—both religious and secular—as important sites for the reworking of social boundaries and racial, gendered, and generational hierarchies (Comaroff 1985; Fernandez 1974, 1977; Myerhoff and Falk Moore 1977; Schieffelin 1976; Tambiah 1981, 1985; see also Bell 1992 on ritualization). Judith Butler became influential in anthropology in the 1990s and was widely used by anthropologists, but performativity theory's reliance on speech acts and on linguistic/semantic interpretation made it insufficient by itself to understand embodied, kinesthetic, and visceral aspects of performative action that escape such linguistic/semantic interpretation, since the effects of ritual are not only brought about by semantics.

These various approaches have been combined in anthropological scholarship on expressive cultures in Latin America in which attention to the performative rather than the ascriptive dimension of cultural and racial categories of belonging has yielded interesting approaches and an impressive count of theoretically sophisticated ethnographies that studies the constitution of society, identity, community, citizenship, and the public sphere through dance performances (Mendoza 2000), musical performances (Bigenho 2012; Tucker 2013), and cultural festivals among migrants in Lima and abroad (Cánepa Koch 2010; Huerta-Mercado 2006). For example, Michelle Bigenho (2012) has usefully shown how one category—that of "Andean music" or "indigenous music"—in the context of circulation between Bolivia and Japan is performed, claimed, and coopted by differently positioned social actors who were all engaged in playing "someone else's music." These actors include Bolivians who identified nationally as mestizos; the Japanese who played Andean music as foreigners but who claimed a closeness with Bolivia's indigenous peoples; and the "gringa anthropologist" who also played while studying the circulation of indigenous music. Similarly, in his study of popular *huayno* music and the way it has been marketed to Peru's emerging middle class, Joshua Tucker has shown that musical creation, performance, and circulation is a key conduit through which Andean migrants and a range of mediators have altered the public culture in Lima and of Peru overall and—through its circulation—segmented the public sphere into distinct social and sonic territories (Tucker 2013:2). Likewise, Alex Huerta-Mercado (2006) discusses how the members of the Primer Movimiento Peruano (First Peruvian Movement—a social organization of Gay Peruvians in New York City—actively work to create and remediate already existing images that circulate of Peru and of Peruvians abroad as they carefully plan their participation in the Heritage of Pride March in New York City's West Village.

The religious procession in which a religious icon is taken to the streets—a central cultural and religious practice all over Latin America and elsewhere in the Catholic world—is a type of public ritual that scholars have found intimately connected to the production of subjectivity, space, and community among diverse immigrant groups in the United States. In *The Madonna of 115th Street*, historian Robert Orsi ([1985] 2002) writes about the multiple meanings of the devotion and annual *festa* honoring Our Lady of Mount Carmel by Catholic Italian immigrants in East Harlem at the turn of the twentieth century. The meanings of the festa as what Orsi calls "lived religion" derive not from the religious symbol, doctrine, or even from ritual itself, but from the hopes, fears, conflicts, expectations, aspirations, and disappointments in the lives of immigrants in that neighborhood. The immigrants in Orsi's study turned to the Madonna to express their sorrows, problems, and particular needs or to request graces. Their participation in the festa, and their devotional practices in general, Orsi suggests, must be seen in the particular social and historical context of Italian immigration to the United States and of life in the particular neighborhoods where these migrants settled and where their everyday lives unfolded.

Scholars working at the intersection of religion and politics have connected religious devotion to the constitution of migrants as political subjects. Alyshia Gálvez (2009) focuses on everyday life among undocumented Mexicans in New York City and shows that it is through devotion to La Virgin de Guadalupe and participation in her yearly procession that many of the undocumented Mexican migrants in her study find not just the strength to endure everyday struggles to provide for their families, but also the courage to demand rights, including fair and just immigration reform, but, above all, dignity and respect. Through devotion and performance, Gálvez argues, their humanity is reshaped. Thomas Tweed (1997) has studied the meanings of devotion among Cuban exiles in Miami who frequent the shrine to the patroness of Cuba, and suggested that this practice is a way for these exiles to express diasporic nationalism and to make sense of themselves as a community in exile. Through rituals and religious artifacts, these Cubans map the landscape and history of the homeland onto the new urban environment and recreate an imagined Cuban nation by positioning themselves ritually in space and time (1997:125–31). Relatedly, Paerregaard (2008) has examined how Peruvian migrants all over the world use the icon of Señor de los Milagros to navigate the borderland between the diasporic link to Peru and their new identity as immigrants. He suggests that Peruvian migrants use what he calls "the globalization of El Señor" as a strategy to achieve two aims: On the one hand, the devotion and the practice of taking the image to the streets is a strategy to access to public spaces in the host country where they—through the sacralization of public space—can make legal and moral claims to political rights as immigrants. On the other hand, the procession also allows them to "anchor their religioscapes" in the host society and in this way "localize" their religious practice in their new life-worlds (Paerregaard 2008:149–50). Finally, in my own visual anthropology work on the Lord of the Miracles among Peruvians in New York City, *Waiting for Miracles* (2003), I show how Peruvians who participate in the annual procession in Manhattan experience their relationship with the image in the new context and mobilize stories and experiences of miracles in relation to the image to articulate and make sense of their experiences as migrants. Many believe, or at least they hope, that their acts of carrying or accompanying this religious icon through the streets of New York can potentially produce important "miraculous" effects in their present everyday lives (Berg 2003).

As public spectacles, processions and parades share important similarities, but also important differences in their occupation of public space. Both are key sites for the mediation of relationships and sites for the production of migrant and (trans)national subjectivities. But whereas religious processions have a strong moral subtext and migrants draw on religious symbols to position themselves universally as humans vis-à-vis other humans in ways that are supposed to undo national borders, boundaries, and/or cultural differences, ethnic or national parades that evoke national identity and mobilize national/civic and cultural/ethnic symbols and boundaries are in the most fundamental sense about how people differ in racial, gendered, and other ways.

The tension between the visibility afforded by spectacular cultural, religious, or national performances and its transformative potential for tangible social, cultural, and political change and recognition in terms of public policies that favor racialized migrant and minority populations has been a central concern of Latino Studies scholars. Pioneering debates on cultural citizenship, Renato Rosaldo (1997) has argued that while cultural citizenship understood as cultural recognition and language democracy may not ultimately alter the juridical or social status of minority citizens (not to mention noncitizens), the claim for cultural citizenship is an assertion of rights, which can contribute to the construction of empowering cultural spaces within a larger society from where, at some later stage, political and social rights can be claimed (cf. Flores and Benmayor 1997).

While advocates of cultural citizenship are generally optimistic about the prospects of political empowerment deriving from the staking of claims to visibility and cultural rights to difference in the public sphere, others are less so. From the perspective of governmentality, Aihwa Ong

critiques the notion of "cultural citizenship" advocated by the proponents of cultural citizenship in the form of apparent cultural recognition. She defines cultural citizenship as "the cultural practices and beliefs
produced out of negotiating the often ambivalent and contested relations with the state and its hegemonic forms that establish the criteria of
belonging within a national population and territory" (1996:738). Ong
contends that while this dimension of citizenship is easily endorsed by
state institutions who then free themselves from further obligations to
actual and tangible social and political enfranchisement of minorities, it
works to contain immigrant communities by preventing them from advancing toward full citizenship in spite of their cultural difference from
mainstream Anglo American society (Ong 1996:737–38). Ong's critique
of cultural citizenship in the context of the U.S. nation-state resonates
with debates about differentiated citizenship in Latin America, which
have been ongoing since neoliberalism became hegemonic in the region
in the 1990s as both economic policy and political ideology. Charles
Hale (2005:12), for example, argues that "collective rights, granted as
compensatory measures to 'disadvantaged' cultural groups, are an integral part of neoliberal ideology." While appearing to be progressive,
the granting of such limited cultural rights, Hale suggests, deepens the
state's ability to shape and neutralize political opposition in the context
of a multiethnic and pluri-cultural society by fragmenting populations
into sectarian groups.

In the U.S. context, however, Latino Studies scholars have argued
that the important role identity politics play, particularly in the relationship between racialized communities and the state, cannot be so
quickly disregarded. Indeed, Linda Alcoff (2006) dismisses critics who
simplistically repudiate identity politics as inherently essentialist and
pathological and who refuse to take serious any political claims made
on the grounds of racial, gendered, or sexual identities. Such identities,
Alcoff potently argues, far from being essentialist, are historical formations, always changing and open to interpretation. Drawing on the political thought of Rousseau, Beltrán (2010) shows that political rallies,
conferences, poetry events, and festivals—as passionate, participatory,
and performative encounters in the public sphere—operated centrally
in the Chicano and Puerto Rican movement of the 1960s to transcend
self-interest and foster emotionally charged practices of identification

Figure 5.1. The Peruvian Parade in Paterson, 2002. (Photo by Author)

with an idealized notion of community. Such practices, Beltrán argues (2010:94–96), can have an intense effect on the way subjects come to understand themselves politically.[5] The memories of intense and emotive, public yet intimate encounters, may sustain political actors through the more disenchanting aspects of political participation, but they also run the risk of idealizing consensus and—in fear of losing it—make political conflict seem undesirable and therefore to be avoided, when in fact, according to Beltrán and other theorists, it is essential to the workings of democracy and to the constitution of democratic publics.

Regardless of the scale of circulation—whether rural to urban within Peru or "Peruvian urban" to "U.S. urban" or "national" to "transnational"—to think critically about public events as ritualized performance offers a productive analytics to understand just how the embodied practices of dancing, cheering, addressing a crowd, or walking along with others—here through the New Jersey towns of Passaic, Clifton, and Paterson and dressed in folklore costumes (*vestuario*) or draped in Peruvian flags—offer particular ways of knowing, remembering, understanding, and reworking the links between here and there and between past and present while also drawing up the horizons of future possibilities. A privileged site where membership and belonging are disputed and demarcated, the parade is also a social space within which emergent and enduring conflicts over race, class, gender, and generation are contested and addressed. A brief consideration of the importance of context in anthropological studies of cultural performance is therefore in order before digging into the ethnography of the event itself.

The Power of Context

Anthropologists who study linguistic and folkloric performances have long evoked "context" as central to understanding how people both generate and interpret meaning (Bauman and Briggs 1990; Dilley 1999; Duranti and Goodwin 1992; Howard-Malverde 1997). The basic point here is that the meaning of a performative action or "text" derives from whatever surrounds and thus potentially informs it (Rockefeller 2010: 206). But, as noted by Bauman and Briggs (1990), it is not always clear what aspects of context should be included in the examination and understanding of a given "text." This is particularly important for ethnographic contextualization in transnational research settings as seen in my earlier discussion of ambulant ethnography. For example, what happens when an event associated with independence in one national context such as *Fiestas Patrias* gets detached or "decontextualized" from its original context, circulated transnationally, and then "entextualized," to use Bauman and Brigg's term, in another national context through a distinct performance register? What context then is the most relevant to consider when trying to understand this process of circulation? Or perhaps better, to which *processes* of "decontextualization" and "entextualization" should we pay attention in such cases? I argue here that multiple processes of Peruvianization, folklorization, Latinization, and Americanization are at play in the relational identifications that variously positioned Parade participants bring to bear on the situation. Anthropologists working on folkloric performance and its relationship to citizenship and the state—a widespread and long-standing relationship in Latin America—have posed exactly this question: What happens to ritual material when it is transposed onto new localities and introduced into new contexts? (Abercrombie 1991, 1998; Harvey 1997; Rockefeller 1998; Turino 1993). Abercrombie (1991), for example, has shown that spectacularized folkloric performances are central to indigenous Bolivians' claims to a place in the nation and that these dynamics play out in the context of rural-to-urban migration and connections where "local" indigenous cultural and ritual practices are transported into new urban settings and staged as spectacles for an audience. Similarly, Stuart Rockefeller (1998) shows how campesinos from the town of San Lucas in Bolivia participate in folklore festivals and argues that it is the format—the conscious bodily performance of "culture" as spectacle—which has incited the campesinos who perform in these festivals to experience their "rural" cultures differently, thus constituting them as new nationally oriented subjectivities. Such spectacularized folkloric performance, then, is central to indigenous Bolivians' claims to a place in the nation (Abercrombie 1991, 2003). This echoes Appadurai's more general suggestion (1996) that nation-states continuously strive to make themselves into the most defining and relevant context for the social reproduction of persons, communities, and neighborhoods. Yet that does not always mean that nation-states get their way, as many scholars have noted, since most people both reproduce but also seek to transform their predicaments.

As with human bodies, cultural forms circulate transnationally but they must be studied in situ. Diana Taylor's definition of performance is useful here because it points to the temporal grounding of performance in particular *situational* contexts. Taylor defines performance as "vital acts of transfer" which are capable of "transmitting social knowledge, memory, and a sense of identity through reiterated behavior, or what Richard Schechner has called 'twice-behaved behavior'" (Taylor 2003:2–3). Performances, Taylor argues, may circulate globally and transnationally yet they are always fundamentally "in situ" and are rendered legible in the context of an immediate social environment (2003:3). In this sense, the acts of commemoration of Fiestas Patrias that form part of the Peruvian Parade in Paterson produce explicit narratives about Peruvian national identity that serve to order and reinterpret the past but, as noted above, the event is equally and importantly *of* Paterson connecting migrants' past experiences in Peru with new identifications in their everyday lives and present concerns as racialized Latin American migrants to the United States.

The Peruvians who arrived in Paterson in the 1960s and 1970s, as discussed in the Introduction, were mostly from working class or lower middle-class backgrounds in Lima. Relatively decent job opportunities and the 1965 immigration reform Act made these Peruvians into residents and U.S. citizens and they quickly became solidly part of the middle class. Factory workers gradually moved out of the factories and they did well as small business owners or in white-collar and professional jobs or in the service economy since many of them also came with some education from Peru (Shaw 1994). Those who could afford to move to bigger homes in affluent towns or suburbs surrounding Paterson pursued suburban lifestyles as consumer-citizens. This does not mean, however, that Peruvians are living outside ethnic neighborhoods, because as Logan et al. (2002) remind us, many such suburban enclaves are indeed ethnic communities in relatively high-status settings. Furthermore, as part of their larger aspirational project they strove to send their children to private schools and college. In the 1980s, these Peruvians became more active in local social and cultural organizations and founded the Peruvian Parade, Inc. in 1986. Some entertained political aspirations in local government.[6] They had been in Paterson long enough to see the changes in the city and for the most part they lamented what they saw and wanted to change things. What in its golden era had been an attractive commercial center and shopping destination for Northern New Jersey, was now a crime- and vice-ridden cluster of urban decay. Many established Peruvians cited the changing social and racial demographics as an explanation for the city's many problems.

Patricia, who had arrived in the mid-1960s from Lima, offered the following view of the newcomers who started to arrive in the 1980s and more prominently in the 1990s: "The majority of people who come to Paterson now are people from *outside* Lima [e.g., the provinces], but who have lived in Lima before coming here." Patricia was referring to the descendants of rural-to-urban migrants who just recently had got access to international destinations and had arrived in Paterson to try to make a living there. Even if many in fact had lived in Lima, sometimes for several generations, Patricia felt strongly that "they are not real Limeños" (e.g., someone living in Lima for generations and who generally self-styles as "white"). She was also convinced that many of Paterson's current problems were due to the arrival of these newcomers, who didn't know how to conform to life in the United States and who sullied the image of decent Peruvians already living there.[7]

Other long-term residents were more generous in their readings of the newcomers and praised their efforts to "salir adelante," but Patricia's statement is particularly important here because it illustrates another aspect of context, namely, the transnational circulation of the trope of the invasion of urban space by the rural indio. This pervasive image of the Andean indigenous subject and its urban cholo counterpart as unfit for moral and civilized urban life and as an instigator of moral decay and social ills is extremely important to understanding the identifications at play in the unfolding of the Peruvian Parade itself. This image in turn is contrasted with that of the assimilated, rule-following Peruvian American (e.g., the long-term resident, according to Patricia), who—in contrast to the newcomers—is knowledgeable and respectful of "American ways of life" and holds to high moral standards. These complex class and racial politics, which are so central to the dynamics of social categorization and distinction in Peru, became a central aspect of the unfolding of social relations during the performance of the parade. Within a relational economy and from the vantage point of the established migrant, it was the mobility of the neophytes which constituted a menace to the social order that others had worked so hard to be a part of.

Self-Styled "Super-Citizens" and the Peruvian American Dream

On the day of the Parade, Main Street, which runs from Passaic to Paterson through the town of Clifton, is blocked off from early on.[8] Around 11 a.m. the street starts to fill with people and the floats line up, one of them serving as the main stage for the inauguration of the parade. The Parade is led by a grand marshal (*Gran Mariscal*). The president of the Peruvian Parade, numerous local businesspeople, dignitaries, New Jersey politicians, and the general public join the grand marshal in marching alongside the floats. The Gran Mariscal is typically elected from a ranked shortlist made by the Parade board, which often comprises celebrities from Peru or well-known Peruvians residing in the United States. Because it was often challenging to secure a grand marshal for the parade, the board has in recent years increasingly proposed accomplished local community leaders, who have "put down roots" and "achieved personal and collective victories for Peruvians in the United States," to serve as grand marshals.

Since I first attended the Parade in 2002, I have gone numerous times with different companions—Peruvians and non-Peruvians—and whereas the weather, the special guests, the Parade presidents, and the embodied experience change from year to year, the format of the event remains pretty much the same. Over the course of the many hours that it takes the Parade to move through this suburban New Jersey landscape— from the Latino city of Passaic over the Arab and Turkish neighbor- hoods of Clifton, finally culminating in the events in front of the city hall in Paterson—the experience of marching and walking together, singing, dancing, photographing, and videotaping, slowly transformed all of us who participate into one multitude that moves collectively through the urban landscape.

The event begins in Passaic with a ceremony in which the toastmas- ter starts to animate the crowd and welcome the distinguished guests, listing their names, titles, and major accomplishments. Every year the Parade grants honorable mention in various categories to such "distin- guished members of the community" who have done something notable and otherwise been a role model for the community. These Peruvians have earned important titles in local and state government and in the local business community, and by virtue of their aspirations, productiv- ity, industriousness, diligence, and ambition they are examples of those who "made it" into the U.S. mainstream. The speeches galvanizing these "Peruvian Americans," which is how they are often presented, as role models for all Peruvians simultaneously produce a standard of citizen- ship and a particular form of immigrant personhood against which all other migrants are measured up: the successful Peruvian immigrant is the professional, business-minded, entrepreneurial, self-motivated, and rule-following individual who strives to "better himself" and assimilate into the U.S. economy, society, and political life. A "super-citizen im- migrant" (Honig 2001), this Peruvian is self-driven, aspirational, and a "no burden to the state" kind of subject who adheres to capitalist and socially normative values including a white-collar career, a heterosexual family with "traditional family values," and a mortgage—in short, the properties of personhood that many immigrants think of as "immigrant values" when evoking the term "the American Dream."[9]

Such narratives of personal achievement (*superación*), upward mobil- ity, progress, and education through which the Peruvian migrant can be redeemed and indeed "become American" are aligned not only with the central tenets of a neoliberal regime of self-discipline, but also with the ideology of the American Dream (cf. Ramos-Zayas 2012). This kind of larger-than-life praise is frequently lavished on people by both local and national politicians who are recurrent participants in the Parade. The Puerto Rican Democrat José "Joey" Torres, who was the mayor of Paterson from 2002 to 2010, is usually in attendance, as is the Democratic member of Congress for the state of New Jersey, Bill Pascrell. Originally from Paterson, Congress member Bill Pascrell frequently uses the occasion to highlight the similarities between Peruvian and American love for freedom and the strong work ethic of both populations. One year, he praised the "strong relationship" between Peru and the United States by saying:

> This is our 17th Parade, celebrating 181 years of freedom. The relationship between Peru and the United States is very strong and will only get stronger. As a member of congress, I salute the Parade, I salute its leaders, and I salute the hardworking Peruvians and Peruvian Americans. God bless the United States and God bless Peru. Viva Perú.

Most local and state politicians welcome the opportunity to march in ethnic and immigrant parades, and often actively pursue it through their aides, because it offers them an opportunity to endorse immigrant populations in an uncompromising and celebratory way without having to deal with some of the more difficult social and economic issues that these communities face.[10] Pascrell's intervention and cooptation of the Parade illustrates the fact that naturalized Latin American migrants and their U.S.-born children have become a valuable resource for local politicians and political parties who work hard during such events to capture what they uniformly (and problematically so, according to Beltrán 2010), conceive of as "the Latino vote."[11] While Pascrell addressed the audience, Democratic Party members were mingling with the crowd and handing out promotional flyers on how to join the local chapter of the Democratic Party.

Naturalized Peruvians who are elected as public officials in the United States are favorite guests during this part of the Parade because their personal stories embody the narratives of success and the ability to overcome all odds that many migrants desire. These Peruvians were frequently held up as examples of how, through discipline and the cultivation of self in the form of education and hard work, migrants could evolve from being simple, clueless, and recently arrived Peruvians to decent, worthy, and hardworking Peruvian Americans deserving of recognition and U.S. citizenship. Felipe Reinoso, a member of the State Assembly of Connecticut and a prominent leader of education, is one example of such good "immigrant citizenship," and he frequently speaks at civic events in Paterson. Reinoso, himself an educator, always emphasizes education when addressing the Parade participants as the most important tool that Peruvian immigrant parents can give their children in order for their community to grow, prosper, develop, and "salir adelante," in this sense echoing the ideology that education is key to any effort at social mobility and self-innovation. On one occasion Reinoso asserted that these children would and should eventually become "active participants in the political and historical processes of the United States," and that it was time for the Peruvian community to stop being "merely observers in U.S. national politics." Reinoso's position bears a strong subtext of incorporation and assimilation through schooling as the desirable track for the children of Peruvian migrants, but it also simultaneously implied that the success of such a project rested on the ability of hardworking Peruvian migrant parents to inculcate in their children the self-discipline to embody these values so central to the process of "becoming American."

Framing Andean Peru: *Un Huaynito, Por Favor!*

Once the Parade is inaugurated with the performance of both the Peruvian and U.S. national anthems, the floats start moving down Passaic Main Street in the direction of Paterson. In 2002, a mix of private local businesses, cultural and civic organizations, and accomplished individuals participated in the Parade, which was made up of between thirty to thirty-five floats accompanied by a large and also actively participating "audience" waving flags, cheering, singing, and walking in the Parade. A giant Peruvian flag, representing "the sovereign territory that unites all Peruvians regardless of their place of residence," as one participant explained, was unfolded and carried in front of the local authorities who marched at the head of the Parade. A local group of folklore dancers performing the *marinera limeña* (marinera dance from Lima) followed suit.

As the local authorities started to walk down Passaic's Main Street to the sound of *música criolla*, a cultural symbol of the Peruvian coastal areas, the hegemony of coastal and Limeño "Peruvianness" was called into question when someone in the crowd shouted: "How about a *huaynito*?" By evoking the distinct Andean musical form *of huayno*, in the diminutive huaynito, as a desirable alternative soundscape, this participant simultaneously contested the hegemonic narrative of Peruvian national identity and the "ranking" of its musical diversity into a social order that continuously features the coast and its inhabitants at the top and indigenous peoples at the bottom of the social order. This colonial and racial order is, as argued in the chapter's introduction, central to the structuring and reproduction of social relationships in Peru and its diaspora and it was evident in many of the images and identifications generated through the Parade.

Scholars have argued that in postindustrial cities the public sphere is dominated by media and corporate enterprises seeking customers for their products and that the campaigns of such a corporate presence often draw on commonsense social and cultural identities and group sentiments to achieve their goal of creating new consumers (Dávila 2004; Tucker 2013). This intersection between culture and economy dominated the general "feel" of the Parade, where many of the floats represented local or corporate enterprises seeking new consumers among the varied participating and contemplating publics. The Parade thus draws not only Peruvians from all class and regional backgrounds, but also other groups who attend in order to consume their dose of "Spanish food," as one Anglo American passerby commented, or in the expectation of experiencing "the culture of Peru" that day, as another person put it.[12]

Every year the Parade organizers debate with renewed passion how to present "Peruvian culture" to the several and sometimes conflicting imagined audiences. These discussions—and the Parade itself—revive images and identifications related to what Peruvian intellectuals long have referred to as Peru's unresolved "cultural conflict" (Quijano 1980), that is, the incorporation of the Andean indigenous population into the national society. This unsettled national dilemma is evidenced in the ambiguities surrounding the Parade organization's efforts to define, through numerous planning meetings and discussions, what constitutes "Peruvian culture," "Peruvian national identity," or "Peruvian diversity." As one board member expressed it:

> [W]e want to represent the traditional clothing and dances from Peru, from the Incas, from *sierra, costa*, and *selva*, so that other Latinos and people in general can see the traditional clothing that represents the Peruvian diversity.

This tripartite division of Peruvian geography into highland, coast, and Amazonian lowlands (*sierra, costa, selva*) referred to by the board member is the classic image of Peruvian geography that all Peruvians since nursery school have been taught to understand as the official national discourse of diversity (Greene 2007). But as discussed in the Introduction, this limited view of diversity as different cultures neatly corresponding to demarcated geographical areas or regions masks some of the more problematic aspects of the long-term exclusionary politics of race, ethnicity, and class which have characterized Peruvian society since the colonial era and been particularly detrimental to subjects who moved, often without authorization, between these environments. Yet it is this dominant vision that is reproduced when "Peruvian culture," "Peruvian national identity," and "Peruvian diversity" are performed, communicated, and circulated during the event.

Folklore organizations were generally invited to perform at the Parade because the organizing committee deemed it important to "represent" Peru as a country with an ethnically and culturally diverse heritage. Yet the presence and performance of Peruvian folkloric dances is subject of recurring tension every year between the different local actors who claim a stake in the Parade. One year this tension broke out in open conflict between several local folklore groups and the Parade's organizing committee when the latter invited a large group of Bolivian dancers from Virginia representing *la morenada*—a very visually evocative and spectacular dance featured in the famous Carnival de Oruro in Bolivia.[13] Local cultural activists, especially those representing cultural organizations in Paterson whose main focus was the diffusion of Peruvian folklore, were scandalized that "Bolivians" and "Bolivian dances" would get such a prominent place in the Peruvian national parade. Instead they thought it should feature dances like huaylash from Huancayo, wititi from the Arequipa region, and marinera norteña from the northern coast, among others. They argued that given that the morenada is a spectacular and impressive dance with elaborate costumes, it was likely to steal attention from the other dances. Others argued that it was exactly this spectacular quality that the Parade should strive for because this was what attracted audiences.

The conflict over the morenada gave rise to a more general debate in the local community about Peruvian identity and culture and what practices could be taken as representative of it. The cultural and folklore activists were not only critical of the inclusion of the morenada as a "foreign" element in the Parade, but they also expressed their discontent over the dominance of non-Andean musical genres including those generally associated with Caribbean nations, such as salsa and merengue, which they argued presented an unbalanced and erroneous view of "Peruvian culture" and "Peruvian identity." Some even criticized the prominent role given to *música criolla* in many of the participating floats.[14] One cultural activist, Carmen, who was also a respected folklore dancer, wrote an open letter in 2005 to the president of the Peruvian Parade, manifesting her frustration with the issues of framing and defining Peruvianness during the Parade that year:

> The parade was full of cacophonic floats, playing very loud music from other Latin countries: *merengue* from the Dominican Republic, *cumbia* and *salsa* from Colombia, *reggetón* from Puerto Rico, and on top of everything, they featured dancers from Bolivia brought from Virginia. I don't have anything against these artistic expressions, but with all the respect they deserve, they are inappropriate for the occasion. Is it that Peruvians don't want a patriotic parade celebrating our music and our dances? Or are we very ashamed of these? What is the identity of Peruvians? I have never heard a huayno or a marinera at the highest volume in a parade of another Latin American country.

Carmen's intervention illustrates the complexity of factors involved in the relationship between social practice and cultural mediation. Carmen had studied folklore at one of the national academies in Lima and was therefore more than familiar with the role of folklore in national identity projects in Peru. She and many other cultural activists in the area were from smaller towns in the Andes, having migrated to Lima to work or study long before coming to the United States. They were acutely aware of their "double" racialization, first as Andean migrants within Lima and second as a result of their position as migrant workers in the United States within a global labor regime. Like Carmen many of them identified nationally as mestizos but were racialized as *provincianos* within the larger national context. For them participation in folkloric performances during the Parade accomplished two things. On the one hand, it accomplished what De la Cadena (2000) in her work among urban "indigenous mestizos" in Cuzco powerfully has referred to as "de-indianization," that is, the detachment of Andean cultural practices from the rural or "Indian" social condition (see also Leinaweaver 2013 for a discussion of "de-Peruvianizing in the transnational context"). This central process is at work in many dance and fiesta performances, as shown by other scholars working in different parts of the Andes. These scholars have established that processes of "folklorization,"—here meaning that particular dance and fiesta elements are taken out of their original contexts and staged in urban environments—are important to local indigenous performers because they help articulate local customs with issues of national belonging and give them a new and powerful dimension (Mendoza 2000:46; Cánepa Koch 2010; Rockefeller 1998).

On the other hand, Carmen and others had lived in the United States long enough to realize that it took substantial effort to distance oneself from the general stigma accorded to Latin American migrant workers in the United States, and from the stigma accorded to previous generations of Peruvians who came from a country that many saw as an epicenter of terrorism, corruption, poverty, and contagion (such as the cholera epidemic that broke out in 1991). Folklore performance here served as a vehicle to produce a more positive image of "Peru" and of Peruvians more generally, enabling a distinction to be made between themselves and other Latin American migrant workers and also between themselves and the image of the Andean poor. Instead—especially when talking to Americans—they could cast themselves as descendants of the Incas and as bearers of a rich history of cultural heritage.

Figure 5.2. Folklore dancers at the Peruvian Parade, 2002. (Photo by Author)

By evoking "Peruvian folklore" as a central expression of Peruvian national identity in contrast to other Latin American nationalities, including Colombians, Dominicans, Puerto Ricans, and Bolivians, Carmen
and others claimed a space for Peruvians within the larger U.S. society
and for Andean Peruvians within Peru itself. Stylized folkloric dance
performances then became an exemplary practice of folkloric citizenship in which membership in the Peruvian nation and in the transnational collectivity of "Peruvians abroad" could be achieved by recasting
and stylizing "indigeneity" as part and parcel of their Peruvian national
identity, but also central to the formation of new transnational subjectivities. Folkloric citizenship practices do the work of framing "Peruvianness" in a positive and nonthreatening light vis-à-vis a spectating and
contemplating public in Paterson and the United States more broadly,
but for racially marked Andean Peruvians in particular it also works as
a way to claim "Peruvian nationality."

National identities are not only affirmed vis-à-vis their internal
other—here people from the Andes with assumed backward and "pri-
mordial" identifications with a rural past—but also vis-à-vis external
others. Carmen and other activists also had a great deal to say about the
fact that the artistic director hired for the Parade that year was a Chilean

national. In a different part of the open letter, Carmen states: "To incre-ment the insult on the Peruvian identity, Peruvian Parade Inc. has as its artistic director a Chilean citizen, as if among us Peruvians there wouldn't be people knowledgeable of our own artistic traditions." This critique is an immediate reminder of historic anti-Chilean sentiments in Peru which followed the Chilean defeat of Peru in the War of the Pacific (1879–1883), but it also operates in the diaspora to produce a sense of Peruvian national unity vis-à-vis this "foreign" Other that can bridge the gap of Peru's own internal cleavages. In Carmen's view, the Peruvian Parade had to remain sovereign (and inclusive for all Peruvians, but only Peruvians), and this required limiting or excluding the influence of "foreign ele-ments," including musical genres from other Latin American countries and cultural producers of other nationalities, particularly Chileans.

These critiques were brushed off by the Parade's organizing commit-tee which argued that it was indeed invested in producing a broad view of "Peruvian culture" combining Peruvian folklore *along* with other musi-cal genres, including salsa and música criolla, and defended the Chilean artistic director by saying that he was "more Peruvian than anyone." The larger public, one board member reasoned when I prompted him, would not distinguish between the Bolivian *Morenada* and Peruvian folkloric dances anyway, a view that further infuriated folklore activists. The pres-ident of the Parade tried to remedy this in his address to the audience in front of Paterson's City Hall, according to which the Parade strove to:

> continue to persevere and show the world and the other communities the culture of us Peruvians . . . our culture . . . and also show Peruvian youth that over here [i.e., in the United States], in faraway lands, we con-tinue to be true to our race, our Indian race, our language that is Spanish, and letting the Latin American and the Peruvian community know that we should preserve that culture, which is the Spanish culture that our ancestors bestowed on us.

This speech reflects the ongoing predicament that affects the produc-tion of subjectivities in a transnational context. It reflects the historical predicament of colonialism, racial mixing, and linguistic and cultural domination which have shaped relational identifications between Peruvians more generally, but it also takes sides in this historical process by locating "Spanish culture" as the ancestral source for Peruvian identity thereby displacing the centrality of Peru's indigenous population both in the colonial encounter and in the formation of modern Peru. These references call for a deeper consideration of Peru's inconclusive and ongoing dilemma of "national integration," which began with colonialism and continues to shape social relations across class and ethnic boundaries today—in Peru and in the diaspora.

But whereas images of a "glorious Inca heritage" that made Peru famous worldwide through tourism and museum displays and the performance of folkloric dances could provide an acceptable and fluid space for "indigeneity" within the ongoing constitution of national identity and in local discussions on how it should be presented to various spectating publics in the United States, the boundary transgressing cholo—as the quintessential "in between" category in the Peruvian social imaginary—could not so easily be fitted in. Despite the fact that Peru is also changing as the growing Andean bourgeoisie stakes its claims to key social spaces previously reserved for elites, the figure of the vice-ridden and transgressive cholo still haunts the reproduction of social relations across class divides in Peru and continues to play out in the processes of identification of Peruvians of different regional and class backgrounds abroad. This figure therefore also makes an almost obligatory "guest appearance" on the day of the Parade.

The *Cholo Malazo* and the Pitfalls of Public Visibility

Parade leaders were very aware that the public visibility the event offered came at a price and that it could be a doubled-edged sword. While the Parade offered an opportunity to display carefully crafted images of "Peruvianness," packaged for consumption by a wider U.S. public, it also opened up a social space of possible transgression (cf. Bakhtin 1968; Stallybrass and White 1986). Parade organizers were well aware that drinking in the streets, signs of aggressive and what was variously deemed "morally inappropriate behavior," and other forms of excess—all of which are typically attributed to the figure of the urban cholo/a in Peru (cf. Weismantel 2001)—could compromise the image of Peruvians as hardworking, self-regulating, and decent citizen-subjects which the Parade organizers had worked so hard to stage and stylize.

To regulate unwarranted and undesirable behavior, Parade organizers established strict guidelines to offset any possible negative stains on the public image produced by the parade. However, most leaders recognized that complete control was not possible, especially during the cultural festival which followed the culmination of the Parade in front of Paterson City Hall. But one statement in particular caught my ethnographic attention: "There is always the bad cholo [el cholo malazo]," said one of the local journalists covering the event, "who embarrasses us as Peruvians, making everything dirty and behaving as if he was in Lima." More than just an indication of the possibility that "someone" could go berserk or even just be slightly inappropriate during this festive occasion, the comment points to a much more fundamental process that operates across a range of social and cultural spaces and borders—and between one country and another. Stallybrass and White (1986) have urged scholars to move beyond what they call "Bakhtin's troublesome *folkloric* approach" and consider the carnivalesque "as an instance of a wider phenomenon of transgression," because—as they argue—"it reveals that the underlying structural features of carnival operate far beyond the strict confines of popular festivity and are intrinsic to the dialectics of social classification as such" (1986:26).

The journalist's statement, not uncommon in social interactions among Peruvians more generally, evoked the figure of the *cholo malazo*—an imaginary but always present social category—and linked it to the always-present possibility of transgression associated with Andean Peruvians in cities. Doomed as the cholo/a is for his/her imagined uncontrollable affects and embodiment of excess, he/she can always potentially "erupt" and thereby interrupt not just the flow of a particular event but that of an entire body politic. This cholo is the antithesis of the decent, "civilized," and self-regulated neoliberal subject—the perfect immigrant—who displays knowledge and mastery of the codes regulating public life in the United States. The comment also carries an important ideological subtext about what racially marked populations had to do to compensate for their perceived "difference"—within and outside social relations between Peruvians—and the forms of racialization to which they were subjected in the United States, especially in recent years as nativist and anti-immigrant rhetoric has intensified. Peruvians simply could not afford to "stain" the image of docile and hardworking immigrants which they had worked so hard to produce and circulate, and in support of which they had to publicly align their bodily performances. "This is a sound presentation (*esto es una presentación sana*)," affirmed María, the president of the Parade in a conversation with me a few days afterwards, as if she wanted to have the final word and erase any possible doubts that I could have had about the decency, morality, and overall merits of the Parade and the worthiness of its organizers.

The pitfalls of public visibility in the United States for racialized populations like Peruvians and other Latin American migrants extend beyond the temporal framing of the performative event itself, and any images it generates—favorable or not—continue to inform how wider publics view "Peruvians" in general. In the days after the event, the Parade and its organizers were targets of both praise and critical scrutiny in the local media. People sent in letters to local newspapers to express their opinions and journalists and community leaders published polemic op eds. At the center of these debates was the question of the effects of the Parade, that is, what it could actually *do* for the community. Many observers agreed that it offered an excellent opportunity to display "Peruvian culture" and that it was important for the Peruvian community to distinguish itself from other groups in Paterson. But others, especially those who were critical of the Parade organizers, did not see the event as accomplishing anything to elevate the image of Peruvians in this city or anywhere else. One local Peruvian journalist, Juan, was extremely critical of the Parade organization and its organizers. In a polemical spirit he wanted to convince me, the anthropologist, that the thousands of visitors who came every year did not do so because the Parade was particularly well organized or offered anything different or novel, or even because it gave them a sense of belonging to a Peruvian community or a sense of shared history. Completely discrediting the efforts of the organizing committee, he insisted that people came because they were looking for something to do, just as they would on any regular Sunday. He claimed that the Parade drew crowds only because this was the nature of such public events:

> This is a spontaneous reaction from the community. It's the law of inertia, the moment happens just because. But they [the leaders] feed a false self-esteem. This is a ghost institution, unable to draw a real constituency,

without real projects to serve the community. They are figurative bodies without any merit. In the end it's an exhibition of a Peruvian image, but purposeless. It's not useful, but it exists. It's an infertile presence. For example, a man that lacks the ability to procreate is sterile, right? Or a sterile woman can have presence and beauty, but being sterile, she doesn't serve any purpose or cause . . . she exists but doesn't reproduce. These institutions are decorative entities that offer only some solace—they say "we are here"—but they don't produce or reproduce anything.

Juan's analogy between the biological and social reproduction of a community, while extreme, is illustrative of the different views of politics at play here and what it means to be a political subject. Juan argued on several occasions that if it did anything, the event filled participants with the illusion of visibility, recognition, progress, and prosperity, but it didn't advance any fundamental social or political rights that could benefit Peruvians in Paterson—symbolically or materially—once the event was over and the curtain was closed. But others disagreed, and one year, when the Parade was in danger of not being held, they stood up to defend it. This illustrates the centrality of parades as key political sites, both for producing national identities and also for potentially transforming them.

Beyond Unity: Folkloric Citizenship and Immigrant Personhood

In the past few decades, the growing presence and visibility of politically active Latin American migrants in the United States—documented and undocumented—has fostered an upsurge in nativist discourse. This has particularly been the case since 9/11 as numerous anti-immigration laws and policies have been proposed and implemented under the pretext of securing U.S. borders against foreign terrorists. These anti-immigration laws and policies have real consequences for Latin American migrants' lives and for their U.S.-born children and grandchildren, constructing them as internal, cultural Others who pose a peril to national stability and continuity (Beltrán 2010; Chávez 2008; Inda 2006; Gonzalez 2014). In this broader context, ethnic parades, like other public manifestations, aquire renewed importance for migrants and local immigrant communities because of their pressing need to access public spaces of visibility from where they can counter pressures from nativist discourses and practices and recast their cultural and racial difference in favorable terms. These terms involve asserting themselves as self-driven, disciplined, entrepreneurial, and docile immigrant workers who embody all the right properties of productive neoliberal personhood to make them legible as nonthreatening under the new post-9/11 national security regime, producing a version of "Peruvianness" and "Peruvian culture" that could be readily consumed by larger U.S. publics. Without being too exotic to be consumable by whites, this image also involves negotiating old notions of difference in relational identifications between Peruvians, now reproduced in the transnational context.[15]

Local migrant communities exploited ethnic parades—and to an extent depended on them—for such an opportunity to create an image of themselves as unthreatening neoliberal-friendly new Americans with a distinct but enriching flavor. When the newly elected African American mayor Jeffery Jones, who was facing looming budget cuts in 2011, demanded that Parade organizers pay for police overtime and the cost of cleanup services after the event—a cost that could easily amount to as much as $100,000 per event—Parade organizers were outraged. They angrily demanded their "right to parade" and their "right to display, and honor our culture and nationality," claims that resonated across immigrant communities in the area. Only the leaders of the African American Day Parade supported Mayor Jeffery Jones's decision and expressed their solidarity with the challenges he faced in resolving the city's economic woes in the wake of the recession following the global financial crisis of 2008.

The organizers of the Peruvian Parade immediately proposed to move their event to the neighboring towns of Passaic and Clifton after Mayor Jones asked them to raise $56,000 to cover the costs of their parade.[16] Parade organizations relied on corporate sponsorship to cover the cost of their events, but the majority of the funds came from small local businesses and was hardly enough to meet the contribution requested by the mayor. And Peruvians were not alone in their indignation. The president of the Dominican Day Parade said in the local media: "If we can pay, we can have a parade; if we can't pay, we can't. How can you put a price on our culture? If the city can do this to us today, what are they then going to do to us tomorrow?"[17] In Paterson, where most parades are organized by Latin American and Caribbean migrants from countries with a strong emphasis on national unity as part of their nation-state projects, these groups took the mayor's demand as an offense and an outright attack on their right to public and civic participation. It revived for a time the historic racial tensions between Latinos and African Americans in the city of Paterson.

Despite the short-lived menace of cancellation, that year Peruvians were able to celebrate their Independence Day in Paterson. As the day progressed and the parade got closer to downtown Paterson where it would culminate in front of City Hall, the sun, the marching, and the multitude of people like any other year seemed to have erased the social boundaries between people of different class and regional backgrounds. I was moved once again by the experience of moving through the landscape and seeing Peruvian flags and the red and white colors everywhere and I remembered the many times I had celebrated Fiestas Patrias in Peru. Events such as the Parade surely have the capacity to evoke a certain "structure of feeling" (Williams 1977) that offers to the participant traces of a particular quality of lived experience in a particular time and place, as Williams suggested when first evoking the term. The sound of the characteristic Peruvian Spanish everywhere and the well-known "feel" of interactional styles made many participants, including myself, the foreign anthropologist, feel momentarily at ease in a social landscape otherwise not of one's own making. Yet, as I had also learned, tensions always simmered beneath the surface and what seemed like an easygoing flow could erupt into full-blown conflict at any moment.

This chapter has examined the yearly Peruvian Parade in Paterson as a significant site in which the migrant body—by marching, dancing, and chanting its way across the New Jersey landscape—creates a palpable frame of selfhood and personhood in both the individual and collective experience of Peruvian migrants in the United States. Scholars interested in the relationship between the human body and social collectivities have long held that the body mediates all social action upon the world and that it simultaneously constitutes the self as well as the myriad of social relations of which it is a part (Comaroff 1985; Ortner 2006; Mascia-Lees 2011). This mediation occurs through concrete and embodied actions in specific environments.

The processes of mediation of "Peruvian culture" and "Peruvianness" and the self-reflexive fashioning of these forms in the Parade performance and at its planning meetings demonstrates how identifications are always already bound up with larger sites, processes, and structures of power. While on the surface parades work to evoke positive images of national unity, their production cracks open and revives centuries-old processes of ethnic, racial, gender, and class cleavages in migrants' countries of origin that are revitalized in the diasporic setting. I have argued that multiple historical and material contexts are relevant and must be considered to fully appreciate the event as a transnational site where Peruvians through performance can produce themselves variously as Peruvian "nationals," as Andean Peruvians, *and* as decent, worthy, and hardworking "immigrants" deserving of recognition and respect by larger U.S. publics.

How Peruvians in Paterson aligned their bodily actions in public space to dominant capitalist and normative values and ideologies to show themselves worthy of citizenship in the United States is in many ways homologous to the way for much of the twentieth century and further back indigenous migrants of rural origin in Latin American cities have been associated as much with the social identities they have not yet mastered as with those they have failed to leave behind. Such a predicament of course is not particular to Peruvian migrants in the U.S. political and racial economy, but is common to migrants of other national origins in the United States and beyond the U.S. context. Yet the swiftness with which working class and indigenous Peruvians over the course of only a few decades have become transnationally mobile in ways unimaginable just a few decades ago has produced "friction" (Tsing 2005) within and between migrants, their families, their communities, and the state. This chapter has shown how Peruvians more generally have attempted to act on and transform their predicament as racialized Latin American migrants in the U.S. public sphere and constitute themselves as full persons worthy of citizenship and with the right to difference. The next and final chapter turns the gaze back to Peru to show how Andean migrants of rural origin attempt to reposition themselves vis-à-vis the Peruvian state from abroad in ways that do not transform them into glamorized diasporic citizens. Instead they become "phantom members" of their rural communities of origin who come back to haunt the state through their claims to justice and recognition.

6

Phantom Citizens in El Quinto Suyo

The community was tired of always being robbed. They stole our animals, everything from guinea pigs to cattle and money too, they entered our houses without anyone seeing them and they took our things, sometimes they left large holes in our walls when they took out the animals. Often you could not leave your house unattended and there have even been cases of rape. . . . We suspected a couple of men from here, they were real criminals and we were also afraid of them. . . . They were not afraid of anyone. But the community, we were tired of them. One day cows and sheep had disappeared, so a delegation led by the president of the Comunidad went to get the suspects. We were around twenty people, including several local authorities. We found the offenders under the roof of a house where they were eating and talking. We told them to come down and they started to laugh at us, saying 'why do you make us come down if you will let us go anyway', they threatened us by saying that as soon as we would let them go, they would kill everyone present in the house, that they already knew who we all were. They had been threatening many people in the community and the majority were afraid of them, so we took them to the central Plaza of the village. The comuneros started to throw water on them, they got completely soaked. . . . The church bell started ringing and everybody came out of their houses and gathered on the Plaza, we started to hit them, they hit them. . . . Well, all of us hit them, but nobody wanted to kill them. It was about 3 or 4 in the morning when we finished punishing the thieves, but then someone had brought gasoline and the thieves were set on fire, they got second and third degree burns, but they were still alive. . . . The next day the police came and took them to Jauja. Nobody had seen who had set the thieves on fire or who had brought the gasoline. Around 11 in the morning the police came back and the governor began to give out names, so people started to protest, especially the local authorities. Basically all of us had participated in the crime. . . . (Member of the Comunidad Campesina in Urcumarca).[1]

A Violent Incident in the Central Andes

In March 1999, two cattle thieves were lynched in the village of Urcumarca—back then already one of the villages in the Mantaro area with significant migration to the United States. The event was an act of communal *ajusticiamiento* in which an angry crowd of local residents attacked and attempted to murder the suspected criminals. The following day the news about the violent incident appeared on the front pages of local and regional news media. The story was also broadcast on national television where it was covered as a new outburst of "barbarian violence" in the Peruvian Andes.[2] The event in Urcumarca and the media coverage it received immediately evoked memories in the national and popular imagination of the violent and brutal massacre in Uchuraccay in 1983. While attempting to enter the area to investigate a massacre committed by the Shining Path in a neighboring town, eight journalists were killed at the hands of local residents in one of the largest and bloodiest massacres of journalists in Peruvian history. The commission that investigated the crime, presided over by the Nobel Prize winning Peruvian writer Mario Vargas Llosa, concluded that the comuneros had acted brutally and savagely in self-defense because they had "confused" the journalists carrying camera equipment with terrorists carrying weapons. The report concluded that the campesinos had acted without rational judgment as a result of the extreme conditions of marginality and lack of civility that characterized their Indian social and cultural conditions. The infamous report said nothing about the responsibility of the Peruvian armed forces in instigating the killings to help defeat the Shining Path in the area, but instead fueled the perception of Andean peasants and their communities as "premodern," unchanging, and incompatible with liberal democratic ideals of modern citizenship (Del Pino 2003; Poole and Renique 1992; Starn 1991).[3]

When the police and various state representatives arrived in Urcumarca the following morning to assess the crime and identify the suspects, the message from the local community was clear and united: "If you take our *Gobernador*, the president of the *Comunidad Campesina* or any other local authority, we will all go to prison with them because we are all guilty."[4] Yet what never made its way into the news coverage, the police reports, or the minutes from the court hearings was that a considerable amount of the money for the legal defense of the accused *comuneros* in Urcumarca came from their migrant relatives in the United States. This part of the story is central to understanding how historically marginalized and racialized Andean Peruvians come to constitute themselves as political actors through transnational migration. The migration process itself has prompted migrants to become more aware of their social and racial positioning, I shall argue, thereby enabling them, as phantom citizens, to effectively challenge the state at the local level and ultimately claim recognition as citizens and "nationals" of Peru.

In previous chapters I analyzed the various realms of communicative and social practice through which migrants strive to facilitate their mobility within larger politicoeconomic contexts. These practices, I have argued, profoundly shape migrants' subjectivities and consciousness and they also importantly make up the historically specific social locations from which they, in M. P. Smith's words, "act back upon structural economic conditions" (2005:236). This final chapter recenters the analytical focus on the racist and paternalistic state as a key "structural condition" which shapes the lives of contemporary migrants within a broader transnational system. I examine the incident of communal violence in the rural community of Urcumarca as variously described to me in ethnographic encounters with Urcumarquinos in Peru and the United States.

As inhabitants of Andean Peru, Urcumarquinos had only exercised second-class citizenship in their country of origin prior to migration. This historical exclusion and lack of recognition as participating citizens in national public life centrally shaped nonelite Andean migrants' exclusion from the current and much celebrated category of the emigrant citizen subject. Over the course of my fieldwork I came to conceptualize these migrants as phantom citizens of a Peruvian nation-state which itself is in a process of transformation as a result of neoliberal economic policies and new forms of governance that circulate globally. By phantom citizens,

I mean those spectral citizens—unpleasant, dreaded, and despised by elites—who have no particular form, but who, facilitated by transnational flows and communications, come back to haunt and challenge the state.

Changing Contours of Citizenship in Peru

Despite the fact that they inhabited one of the most economically dynamic of Peru's highland regions prior to migration, few Urcumar-quinos have exercised full citizenship in their country of origin. Close to two hundred years have passed since the dismantling of the sepa-rate republics of Indian subjects and Spanish citizens. Historians have shown that the liberties and rights promised by the first regimes after independence were slow to materialize for the former "Indians" who, instead of becoming citizens of the new nation-states, became subjects of indirect government by local strongmen and landowning provincial elites, and even lost the relative protection they used to enjoy under the colonial regime (Thurner 1997; Mallon 1995). This history with roots in colonial forms of segregation has engendered stubborn images of first- and second-class citizenship that still prevail in contemporary Peruvian society and politics (Stepputat 2005:61–62).

The "citizenship option" for most indigenous Peruvians during most of the twentieth century (and for Bolivians too; see Lazar 2008) had been that of assimilation as workers or as peasants (*campesinos*). Since the 1990s, sev-eral countries in Latin America have enacted constitutional and legislative reforms that allow for a wider variety of relationships between individuals, communities, and the state (Lazar 2008). But as scholars of indigenous citizenship have noted, the policies of state multiculturalism were "charac-terized by contradictory processes of incorporation and exclusion" (García 2005:4) and in practice assimilation and exclusion continue to exist along-side multiculturalism. Peru has typically been constructed as an anomaly within this scenario in which the indigenous movement was either identi-fied as "largely non-existent" (Yashar 1998) or "utterly marginal" (García 2005:5). However, as De la Cadena (2000) argues, the fact that there is no recognized "ethnic" mobilization doesn't mean that such activism does not exist. Rather, such mobilization might take different forms.

Marginal to the agenda of the modern and developmentalist Peruvian state, the rural communities of the Andean highlands have for the better part of the twentieth century remained largely isolated from national, public life and often been left alone with very scarce resources to resolve local conflicts and problems (Manrique 1987, 1998; Poole 2004). The internal conflict between the Shining Path and the Peruvian state, which lasted from about 1980 to 2000, further exacerbated such precarious citizenship. The violence increased dramatically in the central highlands around 1987 and affected mainly the *puna* communities located in the highest reaches of the mountains of the provinces of Concepción, Jauja, and Huancayo. In January 1988, the first Comité Popular of the PCP-SL, also known as Shining Path, was installed in the highland community of Chongos Alto in the Canipaco area. In Alto Cunas, the SAIS cooperative was destroyed and several public buildings in this and other communities were burned down (CVR 2003; Manrique 1998).[5] Several local community leaders and local state officials, including mayors, governors, and justices of the peace as well as "rich" campesinos, were killed as part of Sendero Luminoso's aggressive and violent strategy of selective and targeted killings to destroy the bureaucratic state and its representatives. In the lower parts of the Mantaro Valley, the impact of Sendero's actions was less severe than in the puna communities, although several local communities across the valley experienced an increase in casualties and subversive activities on behalf of both PCP-SL and the MRTA. In Matahuasi, for example, the vice mayor (*teniente alcalde*) was assassinated. In Urcumarca, the municipal authorities fled the area after their peers had been killed in a neighboring district. In Huancayo, the PCP-SL concentrated their political and military activities at the region's largest public university, La Universidad del Centro del Perú, which they controlled from around 1987 on, and they also recruited supporters in the migrant settlements surrounding the city (CVR 2003).

With the escalation of violence, the state only related to the rural population through the army, which thus became this population's only reference for interaction with state officials (CVR 2003; Guerrero Bravo 2004:206). In 1988, the government declared a state of emergency in all of Junín province and gradually the Peruvian army came to assume complete political control. The casualties further escalated when the national army armed civil defense patrols to assist in the fight against the guerillas. After Fujimori's election in 1990 and later self-coup in 1992, human rights violations such as threats, kidnappings, torture, detentions, extrajudicial executions, and disappearances became part of daily life in the Mantaro Valley. This long history of complicated citizen-state relationships and the uneven distribution of citizenship across the national territory continued to have a profound effect on rural Peruvians' view of the state from abroad.

Peru's relationship with the international community also became tense in this period. Relations with the United States had already been strained since Fujimori's election in 1990 due to his initial reluctance to sign an accord to increase military efforts to eradicate coca fields in the Peruvian lowlands. (Fujimori later signed this accord in order to receive financial aid from Washington.) However, President George H. W. Bush was quick to officially recognize Fujimori as Peru's legitimate leader after the self-coup in 1992 despite continued skepticism among several international organizations. President Bush's endorsement was the result partly of Fujimori's willingness to continue to implement neoliberal economic austerity measures (Roberts 1995), but also because the U.S. government, which had recently launched a media campaign against *Sendero Luminoso*, supported Fujimori's hardline policy toward eradicating the Maoist guerillas. The Peruvian media devoted some attention to emigration in this period but focused mainly on alleged Senderistas in other countries, especially when Fujimori threatened to revoke the citizenship of any Peruvian abroad with connections to the guerillas.[6] As several scholars have pointed out, a culture of fear became predominant and had severe and long-term demobilizing effects on civil society (Bourque and Warren 1989; Burt 2006; Manrique 2002; Poole and Renique 1992). Political repression increased after the coup and the average citizen could no longer publicly contest the regime's economic policies, authoritarian practices, and human rights abuses because the general sentiment was that "Quien habla es terrorista" (Anyone who speaks out [in protest] is [considered] a terrorist) (Burt 2006:34).

Peruvians who left their country during the late 1980s and 1990s suffered a lot of "bad press" both in Peru as well as internationally. In Peru, migrants who left for foreign destinations were accused of "recoiling" from their responsibilities as citizens during a difficult moment in Peru's modern history. For example, in 1989–90, at the height of the crisis, the respected public intellectual and member of the Alianza Popular Revolucionaria Americana (American Popular Revolutionary Alliance—APRA),[7] Luis Alberto Sánchez wrote in a column in the magazine *Caretas*:

We have endured some major crises in our history, one from 1885 to 1890, one from 1930 to 1939, one from 1968 to 1976, and this one that has developed rapidly since 1982, and we will always prevail without recoiling or going abroad, where there is also a crisis and it's difficult to find work.[8] Hence the fact that escaping Peru is such a sad and cowardly option. I hope that the thousands of migrants from Peru who are suffering or enjoying life abroad remember those of us who stayed to face misfortune head-on, for only by confronting it directly can we overcome the severe suffering that affects us collectively.[9]

Migration to international destinations had thus become an ambivalent affair that was easily equated with the abandonment of the national project of the liberal state whose elected officials were left to combat the worst period of political violence in Peru's modern history. Ironically, the view of Peruvians abroad as selfishly seeking out a better life for themselves overseas with little or no consideration for the country they left behind was echoed by PCP-SL and MRTA. Their members saw themselves as leading a popular revolution on behalf of the popular masses, and also regarded elites and middle-class Peruvians who fled the country as traitors—not to a political project of the liberal state which, according to PCP-SL had to be destroyed, but to the people's revolution (CVR 2003). The cholera epidemic, which broke out in 1991, further added to the bad press of Peruvians abroad as citizens of a nation full of potential terrorists, drug traffickers, and cholera-infested outcasts. These images, which circulated widely across the globe, were also central to the desire of migrants living abroad, as discussed in chapter 5, to offer correctives and more positive representations to neutralize this unilaterally negative image.

Finally, this chapter demonstrates that state officials' current discourse of inclusion and glamorization of Peruvians abroad works to exclude indigenous or Andean Peruvians from the celebrated category of the Quinto Suyo emigrant citizen. These migrants have responded to the unrelenting processes of racialization and subordination that have been intrinsic to postcolonial state formation in Peru and that also characterize their present social locations as racialized labor migrants in the United States by returning as "phantom citizens" to stake their claim to citizenship and recognition.

From Traitor to Hero: El Quinto Suyo and the New Transnational Citizen

Along with the decline of political violence in Peru after the capture of Sendero's leader Abimael Guzman in 1992, the public discourse on migration and Peruvians abroad started to shift from condemning migrants abroad to endorsing them as resourceful partners in capitalist and democratic development.[10] Over the course of the following decade, migrants abroad were refashioned in state discourse as highly valuable, independent, entrepreneurial, and self-regulating citizens who supported their families back home, invested in their home country, and served as the state's partner in development while demanding little in return—in short, as ideal neoliberal subjects. There are several reasons for this shift which, I suggest, reflect a global trend in changing migrant-state relationships and shifting boundaries of citizenship under what scholars have variously referred to as late capitalism, neoliberalism, or flexible accumulation.

First, migrant remittances became a key resource through which the Peruvian state could access foreign currency and boost the country's financial sector as its government worked to stabilize the economy in the aftermath of the internal political and economic crisis of the 1980s. As in many other Latin American countries, migrant remittances in Peru make up a significant source of national income, often surpassing official development assistance and several national industries. While the overall percentage of remittances in the GDP has declined in Peru in recent years as a result of the increase of direct foreign investment, it still remains a significant source of national income. In 2012, for example, Peru received U.S. $2.779 billion from Peruvians working abroad that year (IDB 2012).[11] Without a doubt, therefore, the remittance economy was and is a key factor motivating the state to reach out to Peruvians abroad.

Second, since voting is mandatory for all Peruvian citizens between the ages of 18 and 70 regardless of residency, the absentee vote has a potentially significant impact on the outcome of national elections (Berg 2010; Escrivá et al. 2010). Gregory Schmidt (2002) has shown that in the 2000 elections, when Fujimori was reelected for a third term, the foreign vote was decisive. The reasons were, first, because the election was so close in the first round and, second, because the former head of the Peruvian National Intelligence Service (SIN), Vladimiro Montesinos, was said to have attempted to manipulate the results from foreign polling places where there are very few opposition poll watchers to ensure the integrity of the vote. The foreign vote accounted for 754,154 registered voters in the national election of 2011, representing 3.8 percent of all registered voters that year, according to the National Board of Elections (JNE 2011).[12] Of these, 378,792 cast their vote in the second round, with 100,832 in favor of Ollanta Humala and 239,551 voting for Keiko Fujimori (JNE 2011; Levitsky 2011).[13] Most presidential candidates, recognizing the numerical importance of the foreign vote, targeted this constituency directly. During his campaign leading up to the 2011 elections, President Ollanta Humala addressed Peruvians abroad in a video message titled "Message from Ollanta for Peruvians Abroad," which circulated on his YouTube channel NacionalistaTV.[14] Keiko Fujimori also addressed Peruvians abroad in a similar video spot. While attending a community meeting for Peruvians abroad in Paterson in 2011, I met a representative of her party who was campaigning among Peruvian citizens in the United States.

Finally, Peruvians abroad have become more vocal in their demands on the state to act on their behalf and the state has responded by making several important institutional changes in the past decade. One of the most important legislative reforms was the enactment of a law in 1996 to allow dual citizenship for Peruvians residing abroad.[15] Most of the pressure on the state to enact such laws came from Peruvians abroad. Some of them had resided in the United States since the 1980s or before, and were in a position to naturalize as U.S. citizens but did not want to lose their Peruvian nationality as a result. There was pressure on them to naturalize in the United States because of the enactment of anti-immigrant legislation in the country. Beginning with Proposition 187 in California, three major immigration laws followed in 1996: the Illegal Immigration Reform and Immigrant Responsibility Act (IIRIRA), which was designed to address both legal and illegal immigration; the Personal Responsibility Act and Work Opportunity Reconciliation Act (PRWORA), which reduced the level of benefits that immigrants could receive; and finally, the Antiterrorism and Effective Death Penalty Act (AEDPA), which emerged as a response to the 1993 World Trade Center bombings and enabled the United States to detain foreigners accused of committing crimes without bail and deport them after they had served their sentences in U.S. prisons (Escobar 2007). These changes led not only Peru but also other Latin American countries to pass retention-of-nationality laws in the 1990s and to extend extraterritorial political rights to their citizens residing abroad.[16]

Yet it was not until the presidency of Alejandro Toledo (2001–2006) that the Peruvian state's "courtship" of migrant communities abroad fully blossomed and materialized in institutional changes that benefited them. President Toledo needed to recast the migrant figure as a key contributor to the Peruvian economy and society. He himself embodied many of the narratives of migration-driven progress, entrepreneurship, social mobility, and personal success. Through moral and material over-coming, the story goes, Toledo transformed himself from a shoeshine boy in Chimbote to a fearless leader and opponent of a dictator, from a poor kid of Andean origins to a Stanford Ph.D., and from an indigenous migrant to the president of Peru.[17] His entry on the political scene, as several scholars have discussed, triggered multiple forms of racial and class politics in Peru and one of his main challenges remained to con-tinuously prove to traditional elites that he was an acceptable and viable politician despite his Andean and nonelite background (Berg and Tam-agno 2006; De La Cadena 2001; Vich 2007). These experiences, I sug-gest, were key to his almost personal mission of transforming the deeply engrained meaning of the racialized Andean migrant category into a new, modern, and cosmopolitan, mobile indigenous political subject, which found its mirror image in the Andean transnational migrant.

But to reconcile his past biography with his future political aspira-tions, Toledo needed a revised discourse on the values and merits of indigeneity. Already during the electoral campaign leading up to the 2000 presidential elections, Toledo and his outspoken wife, Eliane Karp, a Jewish anthropologist from Belgium and fellow Stanford graduate, had been popularizing a discourse of political change which drew on indig-enous symbols and evoked the glorious past of Tawantinsuyo—the Inca Empire—as the foundation for a new, modern Peruvian nation com-pletely integrated in the global economy. In her writings, Karp de To-ledo (2002) frequently evokes parallels between her "cholo," as she calls the president, and Inca Pachacutec, the ninth Inca ruler of the kingdom of Cusco who initiated the expansionist strategy of the Inca state and ruled the Inca Empire, Tawantinsuyo, from 1438 to 1471. In Quechua *pachakutiq* means "he who shakes the earth," and this Inca ruler was considered an exceptional leader, fearless warrior (he led a military defense in the battle against the Chancas), and an excellent administrator, according to several chronicles (Rostworowski de Diez Canseco 1999). The discourse of Toledo's indigeneity was aimed at capturing the votes of Peru's nonwhite indigenous and mestizo populations by offering an alternative image to the dominant political system controlled by the traditional political elites. At the same time, it also served to compensate for Toledo's lack of elite pedigree and capitalized on his indigenous past to reinvent a new image of a transnational, indigenous, and neoliberal-friendly subject. Toledo lost the 2000 elections to Fujimori and in protest led the national "La Marcha de los Cuatro Suyos" (The March of the Four Regions, in reference to the four regions of the Inca Empire) to denounce the obvious electoral fraud and to demand that Fujimori step down. After the fall of the Fujimori government, an interim president, Valentín Paniagua, was appointed, and Toledo was elected in the 2001 elections.

The transition from Fujimori's authoritarian regime to Toledo's proclaimed return to democracy brought about major shifts in the political opportunity structure in Peru. While it left a major void in the political party structure, the transition also opened up the possibility for various degrees of citizen mobilization and political leverage for nonstate actors (Arce 2008). This "opening up" also reflected a changing relationship between migrants abroad and the Peruvian state and soon after his election, in August 2001 Toledo's government created the Subsecretariat of Peruvian Communities Abroad, which was later elevated to the status of a secretariat under the Ministry of the Presidency in 2005. The goal of this new agency was to "defend the well-being of the Peruvian communities abroad and promote their protection and defend their interests and rights in the countries of destination, under the principles of veracity, legality, celerity, efficiency, simplicity, and above all without discrimination in consular attention" (Ministry of Foreign Affairs 2005: 5–6). Toledo's celebratory approach to Peruvians abroad marked a definite change in migrant-state relationships in which migrants came to be seen as a valuable resource in local development in Peru, and deserving of favorable investment opportunities, political influence, and decent treatment at Peruvian consulates abroad regardless of their racial, ethnic, and class backgrounds.[18]

The attempts by states to reclaim emigrants as transnational citizens are not unique to Peru and have been documented for other Latin American countries as well.[19] Yet in most places migrant citizens—or a certain *kind* of migrant citizen—occupy an ambiguous position in relation to the state. Susan Coutin (2007), for example, has shown that Salvadoran migrants—even when claimed as citizens and "kin" by the Salvadoran state by using terminologies such as "distant brothers" (*hermanos lejanos*) and "absent children" (*hijos ausentes*)—are still positioned as outsiders to the nation-state. State officials refer to them as "las comunidades en el exterior," a terminology, Coutin suggests, that in its reference to national boundaries both reinforces and reconceptualizes the boundaries of the nation-state (2007:74–75).

In the Peruvian case, while discursively cast as inclusion, the state's attempt to "incorporate" emigrant citizens into the body politic and extend symbolic and material membership to these populations mirrors the deep historical antagonism embedded in organized politics in Latin America in which large, racialized sectors of the population, deemed "nonmodern" by the ruling elites, are still widely denied access to basic services and forms of self-representation (De la Cadena 2010:341). Despite state officials' "inclusion" of Peruvians abroad in the national project, the racial and class politics that shape citizenship in Peru continues to condition the possibilities for participation and self-representation of Andean Peruvians who reside abroad. In this sense, not all Peruvians abroad are deemed fit or worthy by the political establishment in Lima for transnational membership in El Quinto Suyo. Indeed, few Peruvians of rural and indigenous origin benefit in any significant way from the new democratic spaces created by the state. Most of these are controlled by better educated, middle-class, and largely urban Peruvians, who have no problem envisioning themselves as an equal partner in dialogue with Peruvian consular officials.

Given this overall panorama of changing migrant-state relationships, how can we understand the decision of U.S.-based migrants to economically support the legal process following the *ajusticiamiento* back in their rural community of origin? To what extent can this particular transnational engagement be taken as evidence of the development of "transnational citizenship" among Urcumarquinos abroad? How is it related to local struggles against economic and juridical marginalization within Peru? Or is it better understood as a continuation of earlier practices of Andean sociability and reciprocity that emphasize the importance of helping one's family and building the community in a strained economy, now aided by transnational connections? In what way, then, is such practice part of Andean migrants' understanding of themselves as makers of their own history?

Andean Socialities and Transnational Connections

The day after the event of 1999, Asunción received a phone call from Urcumarca. It was her older brother Teófilo. She had just got home from her Wednesday cleaning job to the single-family house in Silver Spring where she lived at the time with her youngest son Paulino, his wife, their two daughters, and whoever else might be staying with them at the moment. At first, Asunción took the sudden phone call and her brother Teófilo's account of the event as good news. Like many *comuneros* in Urcumarca, she expressed her satisfaction with the fact that the community finally had got rid of the thieves, as they had been making life impossible for everyone in the village for way too long, depriving them of their most basic livelihoods. Although she had not suffered directly as a result of the robberies, several of her family members had. But Teófilos's intention was not just to inform Asunción. It was also to request her help. Their sister Serafina's husband Jerónimo, who at the time was president of the Comunidad Campesina, had fallen into disgrace as a consequence of the *ajusticiamiento*. Although the whole community had stood up against the police and the provincial authorities from Jauja in defense of the community, Teófilo reported, the police and state representatives had started to accumulate charges against the governor of the village, the president of the Comunidad Campesina, and other local authorities. The Comunidad needed money to cover the expenses of the court case if they wanted to avoid ending up in jail. And who would take care of Serafina if Jerónimo was imprisoned?

Asunción promised to mobilize resources as quickly as she could. The Comunidad had decided to rent out some communal land (*tierras comunales*) to raise funds, but Asunción begged her older brother not to sell any family land to resolve this matter and she promised him she would help as she best could. Together with her two sons, Asunción immediately started to collect monetary contributions (*cuotas*) from all the Urcumarquinos in the Maryland area. Before going to her first cleaning job the next morning, Asunción sent several hundred dollars from a remittance agency in Silver Spring which she had mobilized through her kin and *paisano* network to cover the initial expenses of the upcoming court case. But more support was soon needed. Asunción and her sons decided to organize a fund-raiser in the community to send a more substantial amount. "In Peru, if you don't pay, nothing happens," she said. She was referring to the fact that when there was a court case you needed to have a budget to bribe the judges and pay a lawyer to speed up the judicial process. "Here, in the U.S., you feel protected by the law, but in Peru it is the opposite. The law does not protect you unless you pay." She told me that she had only attached one condition to her support, which was that the community back in Peru was forbidden from mentioning individual names. If anyone asked, she had instructed, they should say that all of them did it. And so it was. Maintaining one's silence is a collectivist strategy of contesting the authority of a state that seeks to ascribe responsibility to single individuals.

In many ways, the engagement of migrants abroad with their home communities mirrors the mutual aid networks that link kin and community together through ties of reciprocity and a sense of obligation to one another. These practices have been documented as a central characteristic of sociality in the Andes in the anthropological scholarship of rural Andean communities (cf. Harris 2000; Isbell 1978). These engagements include frequent remittances, mutual aid of various kinds, and participation in the fiesta cargo system whenever migrants are able to travel back home. To a great extent such relations have also followed migrants abroad and have become the basis of their social worlds in the United States. For example, in the early 1990s, when there were only a few Urcumarquinos in the area, Asunción and her family participated occasionally in the activities of a cultural organization called Centro Cultural Huancayo in Washington, D.C. But as more relatives joined them—and due to some discord with members from the Club Huancayo, who Urcumarquino migrants felt were trying to assert themselves as better and superior because they were from the city of Huancayo—Asunción's family instead founded their own social club in 1994. Over its almost twenty years of existence the club has organized many fund-raisers for numerous projects in their hometown of Urcumarca, including a project to help restore the cemetery of the community and another to rebuild the roof of the village church, which had been damaged when Shining Path made their incursions into the town in the late 1980s. The donations made to the Comunidad Campesina in response to the 1999 *ajusticiamiento* must be seen, I suggest, in light of this prior trajectory of collective remittances which bind the individual to the social collectivity through social practice and the mediation of social relationships.

The Urcumarquinos who manage to legalize their status in the United States enter a second phase of transnational engagement when travel to Peru becomes possible, thus allowing them to participate "face-to-face" in important festive and ritual events in the community. Their un-documented counterparts, meanwhile, continue to participate in these events through fiesta videos that circulate transnationally. Participation in village fiestas, as we saw in chapter 4, allows migrants to rework and redefine their social relationship with the community and its authori-ties after years of "physical" absence. Such fiestas also provide a special context in which migrants can perform their mastery of certain social and cultural competencies acquired abroad, which positions them both as knowledgeable of local understandings of legitimate authority and as models for local aspirations for transnational mobility and cosmopoli-tan sensibilities and style. Returning transnational migrants use festive occasions in the community to simultaneously improve their social po-sition and that of their relatives in the village *and* make claims to new transnational subjectivities. These claims are validated not only in the context of the village fiesta, but also transnationally. Back in the United States, Urcumarquino migrants produce narratives and circulate images of their fiesta sponsorship. Ultimately this serves to boost their social and symbolic capital not only in the context of the U.S.-based migrant collectivity, but also transnationally.

Contrary to other Peruvian organizations in the D.C. and Maryland area that draw on a base of middle-class professional migrants, the Ur-cumarquinos tend to limit their everyday encounters with the U.S. and Peruvian state to the necessary minimum. Nor do they engage in more formal migrant activism by lobbying the central Peruvian government for diasporic recognition (see Berg and Tamagno 2006). Few Urcumarquinos go to the Peruvian embassy in Washington, D.C., and when they do it is simply to renew their Peruvian national identity cards (DNI), obtain certified documents, or to cast their mandatory votes in the Peruvian presidential elections. This limited transactional relationship with Peruvian state officials abroad, however, does not mean that they do not engage "the state" at the local and regional levels in Peru by acting upon new political subjectivities generated through the migration process.

Contesting the State from Abroad

In previous chapters I have argued that over the course of the migration process migrants become increasingly conscious of their social positions within wider social and racial orders. This includes a more critical stance toward the way their home communities have been "left to die" by the state; in turn their heightened consciousness prompts them to act upon their predicament in order to produce social change in their communities. The violent event in Urcumarca ultimately ended with the death of the two accused thieves, one of them in the emergency room of a nearby hospital.[20] The affair stirred up different reactions among people in the area. For one it revived the image of the savage Indian. This was the image that dominated the media coverage of the event in Peru, where it was condemned as a brutal act of violence and an expression of the ignorance and lack of civility of Andean populations, much like the Uchuraccay massacre discussed in the opening of the chapter, despite its minor scale. The event also prompted some people to acknowledge the everyday structural forms of violence and inequalities which shape daily life at the margins of the state in Peru (cf. Poole 2004). Most reactions elicited by journalists in the local newspapers acknowledged that the incident had occurred because of the lack of formal justice in Peru. One woman interviewed in Huancayo by a journalist from the local newspaper *El Correo* remarked: "The first to blame in these massacres are the authorities, there are so many criminals around who steal and who never go to jail, so the people [*el pueblo*] do not have any other alternatives than to do justice with their own hands. Of course it is wrong, but what else can be done?" Another man said: "Justice in this country is a fantasy, so I think the decision of the Comunidad is right. They acted because they were tired of all the robberies. I think that no other justice is possible in Peru."[21] Villagers and transnational migrants alike reiterated their view that it was *because* of the generalized exclusion and the lack of formal justice at all levels in Peruvian society that the Urcumarquinos took "justice into their own hands." Knowing well that their kin and *paisanos* back in Urcumarca could not count on any kind of backing from the Peruvian state and justice system to solve their problems, U.S.-based migrants agreed to help the resident Urcumarquinos achieve social justice for the community through their own efforts and money.

Scholars working in neighboring Andean countries have reported similar scenarios. Daniel Goldstein (2004) demonstrates that in urban neighborhoods in Cochabamba, Bolivia, lynching and attempted lynching as a staged spectacle are instrumental in the struggles of the marginalized urban poor to give themselves public visibility and put them on the agenda of local and national politicians. Lynching, Goldstein argues, is an instrument that marginalized people can employ to call attention to their vulnerability to crime and their lack of access to an official justice system to protect them. At the same time, it is also a demonstration of power in which people can "express their dissatisfaction with a state that seems to be in league with the very criminals it is supposed to combat, and by punishing (or threatening to punish) criminals under their own authority, they push the state toward reform" (2004:216). These lynchings, Goldstein suggests, can be understood as a kind of "neoliberal violence" emerging from the deficiencies and erosion of social provisions of the privatizing state and by transnational capitalism itself. In Ecuador, Andrés Guerrero (2000) shows that the indigenous communities of Cotopaxi and Tunguruhua have taken advantage of radio and television to stage and broadcast spectacular accounts of violence (*ajusticiamientos*) and in this way effectively challenge the state and its neoliberal policies and logics which have had harmful consequences for the local populations. Members of this population, Guerrero argues, then reiterate their "right to kill" and to take justice into their own hands as long as the state "lets them die" (2000:488).[22]

The violent events in Urcumarca illustrate how the modern myth of the state as a superior source of social order and stability is at odds with the everyday experiences of people interacting with state agencies in many parts of the postcolonial world (Blom Hansen and Stepputat 2005). It is commonly assumed in Peru that the absence of the state throughout the national territory is one of the main reasons for the abandonment of the poor rural communities in the Andes. But more recently, scholars have suggested that rather than absence, it is the inefficient character, internal inconsistency, and often violent routines of the state apparatus that, despite its claims to transparency and legitimacy, hinders the proper consolidation of democratic participatory processes (Degregori 2004; Pajuelo 2004; Poole and Renique 2003). Furthermore, for several years the national army was the only "state agency" which had a real presence in the central highlands, and as it manifested itself mostly through violence, disappearances, and unjustified detentions local inhabitants began to look at the state with suspicion at the same time as they were trying to garner its attention. For the *comuneros* of Urcumarca one thing was clear. Knowing that they could not count on any state-conferred entitlements to empower them, they had to deploy other strategies to protect themselves against the inadequacies and injustices of the state. Besides raising a little money on their own through the sale and rental of communal lands, the most immediate resource available to them was their transnational connections with *paisanos* and family members abroad.

Transnational migration and diaspora scholars have argued that the force of diaspora politics often lies in its fund-raising capacity (Laguerre 1998:163).[23] However, migrants' fund-raising activities are seldom devoid of personal or collective interests—and this case is no different. There is little doubt that the initial motivation of the Flores family in supporting fellow *comuneros* in "defense of the community" was their desire to defend their own close kin from falling into disgrace. Likewise, just as Asunción would send money for funerals, fiestas, or life cycle events in the extended family, she also sent money to her brother-in-law and his fellow *comuneros* to prevent them from being incarcerated—an outcome which would have brought disgrace to her sister Serafina. But more importantly, the call for help on behalf of the *comuneros* also provided a special context in which U.S.-migrants could express and perform their loyalty to the community, and consequently improve their social position, achieve status and power, make claims to membership, and refashion themselves as agents of their own history. Moreover, it implicitly challenged the state apparatus and questioned its legitimate authority to distribute "justice" in the aftermath of the event.

The migrants' economic support for the legal process therefore did cast them in a favorable light, but only among some sectors of the local community. "Thanks to the *residentes* in the United States we have been able to solve the problem of the Comunidad [comunidad campesina] and its authorities," one *comunero* remarks. Yet others were less enthusiastic and some even minimized or ignored the importance of U.S.-based migrants' support. The former mayor of Urcumarca, for example, who long had had issues with U.S.-based migrants' involvement in local politics and their participation in the fiesta cargo system, denied the participation of the migrants abroad in the judicial process and said that all the expenses of the judicial process were paid for with public funds and with money from the rent of communal lands. He said: "Our friends in the United States have not supported us, at least, I do not know of any support, maybe Señor Jerónimo has received some help from his son, but they never supported us authorities or the comuneros. I cannot confirm that there has been any support, because there has been no support on behalf of *that* family." The ex-mayor then proceeded to critique how migrants abroad had taken over the fiesta and had organized it without coordinating properly with the locally elected politicians: "They organize the fiesta in the village [the patron saint fiesta] without coordinating with the municipality and that is also wrong. How come that just because they have money they think they can do whatever they want without coordinating with the municipality? They do everything by themselves." The statements by the ex-mayor demonstrate that U.S.-based migrants' activities vis-à-vis the hometown were not without friction, because life in the town was mediated by multiple authorities—the Comunidad Campesina and the municipality representing the state at the local level. Migrants abroad acted according to what they understood as appropriate rules for reciprocity within particular social and familial relationships.

Their actions demonstrate how persons and collectivities whose worlds had been profoundly decentered by violence, state abandonment, and larger forces in the global capitalist system strove to reconstruct themselves, their communities, and their social and moral worlds across both borders and boundaries. To the local state representatives their "phantom appearances" were undesirable, but to migrants and their families they were empowering and motivated them to transform their predicament as Peru's second-class citizens.

Phantom Citizens in a Transnationalized Andes

In May 2013, I participated in the twenty-seventh convention of the Asociación de Instituciones Peruanas en Estados Unidos y Canadá (AIPEUC)—an umbrella organization for Peruvian cultural and political institutions in the United States and Canada, which has as its mission "to stimulate unity between Peruvians, Peruvian Americans and all those who appreciate the culture, history and people of Peru in sharing Peru's heritage and vibrant culture." The convention was held over three days at the elegant J. W. Marriott Hotel on Pennsylvania Avenue in Washington, D.C., and the program offered a mix of cultural events, panel presentations on a variety of topics, and plenary discussions of key political issues of interest to the Peruvian community. This year the proposal to create an electoral district of Peruvians abroad was the central item on the agenda and the convention featured the presence and participation of several members of the Peruvian Congress who had traveled to Washington, D.C., to debate this proposal with "Peruvians in the United States." Such a proposal would enable this imagined collectivity of "Peruvians abroad" ("Peruanos en el exterior") not just to vote for candidates directly representing their "emigrant constituency" through one unified electoral district to be named El Quinto Suyo or "the fifth region," but also to run as candidates for the Peruvian congress representing Peruvians abroad as a separate constituency (cf. Rodrigues Cuadros 2009). Several of the participants I talked to during the AIPEUC convention aspired to run for congress in Peru should such a proposal be approved and made into law.

When I called Paulino, Domitila, Aurelio, and other Urcumarquino informants and friends in the larger Washington and Maryland area to arrange to meet while I was in town for the weekend, they seemed surprised to learn about this "Peruvian event" in their area, since none of them had heard about it or seen it announced anywhere. Domitila expressed interest in attending one of the panels with me on women and health, but when I tried to make arrangements for her to attend I was told by the organizing committee that all attendees had to register in advance for the convention and belong to a member organization. Needless to say, none of the small social and cultural organizations that Urcumarquinos and other Andean migrants had established in D.C. and Maryland were to be found in AIPEUC's membership directory.[24] The AIPEUC convention was an exclusive social space of privileged membership, not a context in which Andean labor migrants could assert themselves as cosmopolitan subjects, claim rights as transnational citizens vis-à-vis visiting Peruvian state officials, or participate in a "unity" among Peruvians. It is no wonder that labor migrants like Domitila, Paulino, Aurelio, or Asunción looked to their local kin-based social networks and to their hometown itself for positive validation of their achievements through migration and for alternative channels to exercise their newfound political agency as transnational subjects.

Historically, in Peru as elsewhere in the postcolonial world, privileged groups have always been citizen members of the nation-state and have done their best to police the boundaries for membership in the national community by preventing indigenous Peruvians from participating as citizens in urban political life. As inhabitants of rural Peru prior to migrating to the United States, few Urcumarquinos have historically exercised full citizenship in their country of origin. Those who were not included in the "citizenship option" that the modern Peruvian nation-state made available to them (i.e., assimilation as urban workers or as rural campesinos) had to find alternative ways of imagining and constituting themselves as political subjects, or remain excluded. This limited scenario for participation as citizens was further aggravated during the period of political violence in the 1980s when the state withdrew almost completely from the area with the exception of its presence through the national army. Local valley residents who did not side with the army were targeted as *terrucos* (terrorists) and those who did not side with the PCP-SL, or remained indifferent, were seen by the PCP-SL as enemies of the people's war to overthrow the bourgeois state. It was during this period that most Urcumarquinos left for the United States. This is the backdrop against which the *ajusticiamiento* in Urcumarca and the U.S.-based Urcumarquino migrants' involvement in the event's aftermath must be seen.

The particular incidence of supporting the legal process financially following the *ajusticiamiento*, I have argued, can be seen as a continuation of historical struggles of nonelite indigenous Peruvians against economic and juridical marginalization within Peru. While this particular incident cannot be taken as evidence of the development of a more sustained form of "transnational citizenship" among Urcumarquinos abroad, it offered U.S.-based migrants, and Urcumarquinos in general, an opportunity to challenge the state in its local and regional manifestations. The violent event and its aftermath, I have argued, momentarily constituted Urcumarquinos abroad as "phantom citizens" that came back to haunt the state, threaten its authority and its sovereign right to kill by taking justice in their own hands, and refuse to be "left to die." For Urcumarquino migrants, the collective remittance to pay for the court proceedings was on the one hand a continuation of traditional Andean practices of sociability and reciprocity aimed at helping family and building community, now aided by transnational connections. But on the other hand, such support must be seen in relation to migrants' heightened social consciousness about their own positionality within a larger racial and political economy—it is fueled by their continuous efforts and aspirational project of transforming themselves into modern, transnational, and cosmopolitan subjects in order to make their own history as "nationals" and as citizens of Peru. While the Peruvian state may not envision these Andean migrants as ideal emigrant citizens, Urcumarquino migrants abroad consider themselves active participants in the vital transformations of the multiple social and political landscapes they inhabit.

Conclusion

In June 2011, I returned to Peru on a short research trip and arrived in Lima a few days before the national elections. Ollanta Humala, a former army officer and son of an indigenous labor lawyer and ethnic national-ist who had lost the previous presidential election in 2006 in a runoff against Alan García, was now in a tight race with Keiko Fujimori, the daughter of former President Alberto Fujimori, then—and still—serving a twenty-five-year prison sentence on charges of human rights abuses and corruption. The cab driver from the airport, a return migrant from Spain, welcomed me back to Lima by cracking a joke. The joke went something like this: During the electoral campaign, Ollanta makes a trip to a rich neighborhood (*barrio pituco*) and sees all the children chanting his name, "Humala, Humala, Humala!" Ollanta is surprised and says, "Wow, I didn't expect the pitucos to support me, that's great," to which one of the children answers: "No, Señor Humala, it's only because our parents say that if Humala wins, we're moving to Miami."

This joke illustrates the historic trend that affluent Peruvian elites for most of the twentieth century have used exile and travel to foreign des-tination as an escape valve in the wake of political changes that threat-ened—or promise to threaten—their class and racial privileges and reflects the reproduction of desire for travel to foreign destinations across generations. Despite his attempts to refashion his image for the 2011 elec-tions as a center left, socially conscious, but unthreatening neoliberal-friendly leader who understood the importance of foreign investment to the Peruvian economy, Humala was still regarded with suspicion by Lima's political and economic elites. His election could indeed prompt some of them to move abroad, as the joke predicted. Yet the joke's repre-sentation of Peruvian migration as elite Peruvians leaving for Miami—long the symbol of an upper-class leisure and shopping destination as well as a hideout for right-wing Latin American politicians—doesn't ac-curately depict the changing Peruvian migration landscape of today.

The Peruvians who travel internationally today are no longer just wealthy and self-styled "white" Peruvians. Since the 1980s Peruvians of all class and regional backgrounds have migrated to foreign destinations. But unlike the elites who historically have accessed foreign destinations and various forms of capital without any significant barriers to their mobility, recent Peruvian labor migrants, as this book has shown, cannot take state-authorized international travel for granted. Often unable to access legally issued official visas because of restrictive immigration policies that have "delocalized" U.S. borders and expanded border regimes into sending countries, these aspiring migrants must instead turn to the services of an ever-growing migration industry whose travel experts assist them in realizing their migration projects outside state-authorized routes. But the outward and upwardly mobility of these Peruvians, as illustrated by the ethnographic vignette about Jorge at the beginning of the book, produces friction and resentment among "white" urban elites in Lima who regard it as a transgression and a menace to the prevailing social and racial order. Similarly, once in the United States, Andean migrants' mobility also risks being morally and affectively coded as suspicious, transgressive, and as a threat to U.S. society and the social order. Only when staging their "Andean culture" in the form of folkloric spectacles for a wider public or when embodying the social identity of the docile and hardworking immigrant worker can Andean migrants seek to have their mobility publicly validated and regain a sense of control over their own representation.

This book has attempted to accomplish three major goals, each of which reflects an important dimension in the study of transnational migration and circulation between Peru and the United States and back. Yet the insights from this case study also speak beyond the specific Peruvian case and the Latin American context. First, it has sought to understand, analyze, and dissect the reasons why people in the central highlands of Peru leave or have to leave their home country. While my findings reveal that there are particular local, material, and historically specific configurations that shape the possible answers to this question—the Sendero Luminoso insurgency and state counterinsurgency and the characteristics of Peru's economic transition since the late 1980s—they also offer more general insights into why people migrate from any place in the world, especially in the case of populations who, like rural and indig-

enous Peruvians, are both centrally and peripherally situated in relation to global capitalism and metropolitan modernity and whose lives
continue to be shaped by the legacies of larger colonial and imperial
projects.

Second, this book has sought to illuminate the conditions under
which contemporary Andean migrants leave, how they fare, what underlying structural constraints shape their lives and experiences, and
how they reimagine their communities and themselves in the process.
It makes clear that the flexibility of capital and the deepened differentiation of global labor markets within and across national boundaries
has produced not only a spatial extention of traditional Andean mobile livelihoods beyond the national borders of Peru, but has also increased the policing of physical borders in destination countries along
with new racialized boundaries that profoundly affect their actions and
experiences of migration and separation. These dynamics of the global
migration process, I have argued, prompt migrants to engage actively
in the production of their own circulation, broadly understood. They
do so by engaging in communicative and performative practices that
use visual, rhetorical, and material resources and cues to produce not
just a set of social relations, but also a set of images of who they are or
how they would like to be seen within the context of these relationships
and social fields. This is not to say that migrants are in control of their
own making; indeed, equally central to the analysis in this book have
been the various structures, institutions, and technologies that make the
personhood of migrant subjects in today's world increasingly uncertain,
questionable, and under siege within always mutating and unevenly distributed fields of power.

Finally, the book and the ethnographic process through which it
was produced propose a particular form of ethnography—"ambulant
ethnography"—which I have found useful both as a metaphor and as a
fieldwork strategy in contexts where mobility increasingly has become
the modus operandi of the ethnographer, given the social and political realities of social and cultural phenomena that most ethnographers
today study. As noted earlier, the Spanish term *ambulante* best conveys
this form of ethnography, because it evokes a highly mobile, creative,
and malleable form which can adapt to unpredictable travel routes and
uncertain payoff and which is attentive to the way movement is em-

bodied, how it is made meaningful in particular contexts, and how it is historically variable for different populations. In what remains of this concluding chapter, I detail the contributions that this case study on transnational migration between the central highlands of Peru and the United States makes to scholarship on migration and circulation more generally, highlighting some of the questions as well as methodological and epistemological dilemmas that it poses for future scholarly work beyond the U.S.-Peruvian/Latin American context.

Transnational Migration and Cosmopolitan Desires

This book has traced the transnational migration projects of migrants from the central highlands of Peru who left their rural villages for Peru's cities and later for the United States during a period in which Peru was going through profound social, economic, and political changes. These changes brought about by recent globalization and, in particular, by transational migration and circulation are vast and inconclusive and intimately tied to a broader historical process and by larger colonial and imperial projects which have molded this region for centuries.

In recent years, new communication infrastructures have altered the rural landscape of the valley and imbued it with new social meaning. Cell phone towers outside the city of Jauja now enable communication between transnational households in Urcumarca and their migrant relatives abroad even if residents sometimes complain that you have to climb the mountain behind the town to get good reception. Traditional adobe houses lie next to large but empty multistory brick homes in the latest construction styles with flashy glass windows in fancy colors and satellite dishes on the roof that migrants have ordered constructed from afar with their migration earnings. These silent empty buildings in the rural landscape stand as monuments to modernity and to the class aspirations and urban and cosmopolitan sensibilities of their owners. Their materiality testifies to what migrants have achieved abroad and how they would like to be perceived at home as a result of their mobility.

The central Plaza of Urcumarca also boasts several modern cement buildings and large signs welcoming the visitor to the town. One sign displays the web address of the municipality with gigantic letters as if to inform visitors that this town is globally connected and represented on the World Wide Web. Another sign celebrates the history, culture, and folklore of Urcumarca. This sign features Paulino, Celestina, and one of their U.S.-born daughters in traditional fiesta outfits; it is used for festive occasions in the town including the patron saint fiesta and carnival. These fiestas have grown larger and more exuberant in the past decade due to increased participation of U.S.-based migrants. They use these occasions to seek acknowledgment, social status, and validation from relatives and *paisanos* back home of their social and economic achievements abroad. The sign significantly honors Paulino's U.S.-based family as valuable "hijos del pueblo" living abroad and their depiction in local fiesta outfit simultaneously adds value to local and regional customs by showing how "modern" migrants living abroad are still committed to such local Andean cultural forms; indeed, migrants often take such practices with them when establishing communities abroad. The visible presence of U.S.-based migrants in the town, even though they are absent for most of the year—or for many years in a row—is significant because it works to raise the overall profile not just of migrant families within local communities, but also of the town itself. Some residents envy the social and symbolic capital of the "hijos del pueblo en el exterior," Paulino notes, illustrating how transnational migration has created new forms of social stratification between Urcumarquino households with migrant members abroad and those without.

Since the end of my long-term fieldwork in 2005, the Peruvian economy has grown on average 7 percent a year and even managed to survive the global financial crisis without any major blow to the economy. The country has become Latin America's fastest growing economy and one of the world's star economies recurrently held up as the posterchild of succesful neoliberal economic development in Latin America.[1] Foreign investments have poured into the country's extractive industries, including mining, hydrocarbons, and big infrastructure projects (Bebbington 2012). The government has reduced national poverty rates by more than half from 59 percent of the population living in poverty in 2004 to 26 percent in 2012 and doubled the size of the middle class to number around half of all Peruvian families, most of them living in urban areas on the coast, but also in Andean cities like Huancayo.

The city of Huancayo has changed considerably since my last long-term fieldwork in the area. When I returned on a short research trip

Figure c.1. A sign encouraging shopping at the new mall in Huancayo, 2011. (Photo by Author)

in 2011, I was surprised to find a huge shopping mall, numerous microcredit agencies, international chain stores, large-scale supermarkets, and auto repair shops outside the city center along La Avenida Real, the city's old commercial street. I learned that a preferred and profitable investment of both return migrants and nonmigrants alike was to purchase vehicles and heavy machinery to rent out on short-term contracts to mining companies in the area—hence the many auto repair shops. These new establishments attest not so much to migration-driven development per se—although the new consumer base certainly includes return migrants and members of transnational families with increased purchasing power through remittances—but to the expansion of the urban middle class in Peru more generally.

Given these developments, it is tempting to assume that many migrants would return to Peru and also that the next generations of Domitilas and Paulinos are more likely to stay in their home country instead of pursuing international migration to "salir adelante." But it is too early to draw such general and far-reaching conclusions. While the government and the mainstream media go the extra mile to carefully interpret statistics about how many Peruvians are returning from abroad in ways that are favorable to their maketing effort to improve Peru's image as a prosperous place in which to invest and to live, a recent report by the International Organization of Migration shows that although Peru has seen an increase in jobs and salaries as a result of its recent economic growth, the rate of return migrants is still relatively small, especially when compared to the number of Peruvians leaving every year, which has seen only a slight reduction (IOM 2012:77).[2] Those in my study who did return from the United States cited personal responsibilities for aging parents; separation from children left behind, deportation, or fulfilled migration goals as the main reasons for returning (cf. Bastia 2011).[3]

Despite Peru's strong macroeconomic performance in recent years, stark social inequalities persist and life is still hard in many parts of the rural and marginally urban Andes. Those households whose small-scale landholdings cannot meet the demands and price levels of the self-regulating markets and who cannot step up to their new responsibilities as consumers in the neoliberal economy, are left to lead ever more precarious lives (Mayer 2002:316–17). In this scenario, transnational migration is likely to remain a desirable strategy for upward mobility for lower-income Andean Peruvians in the years to come.

While the promise of mobility continues to lure people from the Andes to travel to foreign destinations in pursuit of better lives, actualized migration via unauthorized routes and precarious legal circumstances produces entrapments of various kinds. In a housing complex in Broward, Florida, Amparo and her husband José, who recently have become grandparents to two U.S. citizens, are the go-to caregivers for their oldest son and his wife. After more than ten years in the United States, Amparo and José still have no papers, both are underemployed, and they have not been able to accumulate any significant savings for their retirement. Similarly, in 2013, when I last saw Inés, she was still living in a small town in Florida with no papers, struggling to make ends meet through several badly paid jobs, and with a pending order of deportation. She was still yearning to find a white-collar job and someone to marry and thereby move out of the social moratorium of her present situation. But even in the darkest of times she was full of hope for a better future and her night table attests to this admirable existential resourcefulness. Inés has two candles set by a faded printout of a Photoshop collage with an ID-type picture of herself and her son Angel superimposed on a green card. Here, each day she prays to *Diosito* (little God) with the hope that one day He will answer her prayers.

For migrant women such as Inés and Amparo, returning to Peru with no money, no papers, and little or no savings to invest in a business of sorts was equivalent to a failed migration project. Hence they could not return. Instead both women continued to live on, working several jobs at once, all at low pay, and scrambled to get by from day to day hoping that one day their respective papers would materialize and ironically allow them to return home, at least temporarily. Their stories illustrate how Andean migrants want not only to access middle-class lifestyles abroad but also genuinely strive to reposition themselves back home as "nationals" of Peru—a recognition most had not been able to seek in Peru prior to migration. This suggests that when seeking to explain the reasons and motivations for why people migrate, we must consider the central importance of mobility as a social and cultural aspiration not just for Andean Peruvians but for most rural, indigenous, and racialized populations who try to improve their social status through migration.

Those Peruvians who, unlike Inés and Amparo, can return are now able to walk the streets and upscale shopping malls of both Huancayo and Lima and feel that they have successfully reinvented themselves beyond their premigration social condition. Take for instance Paulino, who became a U.S. resident in 2004. He now returns to Peru every year—and sometimes more than that—to participate in the yearly fiesta honoring the patron saint of Urcumarca. But he also always makes sure he spends several days in Lima not just to visit friends and family there, but to take his family to places in the capital that he never dreamed of setting foot in prior to his U.S.-bound migration. This aspiration to belong to a higher-class strata in one's country of origin and ancestry is qualitatively different from the acceptance for which most migrants strive in the United States where claims to citizenship and belonging are more strategically about aiming for opportunities, higher earnings, and equal rights. Their overall goal is decidedly affective and truly an aspirational project of self-invention; one that is central to processes of social becoming, not just in the Peruvian Andes but also far beyond it.

Partial Circulations

The concept of circulation has been central to my framing of migration and mobility in this book as historically grounded multidirectional movements of people, objects, and information. By evoking it I do not imply an actual or assumed ability by migrants to cross international borders at free will; indeed, I have gone to great lengths to analyze the various constraints—structural, technological, institutional, and social—that work to the contrary, requiring mobile people to frame their actions and themselves in particular ways. Existing scholarly works have shown how social consciousness in today's global and interconnected world increasingly spans multiple borders and social contexts (cf. Appadurai 1996); this book has shown that migrants' consciousness about their own social and racial positioning within this wider social field prompts them to act in certain ways.

A central claim of this book has been to show that the intersection of multiple racial and politicoeconomic hierarchies that are characteristic of global migration and circulation processes under late capitalism work to structure migrants' mobile practices. The migration process itself prompts nonelite Andean migrants to engage in various performances of self in which they strive to communicate to others—elite Peruvians, *paisanos* back in the home region, immigration officers, Americans, and other Latin American migrants—an image of what and who they are and how they wish to be seen. These communicative and embodied practices, as shown over various chapters, occur across the many social arenas that traverse transnational migration, circulation, and exchange, and the representations produced through them are always partial. The ID documents that enable international travel are only partial because although they are legal documents, they are not necessarily those of the bearer. Similarly, the letters and phone calls that are exchanged within transnational families are forms of communication that produce and affirm social relations but they often hide the full truth about a person or an event in order to protect other peoples' or one's own feelings. The videos "edit out" aspects of an event to create a representation that the producer is comfortable circulating across borders. Likewise, public events such as the Peruvian Parade in Paterson also seek to produce an image, here of "Peruvianness," which embraces some people as representatives of Peruvians abroad but excludes others, thus resulting in a partial representation of the community to a wider public. And finally, formal politics based on the prototypical citizen figure are not wholly inclusive either, as discussed in the last chapter, leaving Andean migrants to make other kinds of incursions into the political sphere when not formally represented.

The book has demonstrated that over the course of the migration process and through these various kinds of communicative and performative practices migrants become highly self-conscious about their own social positioning within various national and global, social and racial orders and learn to translate themselves between these contexts. This is a reflexivity that many theorists consider a central characteristic of modernity (cf. Bauman 1991). Across the many arenas of mediated communications, circulations, exchange, and face-to-face encounters migrants respond constantly and imperatively at the most basic level of bodily performance to enact the partial representations required to maintain their claims to "legitimate mobility" afloat. And they have good reasons to do so, since "not translating"—or not translating convincingly—can have detrimental consequences for their projects of migration and mobility. Thus they learn to stylize their bodies and move them with ease through a variety of social spaces and over time they acquire the transnational habitus and cosmopolitan competencies that enable them to challenge and circumvent key barriers to social class mobility in Peru. Along with the money earned abroad, when returning to Peru or circulating images of themselves transnationally, these migrants strive to reposition themselves in other, nonmonetary ways, "wearing" their social capital, so to speak, to appear more urban, more cosmopolitan, and therefore less obviously discernable as bearers of a rural or periurban past.

Contemporary global migration and mobility depend on a variety of structures, institutions, technologies, and cultural forms to make circulation possible. The migration processes described in this book have largely coincided with the explosion of new mobile media and communication technologies worldwide which shape how migrants fashion themselves from abroad vis-à-vis family and kinsmen back home and how they produce social relations across borders. A variety of media have become the primary means for the circulation of representations and symbolic forms across time and space and are crucial to the constitution of subjectivities, collectivities, and histories in the contemporary world. For example, the complex webs of circulation and the processes of mediation across multiple platforms and scales exemplify how transnational social relations are mediated by images, objects, practices, and, as in this case, by the expanding reach of Andean cultural forms. Visual and oral forms of communication, I have argued, not only extend but indeed complicate and in their own way expose the inherent tensions and ambiguities of the migrant and the transnational condition of Andean Peruvians. The significance of these dynamics extends well beyond the Andean case and establishes the crucial importance of communicative practices in transnational life more generally. It also demonstrates how the difficulties of maintaining meaningful transnational lives are embedded in the form and process of communication between migrants, their families, their communities, and the state.

The focus on migration and mobility as occurring in a larger context of global circulation has allowed me to critically reassess the contexts which are typically considered in the transnational migration literature as the most relevant; namely, that of the sending and the receiving nation-states. For example, whereas the scientific field of immigration studies in the United States has tended to place the United States as the one unequivocal center, and as the site that dispenses "value" or meaning to the migration journey and process, the transnational approach includes the home country as an important context as well, but still focuses too much on the "national" in the trans*national*. Yet both views are necessarily incomplete because, as I have argued in this book, migrants' actions in the context of the migration process overall derive meaning from multiple social and historical contexts, some of which are located outside the United States, in countries with dense histories of colonial, imperial, and transnational entanglements that complicate assumptions of a unidirectional processes of assimilation, acculturation, and integration that are supposed to make these newcomers into new Americans or into "Latinos." Furthermore, it questions the existence of membership in a national group to begin with. By recentering the analytical gaze not just at the "sending" or the "receiving" end of the migration stream, but instead at the "structured circulation" and at the mediation of migration itself, I have attempted to show that mobility and the values that are imprinted in it at different historical moments and intersections are constitutive of how individuals both accommodate themselves and are accommodated by others as they cross boundaries and social worlds.

I have also striven to continuously highlight the perseverance of race, ethnic, and class hierarchies that derive from colonial and imperial histories and processes and shaped rural-to-urban migration in Peru and now the global movement of Andean Peruvians across national borders, including their life projects abroad. While racial formations and racialization processes in both the home and destination countries can be said to shape all Latin American migrations in critical ways, particularly those that are U.S.-bound, they are especially important to consider in the case of rural, indigenous, and working-class transnational migration because they continue to shape these migrants' reimagining of themselves and their communities from abroad. Thomas and Clarke (2013:307) have recently argued that unlike earlier models of liberal democracy and the vestiges of racial hierarchy and social order that characterized them, new forms of social democracy and rights claims across the globe have made race less explicit (and less central) than other determinants of citizenship tied to labor, mobility, and geographies of national birth. Yet this does not mean that these older hierarchies have disappeared, even if they are not articulated in the explicit language of race.

The Peruvian case exemplifies the complicated relationship between race and global formations today that Thomas and Clarke call upon scholars to consider. This volume illuminates how older colonial racialization models still dominant in Peru today have been reinvigorated by contemporary geographies of migration, citizenship, and new patterns of regulation and immigration governance. By focusing on the experiences and embodied practices of rural and indigenous migrant populations who try to reinvent themselves and their communities through migration, this book has highlighted how centuries-old racial formations in Peru and the subject positions that are produced through migration and transnational practices intersect in significant ways—even when the language of race is not explicitly mobilized. Indeed, the entrance of working-class racialized Peruvians into a global labor market and migration stream has fostered an aspirational class mobility among them. They associate "middle-classness" with material capital, global mobility, and cosmopolitanism. Their strivings are essentially an attempt to wipe off the stigmatizing racialization associated with the rural and what Andean scholars generally have referred to as the "Indian social condition" (De la Cadena 2000; Weismantel 2001). This aspiration prompts Andean Peruvians in the exterior to "become Peruvian" in ways that they could not be prior to migration because of entrenched racism and enduring class bias. Migrants' desire for transnational mobility, as this book has demonstrated, must therefore be seen in relation to—and in active rejection of—the long-lived and pervasive trope of the indio and the urban cholo as the invader of elite social spaces and urban life in Latin America—and now also of foreign destinations previously reserved for traveling elites.

Andean Peruvians' transnational migration practices are therefore much more than just an economic project (even when need in most cases does play a significant role). They also reflect the deep-seated desire for social ascendance, political inclusion, and human dignity. The practices that emerge from the impetus to act upon these desires—sometimes against all odds—are not just performative; they are also generative of new social structures. Within this larger global context of mobility and circulation, old racial and social orders get challenged and redefined, calling for a more dynamic perspective on race and racialization processes in contexts of transnational migration research, because mobility itself—as this book has shown—is constitutive of how individuals both accommodate themselves and are accommodated by others as they cross both borders and boundaries and move between social worlds. For example, when Andean migrants of provincial and rural origin return from abroad to assert their purchasing power and rights to transit in the malls of Lima, like Paulino above, or when they demand inclusion as members of the political community, they also importantly—in Sherry Ortner's words (2006)—"produce the world." Ethnography—and ambulant ethnography in particular—is uniquely suited to study the ways that mobile populations produce the world.

Ambulant Ethnography and the Production of Mobility

The challenge for many anthropologists who study transnational and global migration is how to maintain a sense of fluidity and process from the ground up while also acknowledging the heightened role of nation-states and other regimes of power in ordering and categorizing populations by imposing new forms of governance and control which in turn shape and condition migrants' everyday experiences of mobility. This book has explicitly sought to address this challenge by exposing the productive tension between the lives of Andean migrants, who through the circulation of images, objects, and mediated embodied performances participate in the production of their own mobility, with accounts of the relevant structures, institutions, and technologies that shape and constrain their efforts.

The lives of the transnational migrants studied in this book unfold between rural communities in the Andes, various Peruvian and U.S. cities, and the transit spaces in between, offering the ethnographer an opportunity to notice and follow up on relevant contexts as they emerge in an organic manner rather than making assumptions about the importance or hierarchy of contexts. This includes remaining highly attentive to the assumed homogeneousness of national origin groups often implied in migration studies that take this unit of analysis for granted without seriously scrutinizing nation-state claims to impartiality and representation. This case study shows that there is nothing inherently homogeneous about national categories to begin with—whether "Peruvians," "the Peruvian community abroad," or "Peruvians in the United States"—because people inhabit these categories in radically dissimilar ways and meanings get transformed through mobility. Yet unlike proponents of the transnational approach who criticize other scholars for "methodological nationalism" (Wimmer and Glick Schiller 2002) because they retain a claim on the centrality of the state, I side on this particular point with governmentality scholars who focus not so much on the power of the nation-state *per se* as on the limits of its claims to coherence, impartiality, and legibility (cf. Berg and Tamagno 2013). As we have seen, when migrants turn to the migration industry and its travel experts, their actions reveal the limits of state claims and show how competing forms of legal and political authority, moral reasoning, and concepts of il/legality come into play.

As a form of ethnography that is particularly attentive to mobility as constitutive of persons and communities, ambulant ethnography illustrates what ethnography can bring to migration studies more generally. Social scientists often emphasize migration as a regular and predictable process in which the routes to a destination, the processes that stimulate and motivate migration, and the outcomes that follow when migrants arrive at their destinations can be straightforwardly assessed and understood. As a counterpoint to such views, this book has focused instead on the variable and often surprising pathways of "mediated migrations," and has emphasized the importance of circulation in studies of contemporary migration practices. The longitudinal scope and the spatial reach of this project have allowed me to follow migrants' departure, their time abroad, and importantly, their eventual though seldom permanent returns. In all these contexts I approach ethnographically how mobility is configured at the intersection of multiple places, structures, and histories while also continuing to "loop back" on life in the communities of Peru from where these migrants come, to where they continue to claim membership and belonging, and to where they sometimes although rarely definitively return.

Mobility studies have become an increasingly important field in their own right in recent years with a rapidly expanding scholarship attached to it. By highlighting the importance of mobility, I am not advocating that we adopt what Tim Cresswell (2006) and others critically identify as a "nomadic metaphysics," that is, a metaphysics that has mobility as its center and privileges it over place and attachment, but often in the process ends up naturalizing mobility as unproblematic and given. While I have shown that mobility indeed *is* intrinsic to Andean modernity and to migrant subjectivities, I have also shown that it must be approached as embodied practice and experience and how it is mediated by race, class, and other forms of differentiation produced by larger colonial, imperial, and global projects which historically have drawn the lines between rightful and insurgent mobility. This is still evident today in the way Peruvian state officials, glamorize the mobility and achievements of some Peruvians abroad in El Quinto Suyo and cast it as a virtue whereas the mobility of others is seen as problematic and flawed.

This latter point applies beyond the U.S.-Peruvian divide to a global context in which the hypermobility of global elites whose mobility is a precondition for and an asset to their "higher end" cosmopolitan subjectivities, whereas for the majority of the world's labor migrants—the Domitilas and Amparos of Asia, Africa, and the rest of Latin America—it remains a liability. Nonetheless, from their various latitudes and vantage points, these migrants continue to pursue new ways of reimagining their communities and themselves as they struggle to *salir adelante* in foreign lands. It is the task of the ambulant ethnographer to follow these migrants around and to situate their agency—through ongoing processes of ethnographic contextualization—in the multiple spatial and temporal contexts in which they move, dwell, and perform their mobility. Not all these spatial and temporal contexts involve the crossing of national borders, but all are firmly situated in the larger framework of political and racial economies.

NOTES

INTRODUCTION

1 The Spanish word *miércoles*, literally meaning Wednesday, is a common minced-oath substitute (or euphemism) for *mierda* (shit).

2 See Cresswell (2006) for a discussion of the representations of mobility over the last several centuries in the Western world.

3 Travel licenses to Spain became increasingly difficult to obtain in the late eighteenth century for Peruvian-born *españoles criollos*, including Simon Bolivar, whose frustrations over the loss of his privileges were channeled into several decades of insurgency against the colonial regime, which led to Peru's independence from Spain in 1821 (Abercrombie 1996:89).

4 Scholars typically define neoliberalism not just as a prescription for economic reform, but as a political ideology that posits the supremacy of the market over the state in regulating nearly all domains of social life, making it increasingly hegemonic globally. As a discipline or regime of the self, neoliberalism advocates personal responsibility, entrepreneurial agency, and dependence on family and self-help over social welfare and, above all, it emphasizes contractual relations in the marketplace (Harvey 2007).

5 In 2011, the United States accounted for 31.5 percent of all Peruvian emigrants. The rest are distributed in the following main destinations: Spain (16.0%), Argentina (14.3%), Italy (10.1%), Chile (8.8%), Japan (4.1%), Venezuela (3. 8%) and other countries (11.4%) (IOM 2012).

6 Other participants in this early debate included anthropologists and sociologists like Grasmuck and Pessar (1991); Rouse (1991); Mahler (1995); Kearney (1995); Portes *et al* (1999); Smith and Guarnizo (1998); and Vertovec (1999), among others.

7 The conversations about how immigrants become (or don't become) Americans continue to be debated in sociology even as most U.S. immigration scholarship now recognizes that more and more aspects of migrants' lives take place across borders. New assimilation theory, for example, argues that most migrants over time will achieve socioeconomic parity with their native-born counterparts but that ethnicity and race do matter in this process (Alba and Nee 2005). Segmented assimilation theory, in turn, holds that migrants may take different routes to incorporation, which include 1) becoming part of the (white) mainstream, 2) remaining ethnic, or 3) becoming part of the underclass and experiencing

downward mobility (Portes and Zhou 1993). These trajectories depend on the context of departure in the country of origin, on particular immigrant characteristics, networks, and ethnic enclaves, and on the social, political, and economic situation in the receiving context. See Waters and Jimenez (2005); and Levitt and Jaworsky (2007) for two comprehensive reviews of the immigration and transnationalism literature.

8 Political scientists, on the other hand, criticized the transnational approach for not sufficiently emphasizing the real power of the state to constrain people's lives. See Waldinger and Fitzgerald (2004) for such a critique.

9 For Mauss habitus was central to what makes humans into selves. In his essay, *Techniques of the Body* ([1934] 1992), Mauss used the concept of habitus to refer to the customary habits that are anchored in the body and in the daily practices of individuals and societies.

10 Ortner's entire body of work has focused on advancing practice theory in these directions. Within sociology, Crossley (2001) offers a similar, sympathetic critique of Bourdieu, which is intended to strengthen the concept of habitus by turning to the phenomenological literature (most centrally Maurice Merleau-Ponty and, to a lesser degree, Edmund Husserl).

11 The historiographical record is full of examples of how the Indian population attempted to escape the social status they were accorded by colonial administrators (Glave 1989; Larson 2005; Saignes 1995).

12 Indigenous Amazonians and Afro-Peruvians were largely absent in these turn-of-the-century discussions of national integration because, in contrast to Andeans whose representation and occasional self-representation could at least hinge on the image of being the heirs of an Inca civilization, these populations were considered the very antithesis of cultural beings at the time (Greene 2007:445, see also De la Cadena 2000:21).

13 For a discussion of racialized affect, see Berg and Ramos-Zayas (forthcoming).

14 A number of anthropological studies have analyzed Andean Peruvians in cities, starting with Billie Jean Isbell's now classic monograph *To Defend Ourselves* (1978), which devoted the last chapter to migrants in the city. Other early works include Altamirano (1984, 1988); Gill (1994); Golte and Adams (1987); Matos Mar (2004); Paerregaard (1997); and Roberts (1974).

15 For recent general overviews of South American migration, see Oboler (2005a) and Falconi and Mazzotti (2007). For an in-depth study of Brazilian migration to New York City and Los Angeles, respectively, see Margolis (1994) and Beserra (2003). For studies on Colombian migration to New York City and Los Angeles, see Chaney (1976); Guarnizo and Diaz (1999); and Escobar (2004). Ecuadorian migration has received the most attention, with several book-length studies focusing on different migrant-sending regions in Ecuador and on different aspects of U.S.-bound migration, including networks and economic strategies (Kyle 2000), and gender and family (Miles 2004; Pribilsky 2007).

16 These 2011 numbers are based on the Census Bureau's American Community Survey, which is the largest household survey in the United States.

17 The U.S. Census (2010) only accounts for ca. 60 percent of the number reported by the Peruvian government.

18 Tamagno has also focused on the Mantaro Valley as a migrant-sending region, but focused on transnational migration between this region and Italy (Tamagno 2002a, 2002b, 2003).

19 Peruvians have settled in both traditional immigrant gateway cities as well as in small towns and intermediate cities across the United States. While the largest concentrations of Peruvians are still found in Florida (19%), New Jersey (14%), New York (12%), and California (16%), Peruvians are also increasingly migrating to new destinations away from these traditional locations; this mirrors a broader trend of geographic deconcentration of Latin American, and in particular Mexican migration (Pew Hispanic Center 2013). For an analysis of Mexican migration to new destinations, see Zúñiga and Hernández-León, ed. (2006). For an analysis of Latinos in the "Nuevo South," see Winders and Smith (2012). For a general analysis of the changing immigration landscape and case studies of other national origin migrations, see Massey (2008).

20 Passaic County, where Paterson is located, continued in 2010 to be the largest "Peruvian county" in New Jersey with 19,696 Peruvians, followed by Hudson County (13,533), and Union County (9,446) (Census 2010).

21 See Portes and Stepick (1993) on the transformation of Miami as a result of Latin American migration.

22 Recent statistics show that when averaged and compared to other Hispanics, Peruvians as a whole still have higher levels of formal education and higher average incomes than their Mexican and Central American counterparts. Along with Colombians, Peruvian poverty rates (13%) are slightly below the national poverty rate, which is currently at 16 percent for all groups, including whites (Pew Hispanic Center 2013).

23 Paerregaard has documented the existence of a similar early flow of female Andean working-class migrants from the areas of Ayacucho, Junín, and Ancash, who were brought to Miami in the 1970s by their Peruvian or American employers as domestic workers (2008:57–58).

24 These two phases basically mirror the similar highly gendered flows of Central American migrants to this area when the Central American wars escalated in Guatemala, El Salvador, and Nicaragua in the 1980s (Repak 1995).

25 Marcus suggests that multisited research should be "designed around chains, paths, threads, conjunctions, or juxtapositions of locations in which the ethnographer establishes some form of literal, physical presence; with an explicit, posited logic of association or connection among sites that in fact defines the argument of the ethnography" (1995:105).

26 The fact that participants in my study also had trajectories of internal migration prior to migrating transnationally and that some returned from abroad for

extended periods also makes a case against distinguishing completely between "internal" and "international" and "temporary" versus "permanent" migration (cf. King and Skeldon 2010).

27 This yearlong exchange program (1997–98) in Peru was part of my B.A. degree in anthropology at the University of Copenhagen.

28 I am using a pseudonym for the town's name to protect subject's confidentiality since many of the Urqumarquino migrants I worked with in the United States are still undocumented or only now in process of regularizing their immigration status.

29 "Peru's Roaring Economy: Hold on Tight," *Economist*, February 2, 2013.

CHAPTER 1. *SALIR ADELANTE*

1 Between 1980 and 2000 the violent conflict caused the death and disappearance of some 69,000 Peruvians and displaced more than a million people from their homes (CVR 2003). The Truth and Reconciliation Commission was established in 2001 after the fall of Fujimori to examine the atrocities committed on both sides of the conflict during the 1980s and 1990s.

2 *El Comercio*, May 29, 2004.

3 The Latin American Migration Project (LAMP) and its precursor, the Mexican Migration Project (MMP), is a large-scale data-gathering project established to survey both documented and undocumented migration to the United States from a variety of sending countries in Latin America and the Caribbean. The LAMP survey data from Peru was gathered in the department of Lima in November–December 2001 with another community added in 2005. For more information, see http://lamp.opr.princeton.edu/.

4 Massey and Capoferro (2006:124) have also shown that international migration became less selective after 1987 with respect to human capital (i.e., skills and knowledge). Instead, the likelihood of out-migration became closely related to social capital (i.e., migrant networks).

5 I adapt the term "bootstrap performativity" from Povinelli, who uses the term "bootstrap performative" to characterize the capacity of the oppressed to overcome overwhelming conditions of violence to assume the role of political agents (Povinelli, in Nouvet 2014).

6 This notion is similar to what scholars have referred to as the "sociocentric self," which implies a notion of self where individual interests are subordinated to the good of the collective (Shweder and Bourne 1984:190). The sociocentric self, Shweder and Bourne have argued, is different from the Western conception of self in which "society is imagined to have been created to serve the interests of some idealized autonomous, abstract individual existing free of society yet living in society" (1984:190). See Spiro 1993, for a discussion and critique of the simplified typology of the self and/or its cultural conception as consisting of only two "ideal types," a Western and a non-Western.

7 Aníbal Quijano, a prominent critic of modernity, notes that "although Latin America may have been, in fact, a latecomer to, and almost passive victim of, "modernization," it was, on the other hand, an active participant in the production of modernity" (1993:141).

8 For a comprehensive history of the Inca realm, see Rostworowski de Diez Canseco (1999).

9 All these categories were fiscal ones, but the obligations they entailed changed over time and across different localities. See Robinson (1990:11–12) for a discussion of the regional variation and shifting meanings not only of *forasteros* and other categories assigned to mobile subjects (e.g., *huidos, vagamundos, ausentes, vagabundos, forasteros, yanaconas, mitimaes, fugados, malentretenidos*), but also to subjects for whom place attachment, not mobility, was the principal characteristic of their assigned subject position (e.g., *residentes, originarios,* and *vecinos*).

10 The scholarly literature on seasonal migration in the context of capitalist expansion in agrarian societies in Latin America is extensive. For studies of *campesinos* and relations of production on highland haciendas in Peru, see Martínez Alier (1977); Matos Mar (1976); and Smith (1989). For a study of labor migration to the *selva* and *ceja de selva,* see Collins (1988). For studies of migration to sugar- and cotton-producing haciendas on the coast and the impact on sending communities, see Favre (1977); Klarén (1977); and Matos Mar (1977). For studies of resistance of the valley population to proletarianization as miners, see Bonilla (1974); Long and Roberts (1984); and Mallon (1983).

11 This modernization wave coincided with the first presidency of Agusto B. Leguía, who was twice president of Peru; first as the democratically elected president from 1908 to 1912, and later through a military coup in 1919. His second time in office lasted until his government was overthrown in 1930.

12 Between 1969 and 1979, the Agrarian Reform of 1969 expropriated 9.1 of the total 30 million hectares of available farmland not only from the *haciendas latifundistas* in the highlands, but also from the capitalist plantations on the coast (Matos Mar and Mejía 1980).

13 The environmental impacts of the mining industry have only become worse in the past decade. See "Mantaro River 'in critical condition': Mining residues are the main pollutants" [Río Mantaro 'en situación crítica': Residuos mineros con el principal agente contaminante], *El Comercio,* June 28, 2010.

14 The concept of affect has gained traction among anthropologists interested in emotion, feeling, and sentiments in the past decade. Unlike the psychologically individualistic conception of "emotion" or earlier anthropological conceptions of emotion as grounded, local, and "culturally specific," which were common in the 1970s and 1980s (see Lutz and White 1986 for an overview), the concept of affect allows for a perspective that considers "emotion" as relational and intersubjective, and as a mediator of social and political transformations in particular materialist and historical contexts (see Richard and Rudnyckyj 2009; and Berg and Ramos-Zayas, forthcoming, for such a perspective on affect and political economy).

15 Email correspondence with Inés, October 16, 2000.
16 Doña Rosa already had a multiple entry visa for ten years and could travel back and forth to the United States as she pleased.
17 For a discussion of child-motivated migration, see Pribilsky (2007). See also Leifsen and Tymczuk (2012) on transnational parenting.
18 For a general theory of racialization and racial formation in the United States, see Omi and Winant (1994). For studies of racialization of Latinos and Latin American migrants in the United States, see Chávez (2001, 2008); De Genova (2005); Inda (2006); and Ramos-Zayas (2003, 2012).

CHAPTER 2. PAPER FIXES

1 The U.S. embassy in Lima no longer requires supporting documents, and instead makes decisions largely based on the outcome of visa interviews. See Alpes (2011) for a discussion of how consular staff evaluates visa applicants in Cameroon.
2 Governmentality is a concept first developed by Michel Foucault, most clearly in his work *Security, Territory, Population* (2007), and refers to the various practices through which subjects are governed, including the way governments attempt to produce citizens aligned with its policies.
3 In rural Peru the practice of naming a child after the saint associated with the child's date of birth in the Catholic calendar (*almanaque*) was part of the norms and values imposed by Spanish colonialism, but it is still common today. These names are the ones migration brokers typically associate with "rural backwardness."
4 In the U.S. context, the term "undocumented" is the less derogatory, because it highlights people's inability to obtain proper legal documentation instead of imposing the status of criminals embedded in the terms "illegal" or "illegal alien." Spener (2009:xi) notes; however, that the term "undocumented" is technically also inaccurate, because many migrants possess various kinds of documents that allow them to work in the United States.
5 For an overview of the literature of human trafficking in North America, see Gozdziak and Collett (2005). For the full text of the "Protocol to Prevent, Suppress, and Punish Trafficking in Persons, Especially Women and Children," and "The Protocol against the Smuggling of Migrants by Land, Sea and Air," see http://www.unodc.org/unodc/en/treaties/CTOC/
6 In 2014, the fee was 39 Soles (ca. U.S. $14). Source: http://www.migraciones.gob.pe
7 For analysis and critique of the decentralization reforms, see Arce (2008); Gonzáles de Olarte (2002); and Tanaka (2002).
8 "A thrust at the heart of the Azángaro mafia. One of the masters of falsification was caught," *El Comercio*, 1 de Julio, 2005. This event is also mentioned in Sabogal and Núñez (2010).
9 Señora Pilar's promise of "guaranteed travel" seemed to be a frequent assurance that I heard from other migrants too. Similarly, Coutin reports that she found

several ads in the classified sections of Salvadoran newspapers advertising trips to the United States "with arrival guaranteed" (2005:204).

10 See, for example, headlines like "People smuggler falls in New York" (*Cae traficante de personas en Nueva York*), and "Gang trafficking with Peruvians in Chile is reported [to the police]" (*Denuncia a banda que traficaba con peruanos en Chile*).

11 For an overview of the literature of unaccompanied migrant children to the United States, see Chavez and Menjívar (2010). The migration of unaccompanied minors was also a frequent topic in the headlines of national newspapers: "Fall of mafia trafficking minors to the U.S." (*Cae mafia de tráfico de menores para EE.UU*) and "Peruano took children of illegals to the U.S." (*Peruano lleva hijos de ilegales a EE.UU*).

12 See http://lima.usembassy.gov/visas.html.

13 For a discussion of Peruvian migration to Japan, see Takenaka (1999). For a history of the immigration and racialization of Japanese in Peru, see Takenaka (2004).

14 "Three thousand false 'nikkei' Peruvians work irregularly in Japan" (*La Republica*, June 11, 1991). "False 'Nikkei' undergo surgery to emigrate to Japan" (*La Republica*, June 13, 1991).

15 Peruvians have also migrated to other parts of Asia. Erica Vogel (2011) has examined how Peruvians arrived in Korea in the early 1990s on their way to other destinations including Japan, but ended up staying after finding factory work in Korea. A few of these Peruvians were given visas in the early 2000s, but were later stripped of them and excluded entirely from Korea's 2004 guest worker program.

16 In recent years, a major marketing campaign titled the Peru Brand (Marca Peru) has attempted to change the images of Peru that circulated internationally in previous decades by promoting tourism, gastronomy, and intangible heritage as a national brand (See Canepa Koch 2013 for a discussion of Marca Peru).

17 My own experiences with U.S. consulates confirm the experiences of alienation reported to me by participants in my study despite the fact that my status—first as a graduate student and later as a professor at a well-known U.S. research university—and my intentions were never questioned to the same extent as those of my Peruvian friends and informants.

18 Arguing against Augé's notion of airports as "placeless," Sheller and Urry suggest that airports are indeed "places of material organization and considerable social complexity" (2006:219). They cite, for example, the technological infrastructure and the workers who enable essential airport operations as part of the specific and contingent materiality of airports.

19 See http://travel.state.gov/visa/laws/telegrams/telegrams_1403.html for the complete text of "The Enhanced Border Security and Visa Entry Reform Act of 2002."

20 See http://lima.usembassy.gov/niv/interview.html [Accessed on October 20, 2014].

CHAPTER 3. REMOTE SENSING

1 Chile and Argentina emerged as common destinations in the first half of the 1990s. Paerregaard (2005) has characterized migration from Peru to these Southern Cone countries as "discount migration," to indicate that these less expensive destinations that could be reached by ground transportation were considered by lower-class Peruvians only when other destinations were ruled out. For studies of gendered migration of Peruvian domestic workers to Chile, see Maher and Staab (2005); and Núñez and Holper (2005).

2 For studies focusing on Latin America, see Boehm (2012); Dreby (2010); Hondagneu-Sotelo and Avila (1997); Leinaweaver (2010); Merla (2013). For studies focusing on Asia, mostly the Philippines, see Asis (2008); Fresnoza-Flot (2009, 2013); Isaksen et al. (2008); McKay (2007); Parreñas (2005a); Madianou (2012); Madianou and Miller (2012). For studies focusing on Africa, see Coe (2011); Vidal (2011).

3 The work on transnational parenting has recently expanded beyond mother-child relationships to include the multidirectional exchanges across generations and between genders within the context of transnational families (Baldassar and Merla 2013). This includes greater consideration of "transnational fatherhood" (Pribilsky 2007; Dreby 2010) and of the experience of children (Abrego 2014; Parreñas 2005a, 2005b; Dreby 2010; Boehm 2012; Coe et al. 2011; Leinaweaver 2010).

4 While the data from the Latin American Migration Project (LAMP) overall corroborate the feminization of migration, Durand (2010:17) notes that male emigration continues to be slightly more significant (at 55%) in the Peruvian data.

5 For a different strain of the literature on technology and transnational socialities, which focus on the use of Information and Communication Technologies (ICTs) in the production of diasporic identities and online or virtual social relations, see Bernal 2006; Burrell and Anderson 2008; Collins 2009; Greschke 2010; Wilding 2012.

6 There is an extensive classical literature on kinship and sociality in the Andes, which use formal categories to designate different types of kin relations (see Bolton and Mayer 1977; Ossio Acuña 1992; Smith 1984). These formal studies of kinship have now largely been replaced in favor of notions of kinship as fluid and flexible processes of relatedness (Leinaweaver 2008; Van Vleet 2008; Weismantel 1995; see also Carsten 2000).

7 These affordances include interactivity, reach and visibility, searchability of content, mediated copresence, and materiality, among other qualities (Madianou and Miller 2012:122).

8 See Siems (1992) for a compilation and a brief analysis of letters between undocumented Mexican and Central American immigrants in the United States and their loved ones back home. See also Mahler (2001).

9 Visual communication will be discussed in the next chapter and is therefore largely excluded from the discussion in this chapter.

10 When I did my longer stint of fieldwork in Peru in 2004–05, only 15 out of 100 Peruvians had mobile phones (ITU 2005). Now the rate of mobile cellular subscriptions has reached 100 percent (ITU 2011). Of course, this overall number doesn't account for the fact that some people have two or more mobile phones— one for work and one for private use—while others have none. The ITU core indicators on access to and use of ICTs by households and individuals report that 41.2 percent of all Peruvians have and use a mobile phone. This statistic is based on the latest data available for Peru, which is from 2008 (ITU 2011).

11 There is a growing interdisciplinary literature on cell phones in the reproduction of transnational families (see Horst 2006; Horst and Miller 2006; Wilding 2006; Cabanes and Acedera 2012) and on its use in transnational labor struggles (Barber 2008; Thompson 2009; De Tona and Whelan 2009).

12 In 2007, more than 75 percent of total cell phone subscriptions in Peru were prepaid (Castells et al. 2007:63).

13 During the time of my fieldwork, Osiptel declared that there were 833,209 Internet subscribers in Peru, of which 473,188 were residential; 325,887 were business, only 449 were government offices or educational institutions, and 33,365 were *cabinas públicas*. Of these *cabinas públicas*, 40 percent were located in Lima and the rest (around 18,000) in the provinces (Diaz-Albertini 2006:3). By 2010, the total number of Internet subscribers in Peru had grown to 924,511 (ITU 2011).

14 Migrants in my study mostly refrained from using videoconferences because of their higher cost (cf. Benítez 2006; see also "Abroad at Home," *New York Times*, January 6, 2007). Instead they used Skype and other programs.

15 For elaborations on this Andean kinship ideal, see Leinaweaver (2008); and Van Vleet (2008).

16 Hochschild (1979) sees "feeling rules" as the side of ideology that deals with emotion and feeling. Emotion management, in turn, is the type of work it takes to cope with feeling rules.

17 I rely here on Nelly's narration of the interactions between her and her daughters during their time of separation. Ochs and Capps have shown that narratives provide participants with important resources for socializing emotions, attitudes, and moral stances, for developing interpersonal relationships, and for constituting (or limiting) membership in specific collectivities (Capps and Ochs 1996; Ochs and Capps 2001). Attention to the narrative dimension of transnational communicative practices also illuminates what participants consider reportable in transnational social space and what is better kept to oneself and embargoed from transnational circulation.

18 Studies of language acquisition and language socialization have looked at the acquisition of appropriate emotional responses in children (see Schieffelin 1990; Kulick 1992).

19 Rosaldo coined the term "embodied thought" to challenge the much assumed duality of body and mind (1984:143).

CHAPTER 4. UNFORTUNATE VISIBILITIES

1 See Purnima Mankekar (1999) for a methodological discussion of shared viewing with research subjects.

2 In this chapter, I draw primarily on scholarship about the ways in which media gets produced, circulated, consumed, appropriated, and reinscribed by diverse populations (Ginsburg et al. 2002; Askew and Wilk 2002; Himpele 2008). For studies of videos in the self-making strategies of communities, see Ginsburg 1991; Hammond 1988; Himpele 2002; Kolar-Panov 1996, 1997; and Schein 2002.

3 See Sturken and Cartwright (2001:356) for a definition of genre.

4 According to Poole, a "visual economy" visual economy' involves at least three levels of organization: 1) an organization of production encompassing both the image-makers and the technologies (lithography, engravings, photography, paintings); 2) the circulation of image-objects through which images constitute a social reality of their own, and finally, 3) the cultural and discursive systems through which graphic images are appraised, interpreted, and assigned historical, scientific, and aesthetic worth (1997:11).

5 The indexicality of an image means that this image bears a trace of the real. Peirce distinguishes between different kinds of signs and their relationship to the real: the iconic, the indexical, and the symbolic sign. Iconic signs bear a resemblance to their object, whereas symbolic signs bear no direct or obvious relationship to their object. Indexical signs point to an existential relationship between the signifier and the signified, both being seen as having coexisted at some point in time (Sturken and Cartwright 2001:140).

6 I also tracked the circulation of photographs and other still image-objects and used photo-elicitation as part of my research.

7 Long braided hair is an important marker of indigeneity in the Andes and cutting one's braids is associated with shedding a visible sign of indigeneity and rural identity in favor of a more "urban" look.

8 More immediate problems and issues regarding, for example, the distribution of remittances or coordination about *encomiendas* are hardly ever discussed in the video letters. These matters are handled over the phone via cheap satellite phone cards purchased in the United States, which around the time of my fieldwork allowed for between one and two hours of conversation between the United States and Peru for U.S. $5.

9 See Salazar Parreñas (2005a, 2005b); Dreby (2010); Boehm (2012); Coe et al. (2011); and Leinaweaver (2010) for discussions that focus on the children of global migration, including their emotional responses to the migration of their parents and the bonds they forge with the caregivers who provide substitute parenting while their parents are working abroad.

10 The festive structure of patron saint festivals usually consists of three major events: 1) the *vispera* or *entrada principal* when the dance troupes or *comparsas* make their entries and dance in front of the religious image; 2) the main day (*día*

central) which includes the mass and the procession, and 3) the third day when the *cargos* are passed on to next year's fiesta sponsor called *alférez, prioste,* or *mayordomo* (Cánepa Koch 2001a:227; Mendoza 2000). While many village fiestas are longer than three days, these key moments are included in some form in virtually all patron saint fiestas all over the Andes. In Urcumarca, the fiesta is celebrated during five days starting with the *víspera* on September 14 and culminating on September 18 when the cargos are passed on to next year's *alféreces*. September 15 is the central day (*día central*) when the Virgin of the Nativity is taken out in procession on the central square of Urcumarca.

11 Mauss ([1925] 1967) wanted to present the gift cycle as a theoretical counterpart to Adam Smith's "invisible hand," that is, the term economists use to describe the self-regulating nature of the marketplace and the utilitarian and self-interested dispositions of the so-called *homo economicus*.

12 In *Inalienable Possessions* (1992), Weiner provides a groundbreaking analysis of exchange, which goes far beyond both the functional and structural theory of reciprocity that anthropologists since Malinowski had understood as the basis for social relations in so-called "primitive societies." Reciprocity, Weiner argues, is only the superficial aspect of exchange which involves much more complicated social actions than what the idea of a gift reciprocated with a countergift could account for. She investigates the possessions which must not be given, which, if circulated, must return to the giver.

13 The name of the organization has been modified to protect subjects' confidentiality.

14 While the majority of current members, if not all, are from the district of Urcumarca, the founding members originally envisioned that this organization would grow and eventually encompass migrants from all 33 districts of the Province of Jauja, constituting a kind of umbrella organization of district clubs which would be the sister (and rival) organization to Club Huancayo—the oldest club in D.C. founded by migrants from the city of Huancayo. However, Club Urcumarca never managed to integrate migrants from areas other than the district of Urcumarca itself and remained a very "local" organization based primarily on identification with one neighborhood within the district of Urcumarca. Among the goals listed in their mission statement is to work for "the prosperity and progress of the district of Urcumarca." The club organizes social events for the Urcumarquino collectivity in Maryland, most notably a yearly carnival celebration featuring the traditional *corta monte* dance. At these events U.S.-based migrants raise funds to support small-scale development and civic projects back in Urcumarca.

15 There is an extensive literature in Spanish on popular festivals in Peru—and in the Mantaro Valley in particular. For studies of the fiesta system in the valley and the music and dances that form part of it, see Arguedas (1953); Berg (2001); Cánepa Koch (1998, 2001); Millones and Millones (2003); Ráez Retamozo (2001); Romero (2004); and Vilcapoma (1995), among others.

16 See, for example, Buechler (1980); Guillet and Whiteford (1974); Paerregaard (1997); Roberts (1974).

17 The filmmakers are currently preparing a sequel to this film titled "Transnational Fiesta: Twenty Years Later," which documents the changes to this transnational community over the past twenty years. The film is scheduled for release in 2015.

18 In 2004, El Yanamarquino charged the mayordomo 375 soles (around U.S. $120) to record the four days of the fiesta, including the víspera event.

19 Migrants now request these videos on DVD or as digital files, but in 2004 some local videographers still shot in nondigital formats.

20 While more migrant women have been fiesta sponsors in recent years, traditionally it is the male head of the household who is the primary fiesta sponsor.

21 See Romero (2001) for an explanation of *banda* and *orquesta típica*.

22 The encoding/decoding model of communication was developed by Stuart Hall in 1973. This widely circulated and debated model challenged dominant notions of media messages as static and unchanging through the communication process and of audiences as passive and disempowered. Hall's model implies an agentive view of audience members who are understood to play an active role in "decoding" and in fact in systematically distorting the encoded media messages on the basis of their personal experiences, cultural background, and social contexts from where they interpret such messages (see Hall 1980).

23 Photographs work in much the same way. For a methodological discussion of photo elicitation in anthropological fieldwork, see Bunster (1977), and in social science research more broadly, see Harper (2002).

24 Anthropology has a long-standing interest in the role of gossip as an effective mode of social control in what was perceived as stable, bounded, morally homogeneous, and close-knit societies. For a discussion of anthropological works on gossip, see Engle Merry (1997).

25 Image-and video-based platforms such as Skype also generated the "truth effect" in terms of people claiming to see how the relatives "really" are feeling (Baldassar 2007; Madianou and Miller 2012); however, these technologies still offer the person an opportunity to respond should accusations arise.

26 Anthropologists working with image-making technologies as an integral part of fieldwork often tend to offer up our services as photographers or videographers at community events as a way of giving back. See Poole (1997) on being a "community photographer" in Peru, and Jackson (2004) on the experience of videotaping local events during fieldwork in Harlem.

CHAPTER 5. ENFRAMING PERUVIANNESS

1 I first attended the Peruvian Parade in Paterson in 2002 and have returned many times since. I am drawing on my notes from several different years for this chapter. Whenever appropriate the year has been provided.

2 See also Williams (1977) on performance as a mode of social production.

3 For this particular point, I draw on Judith Butler who from a feminist and poststructuralist standpoint insisted that particular categories, in her case that of women, "produces what it claims to represent" (Butler 1992). See also Beltrán (2010) for a similar analysis of the category of Latino.

4 Durkheim (1965) saw collective representations as arising from ritual enactment in sacred time and essentially through which society becomes aware of itself. The Durkheimian tradition continued to influence ritual studies long after Levi-Straussianism had gone out of fashion. Bellah (2005:185) suggests that its appeal lies in the fact that this approach gives primacy to social and ritual enactment where a ritual cannot be reduced to the symbols that derive from it.

5 See also Gonzalez (2014) for an analysis of the role of the immigrant marches of 2006 in producing this political consciousness.

6 Peruvian migrants in Paterson also mobilize politically in other spaces, including in political parties, labor unions, and non–nationality based grassroots movements focusing on local or single-issue agendas such as schools or the environment.

7 The proliferating regional diversity within the Peruvian community in Paterson is reflected in the many Peruvian associations based on affiliations with places outside Lima. See Altamirano (2000) and Ávila Molero (2003) for an overview and discussion of these organizations. The proliferating socioeconomic diversity is reflected in a greater number of Peruvians who seek aid of various kinds from community organizations, as one pro bono lawyer told me. She herself worked to orient recently arrived Latin American migrants without status, including Peruvians, about their options.

8 Paterson is the third largest city in New Jersey with a total population of 146,199 (Census 2010). It is also the county seat of Passaic County, which is made up of 16 municipalities and a total population of 501,226 (U.S. Census 2010).

9 In her ethnographic study of Newark, Ramos-Zayas (2012) has argued that casting these values as "immigrant values," often in the form of exaggerated praise for hardworking and morally decent immigrants, simultaneously casts and disciplines native-born, racialized groups, including Puerto Ricans, as "delinquent citizens" (Ramos-Zayas 2012:86).

10 "Politicians in step with local parades," *Record*, December 14, 2004.

11 Beltrán (2010) argues that prevailing views of Latinos both as a monolithic voting block and as politically passive—hence "the sleeping giant" metaphor—are problematic because they assume a unity that is not necessarily there. The central contention of her book, very pertinently titled *The Trouble with Unity*, is that "there is no sleeping giant—only political subjects whose variegated actions and intentions are obscured by this limited vision of Latino empowerment" (2010:9).

12 "Spanish food" in the U.S. urban context refers not to a Mediterranean diet, but to the staple foods that Latin American and Caribbean migrants have brought with them to the United States.

13 See Abercrombie (2003) for an analysis of the postcolonial predicaments and the national imaginary at play in the Carnival de Oruro.

14 *Música Criolla* is the overall term for a series of genres associated with the mixture between the musical culture of the Europeans and the enslaved Africans they brought to Peru. Some of the most famous genres include *el vals peruano, la marinera limeña,* and *festejo,* the latter also grouped under the label *música afroperuana.* See Tucker (2013:36–37).

15 See Arlene Dávila (2001) for a discussion of the packaging of Latino culture for a mainstream U.S. audience.

16 *Record,* June 13, 2011. Usually, the Peruvian Parade starts in Passaic, moves through the city of Clifton, and ends in Paterson in front of the City Hall.

17 "Ethnic parades in Paterson likely to be victims of city budget stress," *Record,* June 13, 2011.

CHAPTER 6. PHANTOM CITIZENS IN EL QUINTO SUYO

1 The material in this chapter draws on and updates research that appeared in Berg (2008).

2 Local newspaper headings highlighted this aspect of Andean savagery: "Andean justice in Urcumarca-Jauja: Two thieves burned alive!" (*El Correo,* March 31, 1999) and "When they agonized, they were burned to death" (*El Correo,* April 1, 1999). The real name of the town of Urcumarca as well as all its identifying markers have been changed in all newspaper reports of the *linchamiento.*

3 In a polemical essay, Orin Starn (1991) fiercely attacked the tendency in Andeanist anthropology to overemphasize the continuity between prehispanic and post-conquest cultural, cosmological, social, and political systems. This work, he argues, resulted from a rigid application of a structuralist framework without an eye to social change and transformation, which led researchers to miss the seemingly more modern elements of Andean societies, including migration and poverty that incited desires for political change. This focus, Starn reasoned, had caused anthropologists working in the area to "miss the revolution." For a response, see Mayer (1991). See also Nugent (1994).

4 *El Correo,* Huancayo, March 31, 1999.

5 The particular cases of Canipaco and Alto Cunas (highlands of Chupaca) have been documented by Manrique (1998).

6 In September 1992, the central intelligence bureau SIN prepared a list of alleged Shining Path sympathizers abroad, which was turned over to prosecutors in Peru. This list was quickly dubbed the "Shining Path Ambassadors List" and had devastating consequences for Peruvians living overseas. While several of the 67 names on the list were connected to the Shining Path, many were opponents of the insurgents who had also voiced their criticism of the Fujimori government's human rights abuses (see Kirk and Manuel 1993:4).

7 Founded by Víctor Raúl Haya de la Torre in 1924, the Alianza Popular Revolucionaria Americana (American Popular Revolutionary Alliance—APRA)

is Peru's oldest and best institutionalized party. It is also the only political party that has well-organized political cells abroad.

8 The crises to which Alberto Sánchez is referring here are the period of reconstruction after the War of the Pacific (1879–84), in which Peru and Bolivia were defeated by Chile; the impact on Peru of the world crisis of 1929 and the brutal political repression of members of the APRA Party in the early 1930s (Contreras and Cueto 1999: 207); the military coup of the leftist general Velasco Alvarado in 1968; and finally, the civil war of the 1980s and early 1990s between the Maoist guerilla Sendero Luminoso and the Peruvian state.

9 Alberto Sánchez, who was three times rector of the Universidad Nacional Mayor de San Marcos, an accomplished Aprista politician, and prime minister for a short period in 1989, had himself lived in political exile in Chile, Panama, Colombia, and Mexico for a number of years.

10 The fluctuation between seeing emigrant or diasporic citizens as either threat or promise has been documented for other "emigrant" (Coutin 2007) and "diasporic" (Axel 2001) populations across the world and may be seen as intrinsic to the production of state and national boundaries.

11 While remittances to all of Latin America and the Caribbean fell dramatically at the onset of the global financial crisis, since 2008 they have bounced back (MPI 2010). The 2012 figures for the Andean countries were U.S. $2.451 billion for Ecuador, U.S. $1.094 billion for Bolivia, and U.S. $4.073 billion for Colombia (IDB 2012). For the Andean countries that receive a significant proportion of their remittances from migrants working in Spain, a slowdown in the growth rate of remittances has been observed even as the remittance flow from the United States to Latin America has stabilized (IDB 2012; MPI 2010).

12 This number represents an increase from the close to 450,000 registered voters abroad in the 2006 elections (*El Comercio*, January 3, 2007)

13 Failure to vote in national elections is sanctioned with a U.S. $35 fine, which is enforced upon reentry to Peru.

14 See http://www.youtube.com/watch?v=lmcxgvb1YAU.

15 Peruvian citizenship laws are based upon the Constitution of Peru dated October 31, 1993, and on Nationality Law No. 26574 from January 1996. Peru has recognized dual citizenship since the 1993 modification of the Peruvian constitution, which includes an article (Art. 53) stating that Peruvians by birth who adopt another nationality do not lose their Peruvian nationality unless they explicitly renounce it before a government authority. The United States also accepts, but does not encourage dual citizenship.

16 For an overview of this trend, which links discussion of transnational citizenship across the Americas to discussion about the citizenship effects of neoliberal globalization, see Berg and Rodriguez (2013).

17 "Toledo: Shoeshine boy turned economist," *BBC World News*, Sunday, April 8, 2001.

18 For a discussion of the various policy initiatives that were directed at migrants abroad, including the so-called Advisory Councils (Consejos de Consulta), the

Law on Return Migration in 2005, and the proposal to create an electoral district for Peruvians abroad, see Berg and Tamagno (2006); and Berg (2010).

19 For discussions of similar trends in other Latin American countries, see Fitzgerald (2009) on Mexico; Laguerre (1998) on Haiti; Coutin (2007) on El Salvador; Guarnizo (1994) on the Dominican Republic; and Levitt and de la Dehesa (2003) on Brazil.

20 *El Correo*, Huancayo, April 1, 1999, p. 3.

21 *El Correo*, Huancayo, April 1, 1999, p. 4.

22 It is beyond the scope of this chapter to go into a discussion of the long-term effects of such spectacular violence on state and social justice reforms in Peru. Suffice it to say that since the case of Ilave, Puno, where a three-week long political conflict culminated on April 26, 2004, only a few months before the beginning of my fieldwork in Peru, in the lynching of the mayor, Cirilo Robles, by frustrated Ilaveños, the number of cases reported throughout the Peruvian sierra has increased dramatically. See Cánepa Koch (2004); Degregori (2004); and Pajuelo Teves (2004) for a discussion of the meaning and implication of the events in Ilave.

23 Numerous examples exist in the literature. For a review, see Nyberg-Sørensen et al. (2002); and Nyberg-Sørensen (2012).

24 Originally AIPEUC encompassed only Peruvian organizations in the United States and Canada, but in recent years members of Peruvian organizations in Asia, Europe, and South America have also participated in the AIPEUC conventions. For the organization's mission statement and history, see http://www.aipeuc.net/.

CONCLUSION

1 "Peru's Roaring Economy: Hold on Tight," *Economist*, February 2, 2013.

2 Between 2000 and 2011, a total of 232,559 Peruvians returned from abroad, many of them after the global financial crisis. The majority returned from Chile (34.3%) and others returned from the United States (18.2%), Argentina (10.5%), Spain (8.1%), Bolivia (6.1%), Ecuador (3.6%), Venezuela (3.4%), Colombia (2.2%), Japan (2.0%) and others (11.7%) (IOM 2012:113).

3 See Bastia (2011) for a discussion of migrants' reasons for returning during the economic downturn.

BIBLIOGRAPHY

Abercrombie, Thomas. 1991. "To Be Indian, to Be Bolivian: 'Ethnic' and 'National' Discourses of Identity." In *Nation-States and Indians in Latin America*, edited by Greg Urban and Joel Sherzer, 95–130. Austin: University of Texas Press.

———. 1996. "Q'aqchas and la Plebe in 'Rebellion': Carnival vs. Lent in 18th Century Potosí." *Journal of Latin American Anthropology* 2 (1): 62–111.

———. 1998. *Pathways of Memory and Power: Ethnography and History among an Andean People*. Madison: University of Wisconsin Press.

———. 2003. "Mothers and Mistresses of the Urban Bolivian Public Sphere: Postcolonial Predicaments and National Imaginary in Oruro's Carnival." In *After Spanish Rule: Postcolonial Predicaments of the Americas*, edited by Mark Thurner and Andres Guerrero, 175–220. Durham, N.C.: Duke University Press.

Abrego, Leisy J. 2014. *Sacrificing Families: Navigating Laws, Labor, and Love across Borders*. Stanford, Calif.: Stanford University Press.

Adams, Richard. 1959. *A Community in the Andes: Problems and Progress in Muquiyauyo*. Seattle: University of Washington Press.

Al-Ali, Nadje, and Khalid Koser. 2002. *New Approaches to Migration? Transnational Communities and the Transformation of Home*. London: Routledge.

Alba, Richard D. 1990. *Ethnic Identity: The Transformation of White America*. New Haven: Yale University Press.

Alba, Richard D., and Victor G. Nee. 2005. *Remaking the American Mainstream: Assimilation and Contemporary Immigration*. Cambridge, Mass.: Harvard University Press.

Alberti, Giorgio, and Rodrigo Sánchez. 1974. *Poder y Conflicto en el Valle del Mantaro*. Lima: Instituto de Estudios Peruanos.

Alcoff, Linda Martin. 2006. *Visible Identities: Race, Gender, and the Self*. Oxford: Oxford University Press.

Alicea, Marixsa. 1997. "'A Chambered Nautilus': The Contradictory Nature of Puerto Rican Women's Role in the Social Construction of a Transnational Community." *Gender & Society* 11 (5): 597–626.

Allen, Catherine. 1988. *The Hold Life Has: Coca and Cultural Identity in an Andean Community*. Washington, D.C.: Smithsonian Institution Press.

Alpes, Maibritt Jill. 2011. "Bushfalling: How Young Cameroonians Dare to Migrate." Unpublished Ph.D. dissertation. University of Amsterdam.

Altamirano, Teófilo. 1984. *Presencia Andina en Lima Metropolitana. Un Estudio sobre Migrantes y Clubes de Provincianos*. Lima: Fondo Editorial, PUCP.

———. 1988. *Cultura Andina y Pobreza Urbana: Aymaras en Lima Metropolitana*. Lima: Fondo Editorial, PUCP.

———. 1990. *Los Que Se Fueron: Peruanos en Estados Unidos*. Lima: Fondo Editorial, PUCP.

———. 2000. *Liderazgo y Organizaciones de Peruanos en el Exterior: Culturas Transnacionales e Imaginarios sobre el Desarrollo* (Vol. 1). Lima: PromPeru and Fondo Editorial, PUCP.

———. 2006. *Remesas y Nueva "Fuga de Cerebros": Impactos Transnacionales*. Lima: Fondo Editorial, PUCP.

Appadurai, Arjun. 1996. *Modernity at Large. Cultural Dimensions of Globalization*. Minneapolis: University of Minnesota Press.

Arce, Moíses. 2008. "The Repoliticization of Collective Action after Neoliberalism in Peru." *Latin American Politics and Society* 50 (3): 37–62.

Arguedas, José Maria. 1953. "Folklore del Valle del Mantaro." *Folklore Americano* 1 (1): 101–293.

———. 1975. *Formación de Una Cultura Nacional Indoamericana*. Mexico: Siglo XXI.

———. 1978. *Dos Estudios sobre Huancayo*. Huancayo: Universidad Nacional del Centro del Perú.

Asis, Maruja M. B. 2008. "The Philippines." *Asian and Pacific Migration Journal* 17 (3–4): 349–78.

Askew, Kelly, and Richard Wilk. 2002. *The Anthropology of Media: A Reader*. Oxford: Blackwell Publishers.

Augé, Marc. 1995. *Non-Places: Introduction to an Anthropology of Supermodernity*. London: Verso.

Ávila Molero, Javier. 2003. "Lo Que el Viento de los Andes Se Llevó: Diásporas Campesinas en Lima y en los Estados Unidos." In *Comunidades Locales y Transnacionales: Cinco Estudios de Caso en el Perú*, edited by Carlos Ivan Degregori, 167–261. Lima: Instituto de Estudios Peruanos.

Axel, Brian. 2001. *The Nation's Tortured Body: Violence, Representation, and the Formation of a Sikh "Diaspora."* Durham, N.C.: Duke University Press.

Bakhtin, Mikhail. 1968. *Rabelais and His World*. Cambridge, Mass.: MIT Press.

Baldassar, Loretta. 2007. "Transnational Families and the Provision of Moral and Emotional Support: The Relationship between Truth and Distance." *Identities: Global Studies in Culture and Power* 14 (4): 385–409.

Baldassar, Loretta, and Laura Merla, eds. 2013. *Transnational Families, Migration, and Care Work*. London: Routledge

Baldassar, Loretta, Raelene Wilding, and Cora Baldock. 2007. *Families Caring across Borders: Migration, Ageing and Transnational Caregiving*. Basingstoke, Hampshire: Palgrave Macmillan.

Barber, Pauline Gardiner. 2008. "Cell Phones, Complicity, and Class Politics in the Philippine Labor Diaspora." *Focaal* 51: 28–42.

Barth, Frederik. 1969. *Ethnic Groups and Boundaries. The Social Organization of Culture Difference*. London: Allen & Unwin.

Bastia, Tanja. 2011. "Should I Stay or Should I Go? Return Migration in Times of Crisis." *Journal of International Development* 23 (4): 583–95.

Battaglia, Debbora, ed. 1995. *Rhetorics of Self-Making*. Berkeley: University of California Press.

Bauman, Richard, and Charles Briggs. 1990. "Poetics and Performance as Critical Perspectives on Language and Social Life." *Annual Review of Anthropology* 19: 59–88.

Bauman, Zygmunt. 1991. *Modernity and Ambivalence*. Cambridge: Polity Press.

———. 2000. *Liquid Modernity*. Cambridge: Polity Press.

Bebbington, Anthony. 2012. "Extractive Industries, Socio-Environmental Conflicts and Political Economic Transformations in Andean America." In *Social Conflict, Economic Development and Extractive Industry: Evidence from South America*, edited by Anthony Bebbington, 3–26. Abingdon, U.K.: Routledge.

Beezley, William H., Cheryl English Martin, and William Earl French. 1994. "Introduction: Constructing Consensus, Inciting Conflict." In *Rituals of Rule, Rituals of Resistance: Public Celebrations and Popular Culture in Mexico*, edited by William H. Beezley, Cheryl English Martin, and William Earl French, xiii–xxxii. Wilmington, Del.: Scholarly Resources.

Bell, Catherine. 1992. *Ritual Theory, Ritual Practice*. New York: Oxford University Press.

Bellah, Robert N. 2005. "Durkheim and Ritual." In *The Cambridge Companion to Durkheim*, edited by Jeffrey C. Alexander and Philip Smith, 183–210. Cambridge: Cambridge University Press.

Beltrán, Christina. 2010. *The Trouble with Unity*. Oxford: Oxford University Press.

Benitez, José Luis. 2006. "Transnational Dimensions of the Digital Divide among Salvadoran Immigrants in the Washington D.C. Metropolitan Area." *Global Networks* 6 (2): 181–99.

Ben-Ze'ev, Aaron. 1994. "The Vindication of Gossip." In *Good Gossip*, edited by Robert F. Goodman and Aaron Ben-Ze'ev, 11–24. Lawrence: University of Kansas Press.

Berg, Ulla D. 2001. "Milagros y Castigos: San Sebastián en el Imaginario Popular en la Sierra Central del Perú." In *Perú: El Legado de la Historia*, pp. 235–67, edited by Luis Millones and Villa Rodriguez. Sevilla: Fundación El Monte, PromPerú, and Universidad de Sevilla.

———. 2003. *Waiting for Miracles*. Directed by Ulla D. Berg. New York University's Program in Culture and Media, DVD.

———. 2008. "In Defence of Community? Long-Distance Localism and Transnational Political Engagement between the U.S. and the Peruvian Andes." *Journal of Ethnic and Migration Studies* 34 (7): 1091–1108.

———. 2010. "El Quinto Suyo: Contemporary Nation-Building and the Political Economy of Emigration in Peru." *Latin American Perspectives* 37 (5): 121–36.

Berg, Ulla D., and Karsten Paerregaard. 2005. "Introduction." In *El Quinto Suyo: Transnacionalidad y Formaciones Diaspóricas en la Migración Peruana*, edited by Ulla D. Berg and Karsten Paerregaard, 11–34. Lima: Instituto de Estudios Peruanos.

Berg, Ulla D., and Ana Ramos-Zayas. Forthcoming. "Racializing Affect: A Theoretical Proposition," *Current Anthropology.*

Berg, Ulla D., and Robyn Rodriguez. 2013. "Transnational Citizenship across the Americas." *Identities: Global Studies in Culture and Power* 20 (6): 649–64.

Berg, Ulla D., and Carla Tamagno. 2006. "El Quinto Suyo from Above and from Below: State Agency and Transnational Political Practices among Peruvian Migrants in the US and Europe." *Latino Studies* 4 (3): 258–81.

———. 2013. "Migration Brokers and Document Fixers: The Making of Migrant Subjects in Urban Peru." In *The Migration Industry and the Commercialization of International Migration*, edited by Ninna Nyberg-Sørensen and Thomas Gammeltoft-Hansen, 190–213. London: Routledge.

Berlant, Lauren. 2011. *Cruel Optimism.* Durham, N.C.: Duke University Press.

Bernal, Victoria. 2006. "Diaspora, Cyberspace and the Political Imagination: The Eritrean Diaspora Online." *Global Networks* 6 (2): 161–79.

Beserra, Bernadete. 2003 *Brazilian Immigrants in the United States: Cultural Imperialism and Social Class.* New York: LFB Scholarly Publishing.

Bigenho, Michelle. 2012. *Intimate Distance: Andean Music in Japan.* Durham, N.C.: Duke University Press.

Bigo, Didier, and Elspeth Guild. 2005. "Policing at a Distance: Schengen Visa Policies." In *Controlling Frontiers: Free Movement into and within Europe*, edited by Didier Bigo and Elspeth Guild, 233–62. Aldershot, U.K.: Ashgate.

Blom Hansen, Thomas, and Finn Stepputat. 2005. *Sovereign Bodies: Citizens, Migrants and States in the Postcolonial World.* Princeton, N.J.: Princeton University Press.

Boehm, Deborah. 2012. *Intimate Migrations: Gender, Family, and Illegality among Transnational Mexicans.* New York: NYU Press.

Bolter, Jay David, and Richard Grusin. 2005. *Remediation: Understanding New Media.* 2nd edition. Cambridge, Mass.: MIT Press.

Bolton, Ralph, and Enrique Mayer. 1977. *Andean Kinship and Marriage.* No. 7. American Anthropological Association.

Bonilla, Heraclio. 1974. *El Minero de los Andes: Una Aproximación a Su Estudio.* Lima: Instituto de Estudios Peruanos.

Bonilla-Silva, Eduardo. 1997. "Rethinking Racism: Toward a Structural Interpretation." *American Sociological Review* (1997): 465–80.

Bourdieu, Pierre. 1989. "Social Space and Symbolic Power." *Sociological Theory* 7 (1): 14–25.

———. 1990. *The Logic of Practice.* Cambridge: Polity Press.

Bourque, Susan C., and Kay B. Warren. 1981. *Women of the Andes: Patriarchy and Social Change in Two Peruvian Rural Towns.* Ann Arbor: University of Michigan.

———. 1989. "Democracy without Peace: The Cultural Politics of Terror in Peru." *Latin American Research Review* 24 (1): 7–34.

Bouysse-Cassagne, Thérese, and Thierry Saignes. 1992. "El Cholo: Actor Olvidado de la Historia." In *Etnicidad, Economía y Simbolismo en los Andes: II Congreso Internacio-*

nal de Etnohistoria, Coroico, edited by Silvia Arze and Ana Maria Lorandi, 129–43. La Paz: HISBOL.

Boyd, Monica. 1989. "Family and Personal Networks in International Migration: Recent Developments and New Agendas." *International Migration Review* 23 (3): 638–70.

Brennan, Denise. 2008. "Competing Claims of Victimhood? Foreign and Domestic Victims of Trafficking in the United States." *Sexuality Research and Social Policy* 5 (4): 45–61.

Brubaker, Rogers, and Frederick Cooper. 2000. "Beyond 'Identity.'" *Theory and Society* 29 (1): 1–47.

Buechler, Hans. 1980. *The Masked Media.* The Hague: Mouton de Gruyter.

Bunster, Ximena. 1977. "Talking Pictures: Field Method and Visual Mode." *Signs* 3 (1): 278–93.

Burkitt, Ian. 2002. "Technologies of the Self: Habitus and Capacities." *Journal for the Theory of Social Behaviour* 32 (2): 219–37.

Burns, Kathryn. 2010. *Into the Archive: Writing and Power in Colonial Peru.* Durham, N.C.: Duke University Press.

Burrell, Jenna, and Ken Anderson. 2008. "'I Have Great Desires to Look Beyond My World': Trajectories of Information and Communication Technology Use among Ghanaians Living Abroad." *New Media & Society* 10 (2): 203–24.

Burt, Jo-Marie. 2006. "'Quien Habla Es Terrorista': The Political Use of Fear in Fujimori's Peru." *Latin American Research Review* 41 (3): 32–62.

Butler, Judith. 1992 "Contingent Foundations: Feminism and the Question of 'Postmodernism.'" In *Feminists Theorize the Political*, edited by Judith Butler and Joan Scott, 3–21. New York: Routledge.

Cabañes, Jason Vincent A., and Kristel Anne F. Acedera. 2012. "Of Mobile Phones and Mother-Fathers: Calls, Text Messages, and Conjugal Power Relations in Mother-Away Filipino Families." *New Media & Society* 14 (6): 916–30.

Cánepa Koch, Gisela. 1998. *Máscara, Transformación e Identidad en los Andes.* Lima: Fondo Editorial, PUCP.

———. 2001. "La Fiesta en el Peru." In *Perú: El Legado de la Historia*, edited by Luis Millones and José Villa Rodriguez, 235–67. Sevilla: Fundación El Monte. Perú.

———. 2004. "Los Antropólogos y los Sucesos de Ilave." *Quehacer* 148 (May-June). Lima: DESCO.

———. 2010. "Performing Citizenship: Migration, Andean Festivals, and Public Spaces in Lima." In *Cultures of the City: Mediating Identities in Urban Latin/o America*, edited by Richard Young and Amanda Holmes, 135–50. Pittsburgh: University of Pittsburgh Press.

———. 2012. "Introducción: La Antropología Visual en el Perú." In *Imaginación Visual y Cultura en el Perú*, edited by Gisela Koch Cánepa, 11–60. Lima: Fondo Editorial, PUCP.

———. 2013. "Nation Branding: The Re-Foundation of Community, Citizenship and the State in the Context of Neoliberalism in Perú." *Medien Journal/Visuelle Kulturen* 37 (3): 7–18.

Caplan, Jane, and John Torpey. 2001. *Documenting Individual Identity: The Development of State Practices in the Modern World*. Princeton, N.J.: Princeton University Press.

Capps, Lisa, and Elinor Ochs. 1996. "Narrating the Self." *Annual Review of Anthropology* 25: 19–43.

Carling, Jørgen, Cecilia Menjívar, and Leah Schmalzbauer. 2012. "Central Themes in the Study of Transnational Parenthood." *Journal of Ethnic & Migration Studies* 38 (2): 191–217.

Carsten, Janet. 2000. *Cultures of Relatedness: New Approaches to the Study of Kinship*. Cambridge: Cambridge University Press.

Castells, Manuel. 1996. *The Rise of the Network Society*. Oxford: Blackwell.

Castells, Manuel, Mireia Fernández-Ardèvol, Jack Linchuan Qui, and Araba Sey. 2007. *Mobile Communication and Society: A Global Perspective*. Cambridge, Mass.: MIT Press.

Chaney, Elsa. 1976. "Colombian Migration to the United States" (Part 2). In *The Dynamics of Migration: International Migration*, Occasional Monograph Series, 5 (2): 87–141. Washington, D.C.: Smithsonian Institution, Interdisciplinary Communications Program.

Chávez, Leo. 2001. *Covering Immigration: Popular Images and the Politics of the Nation*. Berkeley: University of California Press.

———. 2008. *The Latino Threat: Constructing Immigrants, Citizens, and the Nation*. Stanford, Calif.: Stanford University Press.

Chavez, Lilian, and Cecilia Menjívar. 2010. "Children without Borders: A Mapping of the Literature on Unaccompanied Migrant Children to the United States." *Migraciones Internacionales* 5 (3): 71–111.

Chu, Julie. 2010. *Cosmologies of Credit. Transnational Mobility and the Politics of Destination in China*. Durham, N.C.: Duke University Press.

Coe, Catie, 2011. "How Children Feel about Their Parents' Migration: A History of the Reciprocity of Care in Ghana." In *Everyday Ruptures: Children, Youth, and Migration in Global Perspective*, edited by Cati Coe, Rachel R. Reynolds, Deborah A. Boehm, Julia Meredith Hess, and Heather Rae-Espinoza, 97–114. Nashville, Tenn.: Vanderbilt University Press.

Coe, Catie, Rachel R. Reynolds, Deborah A. Boehm, Julia Meredith Hess, and Heather Rae-Espinoza. 2011. "Introduction: Children, Youth, and the Everyday Ruptures of Migration." In *Everyday Ruptures: Children, Youth, and Migration in Global Perspective*, edited by Cati Coe, Rachel R. Reynolds, Deborah A. Boehm, Julia Meredith Hess, and Heather Rae-Espinoza, 1–19. Nashville, Tenn.: Vanderbilt University Press.

Cohen, Jeffrey Harris, and Ibrahim Sirkeci. 2011. *Cultures of Migration*. Austin: University of Texas Press.

Cole, Jeffrey. 1985. *The Potosi Mita, 1573–1700: Compulsory Indian Labor in the Andes*. Stanford, Calif.: Stanford University Press.

Collins, Francis Leo. 2009. "Connecting 'Home' with 'Here': Personal Homepages in Everyday Transnational Lives." *Journal of Ethnic and Migration Studies* 35 (6): 839–59.

Collins, Jane. 1988. *Unseasonal Migrations: The Effects of Rural Labor Scarcity in Peru.* Princeton, N.J.: Princeton University Press.

Colloredo-Mansfeld, Rudolf. 1994. "Architectural Conspicuous Consumption and Economic Change in the Andes." *American Anthropologist* 96 (4): 845–65.

Comaroff, Jean. 1985. *Body of Power, Spirit of Resistance: The Culture and History of a South African People.* Chicago: University of Chicago Press.

Condarco, Ramiro. [1971] 1987. "Simbiosis Interzonal." In *La Teoría de la Complementariedad Vertical Eco-Simbiótica*, edited by Ramiro Condarco and John Victor Murra, 7–28. La Paz: Hisbol.

Contreras, Carlos, and Marcos Cueto. 1999. *Historia del Perú Contemporáneo.* Lima: Red para el Desarrollo de las Ciencias Sociales en el Perú.

Cook, Noble David. 1990. "Migration in Colonial Peru." In *Migration in Colonial Spanish America*, edited by David J. Robinson, 41–61. Cambridge: Cambridge University Press.

Coutin, Susan. 2005. "Being En Route." *American Anthropologist* 107 (2): 195–206.

———. 2007. *Nations of Emigrants. Shifting Boundaries of Citizenship in El Salvador and the United States.* Ithaca, N.Y.: Cornell University Press.

Cresswell, Tim. 2006. *On the Move: Mobility in the Modern Western World.* New York: Routledge.

Crossley, Nick. 2001. "The Phenomenological Habitus and Its Construction." *Theory and Society* 30 (1): 81–120.

Cueto, Marcos.1989. "Andean Biology in Peru: Scientific Styles on the Periphery." *Isis* (1989): 640–58.

CVR (Comisión de la Verdad y Reconciliación). 2003. *Informe Final.* Available at: http://cverdad.org.pe [Accessed October 20, 2014].

Dalakoglou, Dimitris, and Penny Harvey. 2012. "Roads and Anthropology: Ethnographic Perspectives on Space, Time, and (Im)Mobility." *Mobilities* 7 (4): 459–65.

Dávila, Arlene. 2001. *Latinos, Inc. The Marketing and Making of a People.* Berkeley: University of California Press.

———. 2004. *Barrio Dreams: Puerto Ricans, Latinos, and the Neoliberal City.* Berkeley: University of California Press.

Debord, Guy. [1967] 1994. *The Society of the Spectacle.* Cambridge, Mass.: Zone Books.

Decena, Carlos Ulises. 2011. *Tacit Subjects: Belonging and Same-Sex Desire among Dominican Immigrant Men.* Durham, N.C.: Duke University Press.

De Genova, Nicholas. 2002. "Migrant 'Illegality' and Deportability in Everyday Life." *Annual Review of Anthropology* 31: 419–47.

———. 2005. *Working the Boundaries: Race, Space, and "Illegality" in Mexican Chicago.* Durham, N.C.: Duke University Press.

———. 2009. "Conflicts of Mobility, and the Mobility of Conflict: Rightlessness, Presence, Subjectivity, Freedom." *Subjectivity* 29 (1): 445–66.

———. 2010. "Antiterrorism, Race, and the New Frontier: American Exceptionalism, Imperial Multiculturalism, and the Global Security State." *Identities: Global Studies in Culture and Power* 17 (6): 613–40.

Degregori, Carlos Iván. 2001. *La Década de la Anti-Política: Auge y Huida de Alberto Fujimori.* Lima: Instituto de Estudios Peruanos.

———. 2004. *Ilave: Desafíos de la gobernabilidad, la democracia participativa y la descentralización.* Lima: Grupo Propuesta Ciudadana.

De la Cadena, Marisol. 2000. *Indigenous Mestizos: The Politics of Race and Culture in Cuzco, Peru, 1919–1991.* Durham, N.C.: Duke University Press.

———. 2001. "Reconstructing Race: Racism, Culture and Mestizaje in Latin America." *NACLA Report on the Americas* 34 (6): 16–23.

———. 2005. "Are Mestizos Hybrids? The Conceptual Politics of Andean Identities." *Journal of Latin American Studies* 37 (2): 259–284.

———. 2010. "Indigenous Cosmopolitics in the Andes: Conceptual Reflections Beyond 'Politics.'" *Cultural Anthropology* 25 (2): 334–70.

Del Pino, Ponciano. 2003. "Uchuraccay: Memoria y Representación de la Violencia Política en los Andes." In *Luchas Locales, Comunidades e Identidades,* edited by Elizabeth Jelin and Ponciano del Pino, 11–62. Madrid: Siglo XXI de España.

De Soto, Hernando. 1986. *El Otro Sendero: La Revolución Informal.* Lima: Editorial El Barranco.

De Tona, Carla, and Andrew Whelan. 2009. "Re-Mediating the Ruptures of Migration: The Use of Internet and Mobile Phones in Migrant Women's Organisations in Ireland." *Translocations: Migration and Social Change* 5 (1): 1–20.

Diaz-Albertini, F. Javier. September 2006. "Diez Años No Son Nada? Internet en el Perú 1996–2005." *Perú Económico,* Lima.

Dijstelbloem, Huub, Albert Meijer, and Michiel Besters. 2011. "The Migration Machine." In *Migration and the New Technological Borders of Europe,* edited by Huub Dijstelbloem, Albert Meijer, and Michiel Besters, 1–21. Basingstoke, U.K.: Palgrave Macmillan.

Di Leonardo, Micaela. 1987. "The Female World of Cards and Holidays: Women, Families and the Work of Kinship." *Signs* 12 (4): 440–53.

Dilley, Roy, ed. 1999. *The Problem of Context* (Vol. 4). London: Berghahn Books.

Douglas, Mary. [1966] 1978. *Purity and Danger: An Analysis of Concepts of Pollution and Taboo.* London: Routledge and Kegan Paul.

Dreby, Joanna. 2009. "Transnational Gossip." *Qualitative Sociology* 32: 33–52.

———. 2010. *Divided by Borders: Mexican Migrants and Their Children.* Berkeley: University of California Press.

Drinot, Paulo. 2011. *The Allure of Labor: Workers, Race, and the Making of the Peruvian State.* Durham, N.C.: Duke University Press.

Drotbohm, Heike. 2009. "Horizons of Long-Distance Intimacies: Reciprocity, Contribution and Disjuncture in Cape Verde." *History of the Family* 14 (2): 132–49.

Durand, Jorge. 2010. "The Peruvian Diaspora: Portrait of a Migratory Process." *Latin American Perspectives* 37 (5): 12–28.

Durand, Jorge, and Douglas S. Massey. 2003. "The Costs of Contradiction: US Border Policy 1986–2000." *Latino Studies* 1 (2): 233–52.

Duranti, Alessandro, and Charles Goodwin, eds. 1992. *Rethinking Context: Language as an Interactive Phenomenon* (Vol. 11). Cambridge: Cambridge University Press.

Durkheim, Emile. [1915] 1965. *The Elementary Forms of Religious Life*. New York: Free Press.

Engle Merry, Sally. 1997. "Rethinking Gossip and Scandal." In *Reputation: Studies in the Voluntary Elicitation of Good Conduct*, edited by Daniel B. Klein, 47–74. Ann Arbor: University of Michigan Press.

Escobar, Christina. 2004. "Dual Citizenship and Political Participation: Migrants in the Interplay of United States and Colombian Politics." *Latino Studies* 2 (1): 45–69.

———. 2007. "Extraterritorial Political Rights and Dual Citizenship in Latin America." *Latin American Research Review* 42 (3): 43–75.

Escrivá, Angeles, Ursula Santa Cruz, and Anastacia Bermúdez. 2010. "Migration, Gender, and Politics: The 2006 Peruvian Elections Abroad." *Latin American Perspectives* 37 (5): 106–20.

Espinoza Soriano, Waldemar. 1973. *Historia del Departamento de Junín*. Huancayo: Editor Enrique Chipoco Tovar.

Falconi, José Luis, and José Antonio Mazzotti, eds. 2007. *The Other Latinos: Central and South Americans in the United States* (Vol. 20). Cambridge, Mass.: Harvard University Press.

Fassin, Didier. 2011. "Policing Borders, Producing Boundaries. The Governmentality of Immigration in Dark Times." *Annual Review of Anthropology* 40: 213–26.

Favre, Henri. 1977. "The Dynamics of Indian Peasant Society and Migration to Coastal Plantations in Central Peru." In *Land and Labor in Latin America: Essays on the Development of Agrarian Capitalism in the Nineteenth and Twentieth Centuries*, edited by Kenneth Duncan and Ian Rutledge, 253–68. Cambridge: Cambridge University Press.

Feller, Erika. 1989. "Carrier Sanctions and International Law." *International Journal of Refugee Law* 1 (1): 48–66.

Fernandez, James. 1974. "The Mission of Metaphor in Expressive Culture." *Current Anthropology* 15: 119–45.

———. 1977. "The Performance of Ritual Metaphors." In *The Social Use of Metaphors*, edited by David J. Sapir and Christopher Crocker, 100–30. Philadelphia: University of Pennsylvania Press.

Fitzgerald, David. 2009. *A Nation of Emigrants: How Mexico Manages Its Migration*. Berkeley: University of California Press.

Flores, William Vincent, and Rina Benmayor, eds. 1997. *Latino Cultural Citizenship: Claiming Identity, Space, and Rights*. Boston, Mass.: Beacon Press.

Flores Galindo, Alberto. 1974. *Los Mineros de la Cerro de Pasco*. Lima: Pontificia Universidad Católica del Perú.

Foucault, Michel. 1979. *Discipline and Punish: The Birth of the Prison*. New York: Vintage Books.

———. 1988a. "Technologies of the Self," in *Technologies of the Self: A Seminar with Michel Foucault*, edited by Luther H. Martin, Huck Gutman, and Patrick H. Hutton, 16–49. Cambridge, Mass.: MIT Press.

———. 1988b. *The Care of the Self: The History of Sexuality, Volume Three*. London: Penguin.

———. 2007. *Security, Territory, Population. Lectures at the Collège de France 1977–1978*. New York: Palgrave Macmillan.

Fresnoza-Flot, Asunción. 2009. "Migration Status and Transnational Mothering: The Case of Filipino Migrants in France." *Global Networks* 9 (2): 252–70.

———. 2013. "Men's Caregiving Practices in Filipino Transnational Families: A Case Study of Left Behind Fathers and Sons." In *Transnational Families, Migration, and Care Work*, edited by Loretta Baldassar and Laura Merla, 170–84. London: Routledge

Gálvez, Alyshia. 2009. *Guadalupe in New York: Devotion and the Struggle for Citizenship Rights among Mexican Immigrants*. New York: NYU Press.

García, María Cristina. 2006. *Seeking Refuge: Central American Migration to Mexico, the United States, and Canada*. Berkeley: University of California Press.

García, Maria Elena. 2005. *Making Indigenous Citizens: Identities, Education, and Multicultural Development in Peru*. Stanford: Stanford University Press.

Gelles, Paul. 2005. "Transformaciones en una Comunidad Andina Transnational." In *El Quinto Suyo: Transnacionalidad y Fornaciones Diasporicas en la Migración Peruana*, edited by Ulla D. Berg and Karsten Paerregaard, 69–96. Lima: Instituto de Estudios Peruanos.

Gilboy, Janet. 1991. "Deciding Who Gets In: Decision-Making by Immigration Inspectors." *Law and Society Review* 25 (3): 571–600.

Gill, Leslie. 1994. *Precarious Dependencies: Gender, Class, and Domestic Service in Bolivia*. New York: Columbia University Press.

Ginsburg, Faye. 1991. "Indigenous Media: Faustian Contract or Global Village?" *Cultural Anthropology* 6 (1): 92–112.

———. 1995. "The Parallax Effect: The Impact of Aboriginal Media on Ethnographic Film." *Visual Anthropology Review* 11 (2): 64–76.

Ginsburg, Faye, Lila Abu-Lughod, and Brian Larkin. 2002. "Introduction." In *Media Worlds: Anthropology on New Terrain*, edited by Faye Ginsburg, Lila Abu-Lughod, and Brian Larkin, 1–36. Berkeley: University of California Press.

Glave, Luis Miguel. 1989. *Trajinantes: Caminos Indígenas en la Sociedad Colonial, Siglos XVI / XVII*. Lima: Instituto de Apoyo Agrario.

Glick Schiller, Nina, Linda Basch, and Christina Blanc-Szanton. 1992. "Transnationalism: A New Analytic Framework for Understanding Migration." *Annals of the New York Academy of Sciences* 645 (1): 1–24.

———. 1995. "From Immigrant to Transmigrant: Theorizing Transnational Migration." *Anthropological Quarterly* 68 (1): 48–63.

Glick Schiller, Nina, and Noel B. Salazar. 2013. "Regimes of Mobility aross the Globe." *Journal of Ethnic and Migration Studies* 39 (2): 183–200.

Gluckman, Max. 1963. "Gossip and Scandal (Papers in Honor of Melville J. Herskovits)." *Current Anthropology* 4 (3): 307–16.

Goffman, Erving. [1955] 2005. "On Face-Work: An Analysis of the Ritual Elements of Social Interaction." In *Interaction Ritual: Essays in Face-to-Face Behavior*, edited by Erving Goffman, 5–46. New Brunswick: Aldine Transaction Publishers.

———. 1959. *The Presentation of Self in Everyday Life*. New York: Anchor Books.

Goldring, Luin. 1998. "The Power of Status in Transnational Social Fields." In *Transnationalism from Below*, edited by Luis Eduardo Guarnizo and Michael Peter Smith, 165–95. New Brunswick: Transaction Publishers.

Goldstein, Daniel. 2004. *The Spectacular City: Violence and Performance in Urban Bolivia*. Durham, N.C.: Duke University Press.

Golte, Jurgen. 1980. *La Racionalidad de la Organización Andina*. Lima: Instituto de Estudios Peruanos.

Golte, Jurgen, and Norma Adams. 1987. *Los Caballos de Troya de los Invasores. Estratégias Campesinas en la Conquista de Gran Lima*. Lima: Instituto de Estudios Peruanos.

Gonzáles de Olarte, Efraín. 2002. "Descentralización a la Peruana." *Debate* 23 (118): 16–20.

———. 2007. "La Economía Política Peruana de la Era Neoliberal 1990–2006." In *Después del Consenso de Washington: Dinámica de Cambios Político-Económicos y Administración de Recursos Naturales en los Países Andinos*, edited by Yusuke Murakami, 11–38.

Gonzalez, Alfonso. 2014. *Reform without Justice. Latino Migrant Politics and the Homeland Security State*. Oxford: Oxford University Press.

Gozdziak, Elzbieta M., and Elizabeth A. Collett. 2005. "Research on Human Trafficking in North America: A Review of Literature." *International Migration* 43: 99–128.

Grasmuck, Sherri, and Patricia R. Pessar. 1991. *Between Two Islands: Dominican International Migration*. Berkeley: University of California Press.

Graubart, Karen B. 2009. "The Creolization of the New World: Local Forms of Identification in Urban Colonial Peru, 1560–1640." *Hispanic American Historical Review* 89 (3): 471–99.

Greene, Shane. 2007. "Entre lo Indio, lo Negro, y lo Incaíco: The Spatial Hierarchies of Difference in Multicultural Peru." *Journal of Latin American and Caribbean Anthropology* 12 (2): 441–74.

Greschke, Heike Mónika. 2010. "Mediated Cultures of Mobility. The Art of Positioning Ethnography in Global Landscapes." COMCAD Working Papers, No. 78.

Guarnizo, Luis. 1994. "Los Dominicanyorks: The Making of a Binational Society." *ANNALS of the American Academy of Political and Social Science* 533 (1): 70–86.

Guarnizo, Luis, and Luz Marina Díaz. 1999. "Transnational Migration: A View from Colombia." *Ethnic and Racial Studies* 22 (2): 397–421.

Guerrero, Andres. 2000. "Los Linchamientos en las Comunidades Indígenas (Ecuador). La Política Perversa de una Modernidad Marginal?" *Bulletin del Instituto Frances de Estudios Andinos* 29 (3): 463–89.

Guerrero Bravo, Juan Carlos. 2004. "Pasado, Presente, y Futuro de las Rondas Campesinas Antisubversivas en Junín, Perú (1990–2001)." CLACSO, Consejo Latinoamericano de Ciencias Sociales. http://bibliotecavirtual.clacso.org.ar/clacso/becas/20110124032438/7Guerrero.pdf

Guillet, David, and Scott Whiteford. 1974. "A Comparative View of the Role of the Fiesta Complex in Migrant Adaptation." *Urban Anthropology* 3 (2): 39–56.

Hale, Charles. 2005. "Neoliberal Multiculturalism: The Remaking of Cultural Rights and Racial Dominance in Central America." *Political and Legal Anthropology Review (POLAR)* 28 (1): 10–19.

Hall, Stuart. 1980. "Encoding/Decoding." In *Culture, Media and Language*, edited by Stuart Hall, Dorothy Hobson, Andrew Love, and Paul Willis, 128–38. London: Hutchinson.

Hammond, Joyce. 1988. "Visualizing Themselves: Tongan Videography in Utah." *Visual Anthropology* 1 (4): 379–400.

Handelman, Don. 1998. *Models and Mirrors: Towards an Anthropology of Public Events.* New York: Berghahn Books.

Harney, Robert F. 1977. "The Commerce of Migration." *Canadian Ethnic Studies/Études Ethniques au Canada* 9: 42–53.

Harper, Douglas. 2002. "Talking about Pictures: A Case for Photo Elicitation." *Visual Studies* 17 (1): 13–26.

Harris, Olivia, ed. 2000. *To Make the Earth Bear Fruit: Ethnographic Essays on Fertility, Work and Gender in Highland Bolivia.* London: Institute of Latin American Studies.

Harvey, David. 1989. *The Condition of Post-Modernity: An Enquiry into the Origins of Cultural Change.* Cambridge, Mass.: Blackwell Publishers.

———. 2007. *A Brief History of Neoliberalism.* Oxford: Oxford University Press.

Harvey, Penelope. 1997. "Peruvian Independence Day: Ritual, Memory, and the Erasure of Narrative." In *Creating Context in Andean Cultures*, edited by Rosaleen Howard-Malverde, 21–44. New York: Oxford University Press.

Harvey, Penelope, and Hannah Knox. 2012. "The Enchantments of Infrastructure." *Mobilities* 7 (4): 521–36.

Hernández-León, Rubén. 2008. *Metropolitan Migrants: The Migration of Urban Mexicans to the United States.* Berkeley: University of California Press.

Hill, Jane H. 1998. "Language, Race, and White Public Space." *American Anthropologist* 100: 680–89.

Himpele, Jeffrey D. 2002. "Arrival Scenes: Complicity and Media Ethnography in the Bolivian Public Sphere." In *Media Worlds: Anthropology on New Terrain*, edited by Faye D. Ginsburg, Lila Abu-Lughod, and Brian Larkin, 301–16. Berkeley: University of California Press.

———. 2008. *Circuits of Culture: Media, Politics, and Indigenous Identity in the Andes.* Minneapolis: University of Minnesota Press.

Hochschild, Arlie. 1979. "Emotion Work, Feeling Rules, and Social Structure." *American Journal of Sociology* 85 (3): 551–75.

———. 2000. "Emotional Care Chains and Emotional Surplus Value." In *On the Edge: Living with Global Capitalism*, edited by Will Hutton and Anthony Giddens. London: Jonathan Cape.

Hondagneu-Sotelo, Pierrette, and Ernestine Avila. 1997. "'I'm Here, But I'm There': The Meanings of Latina Transnational Motherhood." *Gender and Society* 11 (5): 548–71.

Honig, Bonnie. 2001. *Democracy and the Foreigner*. Princeton, N.J.: Princeton University Press.

Horst, Heather A. 2006. "The Blessings and Burdens of Communication: Cell Phones in Jamaican Transnational Social Fields." *Global Networks* 6 (2): 143–59.

Horst, Heather A., and Daniel Miller. 2005. "From Kinship to Link-Up: The Cell Phone and Social Networking in Jamaica." *Current Anthropology* 46 (5): 755–78.

———. 2006. *The Cell Phone: An Anthropology of Communication*. Oxford: Berg Publishers.

Howard-Malverde, Rosaleen. 1997. "Introduction: Between Text and Context in the Evocation of Culture." In *Creating Context in Andean Culture*, edited by Rosaleen Howard-Malverde, 3–18. Oxford: Oxford University Press.

Huayhua, Margarita. 2013. "Racism and Social Interaction in a Southern Peruvian Combi." *Ethnic and Racial Studies* 37 (13): 2399–2417.

Huerta-Mercado, Alex. 2006. "Espejo de los Tiempos: Las Estrategias y Anhelos del Primer Movimiento Gay Peruano en Nueva York." In *Mirando la Esfera Pública desde la Cultura en el Perú*, edited by Gisela Cánepa Koch and María Eugenia Ulfe, 187–201. Lima: CONCYTEC.

Hull, Matthew S. 2012. "Documents and Bureaucracy." *Annual Review of Anthropology* 41: 251–67.

Inda, Jonathan Xavier. 2000. "Foreign Bodies: Migrants, Parasites, and the Pathological Body Politic." *Discourse* 22 (3): 46–62.

———. 2006. *Targeting Immigrants: Government, Technology, and Ethics*. Malden, Mass.: Blackwell.

Instituto Nacional de Estadística y Informatica (INEI). 2013. Accessed on January 21, 2013, at http://www.inei.gob.pe/.

Inter-American Development Bank (IDB). 2012. *Remittances to Latin America and the Caribbean in 2011: Regaining Growth*. Washington D.C.: Inter-American Development Bank.

International Organization for Migration (IOM). 2012. *Perfil Migratório del Perú 2012*. Lima: Organización Internacional para las Migraciones.

International Telecommunication Union (ITU). 2011. World Telecommunication/ICT Indicators Database 2011. Geneva: ITU.

Isaksen, Lise Widding, Sambasivan Uma Devi, and Arlie Hochschild. 2008. "Global Care Crisis: A Problem of Capital, Care Chain, or Commons?" *American Behavioral Scientist* 52 (3): 405–25.

Isbell, Billie Jean. 1978. *To Defend Ourselves: Ecology and Ritual in an Andean Village*. Austin: University of Texas Press.

Jackson, John. 2004. "An Ethnographic Filmflam: Giving Gifts, Doing Research, and Videotaping the Native Subject/Object." *American Anthropologist* 106 (1): 32–42.

Jenkins, Richard. 1996. *Social Identity*. London and New York: Routledge.

Jurado Nacional de Elecciones (JNE). 2011. *Compendio Estadístico Electoral*. Lima: Jurado Nacional de Elecciones.

Karp de Toledo, Eliane. 2002. *Hacia Una Nueva Nación, Kay Pachamanta* [Towards a New Nation, Kay Pachamanta]. Office of the First Lady of the Nation. Lima, Peru.

Kasinitz, Philip, and Judith Freidenberg-Herbstein. 1987. "The Puerto Rican Parade and West Indian Carnival: Public Celebrations in New York City." In *Caribbean Life in New York City: Sociocultural Dimensions*, edited by Constance R. Sutton and Elsa M. Chaney, 327–49. New York: Center for Migration Studies.

Kearney, Michael. 1995. "The Local and the Global: The Anthropology of Globalization and Transnationalism." *Annual Review of Anthropology* 24: 547–65.

Kernaghan, Richard. 2012. "Furrows and Walls, or the Legal Topography of a Frontier Road in Peru." *Mobilities* 7 (4): 501–20.

Khan, Shamus Rahman. 2011. *Privilege: The Making of an Adolescent Elite at St. Paul's School*. Princeton, N.J.: Princeton University Press.

King, Russell, and Ronald Skeldon. 2010. "'Mind the Gap!' Integrating Approaches to Internal and International Migration." *Journal of Ethnic and Migration Studies* 36 (10): 1619–46.

Kirk, Robin, and Anne Manuel. 1993. Human Rights Watch Report on Peru. Available at http://www.hrw.org/reports/pdfs/p/peru/peru a93.pdf [Accessed on January 5, 2013].

Klarén, Peter. 1977. "The Social and Economic Consequences of Modernization in the Peruvian Sugar Industry, 1870–1930." In *Land and Labor in Latin America: Essays on the Development of Agrarian Capitalism in the Nineteenth and Twentieth Centuries*, edited by Kenneth Duncan and Ian Rutledge, 229–52. Cambridge: Cambridge University Press.

Kolar-Panov, Dona. 1996. "Video and the Diasporic Imagination of Selfhood: A Case Study of Croatians in Australia." *Cultural Studies* 10 (2): 288–314.

———. 1997. *Video, War, and the Diasporic Imagination*. London: Routledge.

Kosnick, Kira. 2007. *Migrant Media: Turkish Broadcasting and Multicultural Politics in Berlin*. Bloomington: Indiana University Press.

Kulick, Don. 1992. *Language Shift and Cultural Reproduction. Socialization, Self, and Syncretism in a New Guinean Village*. Cambridge: University of Cambridge.

Kyle, David. 2000. *Transnational Peasants: Migration, Networks, and Ethnicity in Andean Ecuador*. Baltimore: Johns Hopkins University Press.

Kyle, David, and Rey Koslowski. 2001. "Introduction." In *Global Human Smuggling: Comparative Perspectives*, edited by David Kyle and Rey Koslowski, 1–25. Baltimore: Johns Hopkins University Press.

Laguerre, Michel S. 1998. *Diasporic Citizenship: Haitian Americans in Transnational America*. New York: St. Martin's Press.

Laite, Julian. 1984. "Migration and Social Difference amongst Mantaro Valley Peas-
ants." In *Miners, Peasants, and Entrepreneurs. Regional Development in the Central
Highlands of Peru*, edited by Norman Long and Bryan Roberts, 107–39. Cambridge:
Cambridge University Press.

Landolt, Patricia, and Wei Wei Da. 2005. "The Spatially Ruptured Practices of Migrant
Families: A Comparison of Immigrants from El Salvador and the People's Republic
of China." *Current Sociology* 53 (4): 625–53.

Larkin, Brian. 2008. *Signal and Noise: Media, Infrastructure, and Urban Culture in
Nigeria*. Durham, N.C.: Duke University Press.

———. 2013. "The Politics and Poetics of Infrastructure." *Annual Review of Anthropology* 42: 327–43.

Larson, Brooke. 2005. "Redeemed Indians, Barbarized Cholos." In *Political Cultures in
the Andes, 1750–1950*, edited by Nils Jacobsen and Cristóbal Aljovín de Losada, 230–
52. Durham, N.C.: Duke University Press.

Lazar, Sian. 2008. *El Alto, Rebel City: Self and Citizenship in Andean Bolivia*. Durham,
N.C.: Duke University Press.

Leifsen, Esben, and Alexander Tymczuk. 2012. "Care at a Distance: Ukrainian and
Ecuadorian Transnational Parenthood from Spain." *Journal of Ethnic and Migration
Studies* 38 (2): 219–36.

Leinaweaver, Jessaca. 2008. "Improving Oneself: Young People Getting Ahead in the
Peruvian Andes." *Latin American Perspectives* 35 (4): 60–78.

———. 2009. "Raising the Roof in the Transnational Andes: Building Houses, Forging
Kinship." *Journal of the Royal Anthropological Institute* 15 (4): 777–96.

———. 2010. "Outsourcing Care: How Peruvian Migrants Meet Transnational Family
Obligations." *Latin American Perspectives* 37 (5): 67–87.

———. 2013. *Adoptive Migrations: Raising Latinos in Spain*. Durham, N.C.: Duke University Press.

Lessinger, Johanna. 1995. *From the Ganges to the Hudson: Indian Immigrants in New
York City*. New York: Allyn and Bacon.

Levitsky, Steven. 2011. "A Surprising Left Turn." *Journal of Democracy* 22 (4): 84–94.

Levitt, Peggy, and B. Nadya Jaworsky. 2007. "Transnational Migration Studies: Past
Developments and Future Trends." *Annual Review of Sociology* 33: 129–56.

Levitt, Peggy, and Rafael de la Dehesa. 2003. "Transnational Migration and the Redefi-
nition of the State: Variations and Explanations." *Ethnic and Racial Studies* 26 (4):
587–611.

Leys, Ruth. 2011. "The Turn to Affect: A Critique." *Critical Inquiry* 37 (3): 434–72.

Logan, John R., Wenquan Zhang, and Richard D. Alba. 2002. "Immigrant Enclaves and
Ethnic Communities in New York and Los Angeles." *American Sociological Review*
67 (2): 299–322.

Long, Norman, and Bryan Roberts. 1978. *Peasant Cooperation and Capitalist Expansion
in Central Peru*. Austin: University of Texas Press.

———. 1984. *Miners, Peasants and Entrepreneurs: Regional Development in the Central
Highlands of Peru*. Cambridge: Cambridge University Press.

Lund, Sarah. 2001. "Bequeathing and Quest. Processing Personal Identification Papers in Bureaucratic Spaces (Cuzco, Peru)." *Social Anthropology* 9 (1): 3–24.

Lund Skar, Sarah. 1997. "On the Margin: Letter Exchange among Andean Non-Literates." In *Creating Context in Andean Culture*, edited by Rosaleen Howard-Malverde, 185–95. Oxford: Oxford University Press.

Lutz, Catherine, and Geoffrey M. White. 1986. "The Anthropology of Emotions." *Annual Review of Anthropology* 15: 405–36.

Madianou, Mirca. 2012. "Migration and the Accentuated Ambivalence of Motherhood: The Role of ICTs in Filipino Transnational Families." *Global Networks* 12 (3): 277–95.

Madianou, Mirca, and Daniel Miller. 2012. *Migration and New Media: Transnational Families and New Media*. London: Routledge.

Magnet, Shoshana Amielle. 2011. *When Biometrics Fail: Gender, Race, and the Technology of Identity*. Durham, N.C.: Duke University Press.

Maher, Kristen, and Silke Staab. 2005. "Nanny Politics: The Dilemmas of Working Women's Empowerment in Santiago, Chile." *International Feminist Journal of Politics* 7 (1): 71–89.

Mahler, Sarah J. 1995. *American Dreaming: Immigrant Life at the Margins*. Princeton, N.J.: Princeton University Press.

———. 2001. "Transnational Relationships: The Struggle to Communicate across Borders." *Identities: Global Studies in Culture and Power* 7 (4): 583–619.

Malkin, Victoria. 2004. "We Go to Get Ahead: Gender and Status in Two Mexican Migrant Communities." *Latin American Perspectives* 31: 75–99.

Mallon, Florencia. 1983. *The Defense of Community in Peru's Central Highlands: Peasant Struggle and Capitalist Transition, 1860–1940*. Princeton, N.J.: Princeton University Press.

———. 1995. *Peasant and Nation: The Making of Postcolonial Mexico and Peru*. Berkeley: University of California Press.

Mankekar, Purnima. 1999. *Screening Culture, Viewing Politics: An Ethnography of Television, Womanhood, and Nation in Postcolonial India*. Durham, N.C.: Duke University Press.

Manrique, Nelson. 1987. *Mercado Interno y Region. La Sierra Central 1820–1930*. Lima: Desco.

———. 1998. "The War for the Central Sierra." In *Shining and Other Paths: War and Society in Peru, 1980–1995*, edited by Steve Stern, 193–223. Durham, N.C.: Duke University Press.

———. 2002. *El Tiempo del Miedo: La Violencia Política en el Perú, 1980–1996*. Lima: Fondo Editorial Congreso de la República.

Marcus, George. 1995. "Ethnography in/of the World System: The Emergence of Multi-Sited Ethnography." *Annual Review of Anthropology* 24: 95–117.

Margolis, Maxine L. 1994. *Little Brazil: An Ethnography of Brazilian Immigrants in New York City*. Princeton, N.J.: Princeton University Press.

Marston, Sallie. 2002. "Making Difference: Conflict over Irish Identity in the New York City St. Patrick's Day Parade." *Political Geography* 21 (3): 373–92.

Martinez Alier, Joan. 1977. *Haciendas, Plantations and Collective Farms. Agrarian Class Societies—Cuba and Peru*. London: Frank Cass.

Mascia-Lees, Frances E. 2011. *Companion to the Anthropology of the Body and Embodiment*, edited by Frances E. Mascia-Lees. West Sussex, U.K.: Wiley-Blackwell.

Massey, Douglas S., ed. 2008. *New Faces in New Places: The Changing Geography of American Immigration*. New York: Russell Sage Foundation.

Massey, Douglas S., and Chiara Capoferro. 2006. "Sálvese Quién Pueda: Structural Adjustments and Emigration from Lima." *Annals of the American Academy of Political and Social Science* 606 (1): 116–27.

Massey, Douglas S., Joaquin Arango, Graeme Hugo, Ali Kouaouci, Adela Pellegrino, and J. Edward Taylor. 1993. "Theories of International Migration: A Review and Appraisal." *Population and Development Review* 19 (3): 431–66.

Massey, Douglas S., Jorge Durand, and Nolan J. Malone. 2003. *Beyond Smoke and Mirrors: Mexican Immigration in an Era of Economic Integration*. New York: Russell Sage Foundation.

Matos Mar, José. 1976. *Hacienda, Comunidad y Campesinado en el Perú*. Lima: Instituto de Estudios Peruanos.

———. 1977. "Sharecropping on the Peruvian Coast." In *Haciendas and Plantations in Latin American History*, edited by Robert G. Keith. New York: Holmes & Meier.

———. [1984] 2004. *Desborde Popular y Crisis del Estado: Veinte Años Después*. Lima: Fondo Editorial del Congreso del Perú.

Matos Mar, José, and José Manuel Mejía. 1980. *La Reforma Agraria en el Perú*. Lima: Instituto de Estudios Peruanos.

Mauss, Marcel. [1925] 1967. *The Gift: Forms and Functions of Exchange in Archaic Societies*. New York: Norton.

———[1934] 1992. "Techniques of the Body." In *Incorporations*, edited by Jonathan Crary and Sanford Kwinter, 455–77. New York: Zone.

Mayer, Enrique. 1991. "Peru in Deep Trouble: Mario Vargas Llosa's 'Inquest in the Andes' Reexamined." *Cultural Anthropology* 6 (4): 466–504.

———. 2002. *The Articulated Peasant: Household Economies in the Andes*. Boulder: Westview Press.

———. 2009. *Ugly Stories of the Peruvian Agrarian Reform*. Durham, N.C.: Duke University Press.

Mazzarella, William. 2006. "Internet X-Ray: E-Governance, Transparency, and the Politics of Immediation in India." *Public Culture* 18: 473–505.

McClintock, Cynthia, and Fabian Vallas. 2003. *The United States and Peru: Cooperation at a Cost*. London: Routledge.

McKay, Deirdre. 2007. "'Sending Dollars Shows Feeling'—Emotions and Economies in Filipino Migration." *Mobilities* 2 (2): 175–94.

Méndez, Cecilia. 2011. "De Indio a Serrano: Nociones de Raza y Geografía en el Perú (siglos XVIII-XXI)." *Histórica* 35 (1): 53–102.

Mendoza, Zoila. 2000. *Shaping Society through Dance: Mestizo Ritual Performance in the Peruvian Andes*. Chicago: University of Chicago Press.

Menjívar, Cecilia. 2000. *Fragmented Ties: Salvadoran Immigrant Networks in America.* Berkeley: University of California Press.

Menjívar, Cecilia, and Leisy Abrego. 2009. "Parents and Children across Borders: Legal Instability and Intergenerational Relations in Guatemalan and Salvadoran Families." In *Across Generations: Immigrant Families in America,* edited by Nancy Foner, 160–89. New York: NYU Press.

Merla, Laura. 2013. "Salvadoran Transnational Families, Distance and Eldercare: Understanding Transnational Care Practices in Australia and Belgium." In *Migration, Familie und Soziale Lage: Beiträge zu Bildung, Gender und Care,* edited by Thomas Geisen, Tobias Studer, and Erol Yildiz, 295–312. VS Verlag für Sozialwissenschaften.

Miles, Ann. 2004. *From Cuenca to Queens: An Anthropological Story of Transnational Migration.* Austin: University of Texas.

Miller, Daniel. 2007. "What Is a Relationship? Kinship as Negotiated Experience." *Ethnos* 72 (4): 535–54.

Miller, Daniel, and Don Slater. 2000. *The Internet: An Ethnographic Approach.* London: Berg.

Millones, Luis, and Renata Millones. 2003. *Calendario Tradicional Peruano.* Lima: Fondo Editorial del Congreso del Perú.

Ministry of Foreign Affairs of Peru. 2005. *Reglamento Consular 2005.* Lima: Ministerio de Relaciones Exteriores.

Mintz, Sidney W. 1998. "The Localization of Anthropological Practice: From Area Studies to Transnationalism." *Critique of Anthropology* 18 (2): 117–33.

Mitchell, Timothy. 2002. *Rule of Experts: Egypt, Techno-Politics, Modernity.* Berkeley: University of California Press.

Mörner, Magnus. 1985. *The Andean Past: Land, Society, and Conflicts.* New York: Columbia University Press.

Mujica, Jaris. 2011. *Micropolíticas de la Corrupción. Redes de Poder y Corrupción en el Palacio de Justicia.* Lima: Asamblea Nacional de Rectores.

Murra, John V. [1972] 1987. "El 'Control Vertical' de un Máximo de Pisos Ecológicos en la Economia de las Sociedades Andinas." In *La Teoría de la Complimentariedad Vertical Eco-Simbiótica,* edited by Ramiro Condarco and John Victor Murra, 29–85. La Paz: Hisbol.

Myerhoff, Barbara, and Sally Falk Moore. 1977. *Secular Ritual.* Assen, The Netherlands: Uitgeverij Van Gorcum.

Naficy, Hamid. 1993. *The Making of Exile Cultures: Iranian Television in Los Angeles.* Minneapolis: University of Minnesota Press.

Nelson, Diane M. 1999. *A Finger in the Wound: Body Politics in Quincentennial Guatemala.* Berkeley: University of California Press.

Nouvet, Elysée. 2014. "Some Carry On, Some Stay in Bed: (In)convenient Affects and Agency in Neoliberal Nicaragua." *Cultural Anthropology* 29 (1): 80–102.

Noyes, Dorothy. 2004. "Folklore and Myth." In *Social Science Encyclopedia,* 3rd edition, edited by Adam Kuper and Jessica Kuper, 375–78. New York: Routledge.

Nugent, David. 1994. "Rethinking the Politics of Anthropology: The Case of the Andes [and Comments and Reply], Orin Starn, Olivia Harris, David Nugent, Stephen Nugent, Benjamin S. Orlove, S. P. Reyna and Gavin Smith." *Current Anthropology* 35 (1): 13–38.

Núñez, Lorena Carrasco, and Dany Holper. 2005. "'En el Perú, Nadie se Muere de Hambre': Pérdida de Peso y Prácticas de Alimentación entre Trabajadoras Dómesticas Peruanas en Chile." In *El Quinto Suyo: Transnacionalidad y Formaciones Diasporicas en la Migración Peruana*, edited by Ulla D. Berg and Karsten Paerregaard, 291–313. Lima: Instituto de Estudios Peruanos.

Núñez Carrasco, Lorena. 2010. "Transnational Family Life among Peruvian Migrants in Chile: Multiple Commitments and the Role of Social Remittances." *Journal of Comparative Family Studies* 41 (2): 187–204.

Nyberg-Sørensen, Ninna. 2012. "Revisiting the Migration–Development Nexus: From Social Networks and Remittances to Markets for Migration Control." *International Migration* 50 (3): 61–76.

Nyberg-Sørensen, Ninna, and Thomas Gammeltoft-Hansen. 2013. "Introduction." In *The Migration Industry and the Commercialization of International Migration*, edited by Ninna Nyberg-Sørensen and Thomas Gammeltoft-Hansen, 1–23. London: Routledge.

Nyberg–Sørensen, Ninna, Nicholas Van Hear, and Poul Engberg–Pedersen. 2002. "The Migration–Development Nexus: Evidence and Policy Options." *International Migration* 40 (5): 3–47.

Oboler, Suzanne. 2005a. "Introduction: Los Que Llegaron: 50 Years of South American Immigration (1950–2000)—An Overview." *Latino Studies* 3 (1): 42–52.

———. 2005b. "The Foreignness of Racism: Pride and Prejudice among Peru's Limeños in the 1990s." In *Neither Enemies Nor Friends*, edited by Anani Dzidzienyo and Suzanne Oboler, 75–100. New York: Palgrave MacMillan.

Oboler, Suzanne, and Anani Dzidzienyo. 2005. "Flows and Counterflows: Latinas/os, Blackness, and Racialization in Hemispheric Perspective." In *Neither Enemies Nor Friends*, edited by Anani Dzidzienyo and Suzanne Oboler, 3–35. New York: Palgrave MacMillan.

Ochs, Elinor, and Lisa Capps. 2001. *Living Narrative: Creating Lives in Everyday Storytelling*. Cambridge: Harvard University Press.

Olwig, Karen Fog. 2003. "Transnational Socio-Cultural Systems and Ethnographic Research: Views from an Extended Field Site." *International Migration Review* 37 (3): 787–811.

Omi, Michael, and Howard Winant. 1994. *Racial Formations in the United States: From the 1960s to the 1980s*. 2nd edition. New York: Routledge.

Ong, Aihwa. 1996. "Cultural Citizenship as Subject Making: Immigrants Negotiate Racial and Cultural Boundaries in the United States." In *Race, Identity, and Citizenship*, edited by Rodolfo D. Torres, Louis F. Miron, and Jonathan Xavier Inda, 262–93. New York: Blackwell.

Orlove, Benjamin. 1993. "Putting Race in Its Place: Order in Colonial and Postcolonial Peruvian Geography." *Social Research* 60 (2): 301–36.

———. 1998. "Down to Earth: Race and Substance in the Andes." In *Bulletin of Latin American Research* 17 (2): 207–22.

———. 2002. *Lines in the Water: Nature and Culture at Lake Titicaca.* Berkeley: University of California Press.

Orsi, Robert A. [1985] 2002. *The Madonna of 115th Street: Faith and Community in Italian Harlem, 1880–1950.* New Haven, Conn.: Yale University Press.

Ortner, Sherry B. 1984. "Theory in Anthropology since the Sixties." *Comparative Studies in Society and History* 26 (1): 126–66.

———. 2006. *Anthropology and Social Theory: Culture, Power, and the Acting Subject.* Durham, N.C.: Duke University Press.

Ossio Acuña, Juan. 1992. *Parentesco, Reciprocidad y Jerarquía en los Andes. Una Aproximación a la Organización Social de la Comunidad de Andamarca.* Lima: Fondo Editorial Pontificia Universidad Católica del Perú.

Paerregaard, Karsten. 1997. *Linking Separate Worlds: Urban Migrants and Rural Lives in Peru.* Oxford: Berg.

———. 2005. "Callejón sin Salida: Estrategias e Instituciones de los Peruanos en Argentina." In *El Quinto Suyo: Transnacionalidad y Formaciones Diasporicas en la Migración Peruana,* edited by Ulla Berg and Karsten Paerregaard, 231–60. Lima: Instituto de Estudios Peruanos.

———. 2008. *Peruvians Dispersed: An Ethnography of Global Migration.* Lexington, Mass.: Lexington Books.

———. 2010. "The Show Must Go On: The Role of Fiestas in Andean Transnational Migration." *Latin American Perspectives* 37 (5): 50–66.

Pajuelo Teves, Ramón. 2004. "Perú: Crisis Politica Permanente y Nuevas Protestas Sociales." *OSAL* 5 (14), Mayo-Agosto. Lima.

Parreñas, Rhacel Salazar. 2000. "Migrant Filipina Domestic Workers and the International Division of Reproductive Labor." *Gender & Society* 14 (4): 560–80.

———. 2001. *Servants of Globalization: Women, Migration, and Domestic Work.* Stanford, Calif.: Stanford University Press.

———. 2002. "The Care Crisis in the Philippines: Children and Transnational Families in the New Global Economy." In *Global Woman: Nannies, Maids, and Sex Workers in the New Economy,* edited by Barbara Ehrenreich and Arlie Hochschild, 39–54. New York: Metropolitan/Owl Books.

———. 2005a. "Long Distance Intimacy: Class, Gender and Intergenerational Relations between Mothers and Children in Filipino Transnational Families." *Global Networks* 5 (4): 317–36.

———. 2005b. *Children of Global Migration.* Stanford: Stanford University Press.

Pellegrino, Adela. 2003. *La Migración Internacional en América Latina y el Caribe: Tendencias y Perfiles de los Migrantes.* Santiago de Chile: United Nations Publications.

Peutz, Nathalie, and Nicholas De Genova. 2010. *The Deportation Regime: Sovereignty, Space, and the Freedom of Movement.* Durham, N.C.: Duke University Press.

Pew Hispanic Center. 2013. "Hispanic of Peruvian Origin in the United States, 2011." Washington, D.C.: Pew Hispanic Center.

Pinilla, Carmen María. 2004. *Arguedas en el Valle del Mantaro*. Lima: Fondo Editorial, PUCP.

Poole, Deborah. 1997. *Vision, Race, and Modernity: A Visual Economy of the Andean Image World*. Princeton, N.J.: Princeton University Press.

———. 2000. "Videos, Corrupción y Ocaso del Fujimorismo." In *Ideele*, No. 134 (Dec.). Lima.

———. 2004. "Between Threat and Guarantee: Justice and Community in the Margins of the Peruvian State." In *Anthropology in the Margins of the State*, edited by Veena Das and Deborah Poole, 35–65. Santa Fe, N. Mex.: School of American Research Press.

Poole, Deborah, and Gerardo Renique. 1992. *Peru: Time of Fear*. London: Latin American Bureau.

———. 2003. "Terror and the Privatized State: A Peruvian Parable." *Radical History Review* 85: 150–63.

Portes, Alejandro, Luis E. Guarnizo, and Patricia Landolt. 1999. "The Study of Transnationalism: Pitfalls and Promise of an Emergent Research Field." *Ethnic and Racial Studies* 22 (2): 217–37.

Portes, Alejandro, and Alex Stepick. 1993. *City on the Edge: The Transformation of Miami*. Berkeley: University of California Press.

Portes, Alejandro, and Min Zhou. 1993. "The New Second Generation: Segmented Assimilation and Its Variants." *Annals of the American Academy of Political and Social Science* 530 (1): 74–96.

Portocarrero, Gonzalo. 1993. "Introducción." In *Los Nuevos Limeños: Sueños, Fervores, y Caminos en el Mundo Popular*, edited by Gonzalo Portocarrero, 9–37. Lima: TEMPO/Casa SUR.

Pratt, Mary Louise 1992. *Imperial Eyes: Travel Writing and Transculturation*. New York: Routledge.

Pribilsky, Jason. 2004. "'Aprendemos a Convivir': Conjugal Relations, Co-Parenting, and Family Life among Ecuadorian Transnational Migrants in New York and the Ecuadorian Andes." *Global Networks* 4 (3): 313–34.

———. 2007. *La Chulla Vida: Gender, Migration, and the Family in Andean Ecuador and New York City*. Syracuse, N.Y.: Syracuse University Press.

Quijano, Aníbal. 1980. *Dominación y Cultura: Lo Cholo y el Conflicto Cultural en el Perú*. Lima: Mosca Azul.

———. 1993. "Modernity, Identity, and Utopia in Latin America." *Boundary 2* 20 (3): 140–55.

———. 2007. "Coloniality and Modernity/Rationality." *Cultural Studies* 21(2–3): 168–78.

Rae-Espinoza, Heather. 2011. "The Children of Emigrés in Ecuador: Narratives of Cultural Reproduction and Emotion in Transnational Social Fields." In *Everyday Ruptures: Children, Youth, and Migration in Global Perspective*, edited by Cati Coe,

Rachel Reynolds, Deborah A. Boehm, Julia Meredith Hess, and Heather Rae-Espinoza, 115–38. Nashville, Tenn.: Vanderbilt University Press.

Ráez Retamozo, Manuel. 2001. "Generos Representados. Construcción y Expression de los Generos de las Dramatizaciones Campesinas de Semana Santa en Yanamarca, Junin." In *Identidades Representadas: Performance, Experiencia, y Memoria en los Andes,* edited by Gisela Cánepa Koch and Michelle Bigenho, 281–307. Lima: Fondo editorial, PUCP.

Ramos-Zayas, Ana. 2003. *National Performances. The Politics of Class, Race, and Space in Puerto Rican Chicago.* Chicago: University of Chicago Press.

———. 2012. *Street Therapists: Race, Affect, and Neoliberal Personhood in Latino Newark.* Chicago: University of Chicago Press.

Rappaport, Joanne, and Tom Cummins. 2012. *Beyond the Lettered City: Indigenous Literacies in the Andes.* Durham, N.C.: Duke University Press.

Repak, Terry. 1995. *Waiting on Washington: Central American Workers in the Nation's Capital.* Philadelphia: Temple University Press.

Richard, Analiese, and Daromir Rudnyckyj. 2009. "Economies of Affect." *Journal of the Royal Anthropological Institute* 15 (1): 57–77.

Rimachi, Edith. 2003. "Evento y Discurso: La Práctica Andina del Jubeo o 'Limpia con Cuy.'" In *Tradición Oral, Culturas Peruanas: Una Invitación al Debate,* edited by Gonzálo Espino, 277–83. Lima: Fondo Editorial UNMSM.

Roberts, Bryan. 1974. "The Interrelationships of City and Provinces in Peru and Guatemala." *Latin American Urban Research* 4: 207–35.

Roberts, Kenneth. 1995. "Neoliberalism and the Transformation of Populism in Latin America: The Peruvian Case." *World Politics* 48 (1): 82–116.

Robinson, David. 1990. *Migration in Colonial Spanish America.* Cambridge: Cambridge University Press.

Rockefeller, Stuart A. 1998. "'There Is Culture Here': Spectacle and the Inculcation of Folklore in Highland Bolivia." *Journal of Latin American Anthropology* 3 (2): 118–49.

———. 2010. *Starting from Quirpini: The Travels and Places of a Bolivian People.* Bloomington: Indiana University Press.

———. 2011. "Flow." *Current Anthropology* 52 (4): 557–78.

Rodrigues Cuadros, Manuel. 2009. "Derechos de las Comunidades Peruanas en el Exterior." Op-ed, *La Primera,* October 19, 2009. Lima.

Romero, Mary. 1992. "Life as the Maid's Daughter: An Exploration of the Everyday Boundaries of Race, Class, and Gender." In *Feminisms in the Academy,* edited by Donna C. Stanton and Abigail J. Stewart, 157–79. Ann Arbor: University of Michigan Press.

———. 2008. "Crossing the Immigration and Race Border: A Critical Race Theory Approach to Immigration Studies." *Contemporary Justice Review* 11 (1): 23–37.

———. 2012. *The Maid's Daughter: Living Inside and Outside the American Dream.* New York: NYU Press.

Romero, Raúl R. 2001. *Debating the Past: Music, Memory, and Identity in the Andes.* Oxford: Oxford University Press.

———. 2004. *Identidades Múltiples: Memoria, Modernidad, y Cultura Popular en el Valle del Mantaro*. Lima: Fondo Editorial del Congreso del Perú.

Rosaldo, Michelle. 1984. "Toward an Anthropology of Self and Feeling." In *Culture Theory: Essays on Mind, Self and Emotion*, edited by Richard A. Shweder and Robert LeVine, 137–57. Cambridge: Cambridge University Press.

Rosaldo, Renato. 1997. "Cultural Citizenship, Inequality, and Multiculturalism." In *Latino Cultural Citizenship: Claiming Identity, Space, and Rights*, edited by William V. Flores and Rina Benmayor, 27–38. Boston: Beacon Press.

Rostworowski de Diez Canseco, María. 1999. *History of the Inca Realm*. Cambridge: Cambridge University Press.

Rouse, Roger. 1991. "Mexican Migration and the Social Space of Postmodernism." *Diaspora: A Journal of Transnational Studies* 1 (1): 8–23.

———. 1995. "Questions of Identity: Personhood and Collectivity in Transnational Migration to the United States." *Critique of Anthropology* 15 (4): 351–80.

Sabogal, Elena. 2005. "Viviendo en la Sombra. The Immigration of Peruvian Professionals to South Florida." *Latino Studies* 3 (1): 113–31.

Sabogal, Elena, and Lorena Núñez. 2010. "Sin Papeles: Middle- and Working-Class Peruvians in Santiago and South Florida." *Latin American Perspectives* 37 (5): 88–105.

Saignes, Thierry. 1995. "Indian Migration and Social Change in Seventeenth Century Charcas." In *Ethnicity, Markets, and Migration in the Andes*, edited by Brooke Larson, Olivia Harris, and Enrique Tandeter, 167–95. Durham, N.C.: Duke University Press.

Salazar, Noel B., and Allan Smart. 2011. "Anthropological Takes on (Im)mobility." *Identities* 18 (6): i–ix.

Salomon, Frank. 2004. *The Cord Keepers: Khipus and Cultural Life in a Peruvian Village*. Durham, N.C.: Duke University Press.

Salomon, Frank, and Mercedes Niño-Murcia. 2011. *The Lettered Mountain: A Peruvian Village's Way with Writing*. Durham, N.C.: Duke University Press.

Salt, John, and Jeremy Stein. 1997. "Migration as Business: The Case of Trafficking." *International Migration* 35 (4): 467–94.

Salter, Mark B. 2004. "Passports, Mobility, and Security: How Smart Can the Border Be?" *International Studies Perspectives* 5 (1): 71–91.

———. 2006. "The Global Visa Regime and the Political Technologies of the International Self: Borders, Bodies, Biopolitics." *Alternatives: Global, Local, Political* 31 (2): 167–89.

———. 2008. "When the Exception Becomes the Rule: Borders, Sovereignty, and Citizenship." *Citizenship Studies* 12 (4): 365–80.

Sassen, Saskia. 1998. *Globalization and Its Discontents: Essays on the New Mobility of People and Money*. New York: New Press.

Schein, Louisa. 2002. "Mapping Hmong Media in Diasporic Space." In *Media Worlds: Anthropology on New Terrain*, edited by Faye Ginsburg, Lila Abu-Lughod, and Brian Larkin, 229–44. Berkeley: University of California Press.

Schieffelin, Bambi. 1990. *The Give and Take of Everyday Life: Language Socialization of Kaluli Children*. Cambridge: Cambridge University Press.

Schieffelin, Edward. 1976. *The Sorrow of the Lonely and the Burning of the Dancers*. New York: St. Martin's Press.

Schmidt, Gregory D. 2002. "The Presidential Election in Peru, April 2000." *Electoral Studies* 21 (2): 346–57.

Schneider, Jo-Anne. 1990. "Defining Boundaries, Creating Contacts: Puerto Rican and Polish Representation of Group Identity through Ethnic Parades." *Journal of Ethnic Studies* 18: 33–57.

Scott, James C. 1998. *Seeing Like a State: How Certain Schemes to Improve the Human Condition Have Failed*. New Haven, Conn.: Yale University Press.

Shaw, Douglas V. 1994. *Immigration and Ethnicity in New Jersey History*. Trenton: New Jersey Historical Commission, U.S. Department of State.

Sheller, Mimi, and John Urry. 2006. "The New Mobilities Paradigm." *Environment and Planning A* 38 (2): 207–26.

Shweder, Richard A., and Edmund J. Bourne. 1984. "Does the Concept of the Person Vary Cross-Culturally?" In *Culture Theory: Essays on Mind, Self and Emotion*, edited by Richard A. Shweder and Robert A. LeVine, 158–99. Cambridge: Cambridge University Press.

Siems, Larry. 1992. *Between the Lines: Letters between Undocumented Mexican and Central American Immigrants and Their Families and Friends*. Tucson: University of Arizona Press.

Skrabut, Kristin. 2014. *"Extreme Lives: The Unruly Domestication of Peruvian Poverty."* Unpublished Ph.D. dissertation, Brown University.

Smith, Gavin. 1989. *Livelihood and Resistance: Peasants and the Politics of Land in Peru*. Berkeley: University of California Press.

Smith, Michael P. 2005. "Transnational Urbanism Revisited." *Journal of Ethnic and Migration Studies* 31 (2): 235–44.

Smith, Michael Peter, and Luis Eduardo Guarnizo, eds. 1998. *Transnationalism from Below* (Vol. 6). New Brunswick, N.J.: Transaction Publishers.

Smith, Raymond Thomas, 1984. *Kinship Ideology and Practice in Latin America*. Chapel Hill: University of North Carolina Press.

Smith, Robert C. 1998. "Transnational Localities. Community, Technology, and the Politics of Membership within the Context of Mexico and U.S. Migration." In *Transnationalism from Below*, edited by Michael Peter Smith and Luis Eduardo Guarnizo, 196–238. New Brunswick, N.J.: Transaction Publishers.

———. 2005. *Mexican New York: Transnational Lives of New Immigrants*. Berkeley: University of California Press.

Sneath, David, Martin Holbraad, and Morten Axel Pedersen. 2009. "Technologies of the Imagination: An Introduction." *Ethnos* 74 (1): 5–30.

Spalding, Karen. 1970. "Social Climbers: Changing Patterns of Mobility among the Indians of Colonial Peru." *Hispanic American Historical Review* 50 (4): 645–64.

Spener, David. 2009. *Clandestine Crossings: Migrants and Coyotes on the Texas-Mexico Border*. Ithaca, N.Y.: Cornell University Press.

Spiro, Melford E. 1993. "Is the Western Conception of the Self 'Peculiar' within the Context of the World Cultures?" *Ethos* 21 (2): 107–53.

Sreberny-Mohammadi, Annabelle, and Ali Mohammadi. 1994. *Small Media, Big Revolution*. Minneapolis: Minnesota University Press.

Stallybrass, Peter, and Allon White. 1986. *The Politics and Poetics of Transgression*. Ithaca: Cornell University Press.

Starn, Orin. 1991. "Missing the Revolution: Anthropologists and the War in Peru." *Cultural Anthropology* 6 (1): 63–91.

Stefoni, Carolina. 2005. "Inmigrantes Transnacionales: La Formación de Comunidades y la Transformación en Ciudadanos." In *El Quinto Suyo: Transnacionalidad y Formaciones Diasporicas en la Migración Peruana*, edited by Ulla Berg and Karsten Paerregaard, 261–89. Lima: Instituto de Estudios Peruanos.

Stephen, Lynn. 2007. *Transborder Lives: Indigenous Oaxacans in Mexico, California, and Oregon*. Durham, N.C.: Duke University Press.

Stepputat, Finn. 2004. "Marching for Progress: Rituals of Citizenship, State and Belonging in a High Andes District." *Bulletin of Latin American Research* 23 (2): 244–59.

———. 2005. "Violence, Sovereignty, and Citizenship in Postcolonial Peru." In *Sovereign Bodies: Citizens, Migrants, and States in the Postcolonial World*, edited by Thomas Blom Hansen and Finn Stepputat, 61–81. Princeton, N.J.: Princeton University Press.

Stern, Steve. 1982. *Peru's Indian People and the Challenges of the Spanish Conquest*. Madison: University of Wisconsin Press.

Stewart, Kathleen. 2007. *Ordinary Affects*. Durham, N.C.: Duke University Press.

———. 2010. "Afterword: Worlding Refrains." In *The Affect Theory Reader*, edited by Melissa Gregg and Gregory J. Seigworth, 339–54. Durham, N.C.: Duke University Press.

Sturken, Marita, and Lisa Cartwright. 2001. *Practices of Looking: An Introduction to Visual Culture*. Oxford: Oxford University Press.

Takenaka, Ayumi. 1999. "Transnational Community and Its Ethnic Consequences: The Return Migration and the Transformation of Ethnicity of Japanese Peruvians." *American Behavioral Scientist* 42 (9): 1459–74.

———. 2004. "The Japanese in Peru: History of Immigration, Settlement, and Racialization." *Latin American Perspectives* 31 (3): 77–98.

Takenaka, Ayumi, and Karen A. Pren. 2010. "Determinants of Emigration: Comparing Migrants' Selectivity from Peru and Mexico." *Annals of the American Academy of Political and Social Science* 630: 178–93.

Takenaka, Ayumi, Karsten Paerregaard, and Ulla Berg. 2010. "Peruvian Migration in a Global Context." *Latin American Perspectives* 37 (5): 3–11.

Tamagno, Carla. 1998. *"Abriendo Espacios, Tejiendo Redes: Desplazamiento y Reconstrucción en la Region Central."* M.A. thesis. Lima: Pontificia Universidad Católica del Perú.

———. 2002a. "'You Must Win Their Affection . . .' Migrants' Social and Cultural Practice between Peru and Italy." In *Work and Migration: Life and Livelihoods in a Globalizing World*, edited by Karen Fog Olwig and Ninna Nyberg Sørensen, 106–25. London: Routledge.

———. 2002b. "La Plaza del Duomo. Políticas de Identidad y Producción de Localidad, el Caso de los Peruanos en Milán." In *Transnational Identities. A Concept Explored. The Andes and Beyond*, edited by Ton Salman and Annelies Zoomers, 9–60. Antropologische Bijdragen 16. Amsterdam: CEDLA.

———. 2003. "*Entre Acá y Allá: Vidas Transnacionales y Desarrollo. Peruanos entre Italia y Peru*." Unpublished Ph.D. dissertation. Wageningen University, the Netherlands.

———. 2005. "'Entre Celulinos y Cholulares': Prácticas Comunicativas y la Construcción de Vidas Transnacionales entre Perú e Italia." In *El Quinto Suyo: Transnacionalidad y Formaciones Diasporicas en la Migración Peruana*, edited by Ulla Berg and Karsten Paerregaard, 173–204. Lima: Instituto de Estudios Peruanos.

Tambiah, Stanley. 1981. *A Performative Approach to Ritual.* Oxford: Oxford University Press.

———. 1985. *Culture, Thought, and Social Action: An Anthropological Perspective.* Cambridge, Mass.: Harvard University Press.

Tanaka, Martín. 2002. "La Dinámica de los Actores Regionales y el Proceso de Decentralización: ¿El Despertar del Letargo?" Working Paper no. 125. Lima: Instituto de Estudios Peruanos.

Tapia, Rafael. 1998. "Individuación y Comunidad en la Cultura Empresarial Chola Peruana." In *Las Clases Medias: Entre la Pretención y la Incertidumbre*, edited by Gonzalo Portocarrero, 339–55. Lima: Oxfam and Casa SUR.

Taylor, Diana. 2003. *The Archive and the Repertoire: Performing Cultural Memory in the Americas.* Durham, N.C.: Duke University Press.

Thomas, Deborah A., and M. Kamari Clarke. 2013. "Globalization and Race: Structures of Inequality, New Sovereignties, and Citizenship in a Neoliberal Era." *Annual Review of Anthropology* 42 (2013): 305–25.

Thomas, William, and Florian Znaniecki. 1996. *The Polish Peasant in Europe and America: A Classic Work in Immigration History*, edited by Eli Zaretsky. Urbana: University of Illinois Press.

Thompson, Eric C. 2009. "Mobile Phones, Communities and Social Networks among Foreign Workers in Singapore." *Global Networks* 9 (3): 359–80.

Thurner, Mark. 1997. *From Two Republics to One Divided: Contradictions of Postcolonial Nation-Making in Andean Peru.* Durham, N.C.: Duke University Press.

Tienda, Martha, and Susana M. Sánchez. 2013. "Latin American Immigration to the United States." *Daedalus* 142 (3): 48–64.

Torpey, John. 2000. *The Invention of the Passport: Surveillance, Citizenship, and the State.* Cambridge: Cambridge University Press.

Trouillot, Michel-Rolph. 2001. "The Anthropology of the State in the Age of Globalization: Close Encounters of the Deceptive Kind." *Current Anthropology* 42 (1): 125–38.

Tsing, Anna. 2005. *Friction: An Ethnography of Global Connection*. Princeton, N.J.: Princeton University Press.

Tucker, Joshua. 2013. *Gentleman Troubadours and Andean Pop Stars: Huayno Music, Media Work, and Ethnic Imaginaries in Urban Peru*. Chicago: University of Chicago Press.

Turino, Thomas. 1993. *Moving Away from Silence: Music of the Peruvian Altiplano and the Experiment of Urban Migration*. Chicago: University of Chicago Press.

Turner, Victor. 1967. *The Forest of Symbols: Aspects of Ndembu Ritual*. Ithaca, N.Y.: Cornell University Press.

———. 1974. *The Ritual Process: Structure and Anti-Structure*. New York: Aldine de Gruyter.

Tweed, Thomas A. 1997. *Our Lady of the Exile: Diasporic Religion at a Cuban Catholic Shrine in Miami*. Oxford: Oxford University Press.

Urciuoli, Bonnie. 1996. *Exposing Prejudice: Puerto Rican Experiences of Language, Race, and Class*. Boulder, Colo.: Waveland Press.

Urry, John. 2003. "Social Networks, Travel, and Talk." *British Journal of Sociology* 54 (2): 155–75.

———. 2007. *Mobilities*. Cambridge: Polity Press.

Urton, Gary. 2003. *Signs of the Inka Khipu: Binary Coding in the Andean Knotted-String Records*. Austin: University of Texas Press.

U.S. Census Bureau. 2010. Accessed at http://www.census.gov/

Van der Ploeg, Irma. 1999. "The Illegal Body: 'Eurodac' and the Politics of Biometric Identification." *Ethics and Information Technology* 1 (4): 295–302.

Van der Ploeg, Irma, and Isolde Sprenkels. 2011. "Migration and the Machine-Readable Body: Identification." In *Migration and the New Technological Borders of Europe*, edited by Huub Dijstelbloem, Albert Meijer, and Michiel Besters, 68–104. Basingstoke, U.K.: Palgrave Macmillan.

Van Vleet, Krista. 2003. "Partial Theories: On Gossip, Envy and Ethnography in the Andes." *Ethnography* 4: 491–519.

———. 2008. *Performing Kinship: Narrative, Gender, and the Intimacies of Power in the Andes*. Austin: University of Texas Press.

Vasquez del Aguila, Ernesto. 2013. *Being a Man in a Transnational World: The Masculinity and Sexuality of Migration*. Vol. 13. New York: Routledge.

Vertovec, Steven. 1999. "Conceiving and Researching Transnationalism." *Ethnic and Racial Studies* 22 (2): 447–62.

———. 2004. "Cheap Calls: The Social Glue of Migrant Transnationalism." *Global Networks* 4 (2): 219–24.

Vich, Victor. 2007. "Magical, Mystical: 'The Royal Tour' of Alejandro Toledo." *Journal of Latin American Cultural Studies: Travesia* 16 (1): 1–10.

Vidal, Núria Empez. 2011. "The Transnationally Affected: Spanish State Policies and the Life-Course Events of Families in North Africa." In *Everyday Ruptures: Children, Youth, and Migration in Global Perspective*, edited by Cati Coe, Rachel R. Reynolds, Deborah A. Boehm, Julia Meredith Hess, and Heather Rae-Espinoza, 174–188. Nashville, Tenn.: Vanderbilt University Press.

Vigh, Henrik. 2009. "Wayward Migration: On Imagined Futures and Technological Voids." *Ethnos* 74 (1): 91–109.

Vilcapoma, José Carlos. 1995. *Waylarsh: Amor y Violencia de Carnaval*. Lima: Pakarina.

Vogel, Erica. 2011. "*Converting Dreams: Money, Religion and Belonging among Peruvian Migrant Laborers in South Korea*." Unpublished Ph.D dissertation, University of California, Irvine.

Waldinger, Roger, and David Fitzgerald. 2004. "Transnationalism in Question." *American Journal of Sociology* 109 (5): 1177–95.

Walker, Charles. 1999. *Smoldering Ashes: Cuzco and the Creation of Republican Peru, 1780–1840*. Durham, N.C.: Duke University Press.

Waters, Mary C., and Tomás R. Jiménez. 2005. "Assessing Immigrant Assimilation: New Empirical and Theoretical Challenges." *Annual Review of Sociology* 31: 105–25.

Weiner, Annette. 1992. *Inalienable Possessions: The Paradox of Keeping—While Giving*. Berkeley: California University Press.

Weismantel, Mary. 1995. "Making Kin: Kinship Theory and Zumbagua Adoptions." *American Ethnologist* 22 (4): 685–704.

———. 2001. *Cholas and Pishtacos: Stories of Race and Sex in the Andes*. Chicago: University of Chicago Press.

Werbner, Pnina, ed. 2008. *Anthropology and the New Cosmopolitanism: Rooted, Feminist and Vernacular Perspectives* (Vol. 45). Oxford: Berg.

Wilding, Raelene. 2006. "'Virtual' Intimacies: Families Communicating across Transnational Contexts." *Global Networks* 6 (2): 125–42.

———. 2012. "Mediating Culture in Transnational Spaces: An Example of Young People from Refugee Backgrounds." *Continuum* 26 (3): 501–11.

Williams, Raymond. 1973. *The Country and the City*. Oxford: Oxford University Press.

———. 1977. *Marxism and Literature*. Oxford: Oxford University Press.

Wilson, Fiona. 2001. "In the Name of the State? Schools and Teachers in an Andean Province." In *States of Imagination: Ethnographic Explorations of the Postcolonial State*, edited by Thomas Blom Hansen and Finn Stepputat, 313–44. Durham, N.C.: Duke University Press, 2001.

———. 2004. "Indian Citizenship and the Discourse of Hygiene/Disease in Nineteenth-Century Peru." *Bulletin of Latin American Research* 23 (2): 165–80.

Wimmer, Andreas, and Nina Glick Schiller. 2002. "Methodological Nationalism and Beyond: Nation-State Building, Migration and the Social Sciences." *Global Networks* 2: 301–34.

Winders, Jamie, and Barbara Ellen Smith. 2012. "Excepting/Accepting the South: New Geographies of Latino Migration, New Directions in Latino Studies." *Latino Studies* 10 (1): 220–45.

Yashar, Deborah. 1998. "Contesting Citizenship: Indigenous Movements and Democracy in Latin America." *Comparative Politics* 31 (1): 23–42.

Yngvesson, Barbara, and Susan Bibler Coutin. 2006. "Backed by Papers: Undoing Persons, Histories, and Return." *American Ethnologist* 33 (2): 177–90.

Young, Grace Esther. 1987. "The Myth of Being 'Like a Daughter.'" *Latin American Perspectives* 14 (3): 365–80.

Zilberg, Elana. 2011. *Space of Detention: The Making of a Transnational Gang Crisis between Los Angeles and El Salvador*. Durham, N.C.: Duke University Press.

Zúñiga, Víctor, and Rubén Hernández-León, eds. 2006. *New Destinations: Mexican Immigration in the United States*. New York: Russell Sage Foundation.

INDEX

Abandonment, 128, 132

Abercrombie, Thomas, 16

Abrego, Leisy, 133

Absentee voting, 216–17

Affect, 140–41, 251n14; economies of, 137–39; mobilizations of, 57; transnational families and, 124; transnational forms of, 108

Affective labor, 122, 138

Affective responses to migration, 68

African-Americans, Latinos and, 207

Afro-Peruvians, 248n12

Agency, 10, 31, 158

Agrarian Reform, 251n12

Agriculture, 56–57

AIPEUC. *See* Asociación de Instituciones Peruanas en Estados Unidos y Canadá

Airplane travel, 87; migration control and, 94

Airport habitus, 93

Ajusticiamiento, 210, 220, 221; Comunidad Campesina's response to, 223

Alberto Sánchez, Luis, 214–15, 261n8

Altamirano, Teófilo, 26

Ambulant ethnography, 29–30, 233–34, 244–46

American-born Spaniard. See *Criollo*

American Dream, 69; Peruvian, 192–95

Americanization, 9

Andean civilizations, 49–50, 202

Andean Peru, framing, 195–202

Andean Peruvians, 2, 200; cosmopolitan, 218; and Cosmopolitanism, 2; image

of, 224; international migration of, 5–7; mobility of, 15–18; as phantom citizens, 209–30; race and, 243; racialization of, 199; rural-to-urban migration of, 17; sociality, 221–24; Spanish and, 50–52; transnational migration of, 2, 243–44; transnational mobility of, 2, 4, 8–9; in U.S., 62–63

Anthropologist, 183, 244; as videographer, 171–73, 258n26

Anthropology, visual, 171–74

Antifalsification campaign, 82

Anti-immigration, 203, 205

Anti-Latino narrative, 23

Antiterrorism and Effective Death Penalty Act, 217–18

Appadurai, Arjun, 143, 190

Arguedas, José Maria, 21

Asociación de Instituciones Peruanas en Estados Unidos y Canadá (AIPEUC), 228–29

Aspiration, 149; to mobility, 5, 59

Assimilation, 10–11, 192; theory, 247n7

Audiocassette communication, 113–14, 123

Azángaro, 74, 81–82

Bad cholo. See *Cholo malazo*

Bauman, Richard, 32, 169, 189

Bauman, Zygmunt, 43, 61

Belonging, 70; ambiguity and national, 177; public performances and, 183

Berlant, Lauren, 97

Biometrics, 94–97

Bonilla-Silva, Eduardo, 24–25

ABOUT THE AUTHOR

Ulla D. Berg is Associate Professor of Anthropology and Latino Studies at Rutgers University. She has conducted extensive ethnographic research in the central highlands of Peru and among migrants from this area in the United States. She is the co-editor of *Transnational Citizenship across the Americas.*